My own from New life

20/7/02.

More Gathered Gold

More GATHERED GOLD

A treasury of quotations for Christians

compiled by
JOHN BLANCHARD

 EVANGELICAL PRESS

EVANGELICAL PRESS
16/18 High Street, Welwyn, Hertfordshire, AL6 9EQ, England

First published 1986
Reprinted 1988

ISBN 0 85234 218 7 (Hardback)
ISBN 0 85234 219 5 (Paperback)

British Library Cataloguing in Publication Data

Blanchard, John, *1932–*
    More Gathered Gold: a treasury of quotations for Christians.
    1. Christianity – Quotations, maxims, etc.
    I. Title
    808.88′2   PN6084.C52

Other books by John Blanchard

Read Mark Learn
Right With God
Learning and Living
What in the World is a Christian?
Truth for Life
Pop Goes the Gospel
How to Enjoy Your Bible
Gathered Gold
Ultimate Questions
Luke Comes Alive

Printed and bound in Great Britain by The Bath Press, Avon

Affectionately dedicated to

PAUL CANTELON

*my father in God and a brother
in Christ*

Introduction

As its title indicates, this volume has a predecessor. *Gathered Gold* was published in 1984, and has had such an enthusiastic reception that I have accelerated the process of compiling a second volume.

The background to the gathering of the material and the promptings which led to its publication were both explained in the Introduction to *Gathered Gold* and need not be repeated here, but it may be helpful if I underlined a few relevant facts about the contents I have chosen.

Firstly, the inclusion of any quotation does not mean that I endorse the author's stance on any other issue of faith or practice. It does not even mean that the author is a Christian; readers with raised eyebrows are referred to Acts 17:28 as a precedent!

Secondly, not all the quotations have the same depth or tone. Some are technical explanations; others make a serious devotional or practical point; but in some cases the quotation is in the form of a witty or humorous comment.

Thirdly, I have not taken up space with titles, ranks, positions and dates, preferring to let the quotations stand on their own. However, a subject index has been provided, including cross-references where it was thought these would be helpful.

Fourthly, a limited number of quotations from my own written and spoken ministry have been included where it was felt that they had a contribution to make (though I do not claim that they qualify as 'gold'!) These always appear in italics at the beginning of a section.

This second collection (a third is not intended!) is sent out in the hope that it will prove a useful source of quotations for preachers, teachers and other Christian communicators, but also a means of direction, inspiration, insight, encouragement and help to countless other people seeking to live effective Christian lives in today's world. Above all, I pray that for all their limitations these words from mortal men may point their readers to the one 'in whom are hidden all the treasures of wisdom and knowledge' (Colossians 2:3).

John Blanchard
Banstead,
Surrey.
February 1986

ABANDONMENT

(See also: Consecration; Submission; Zeal)

Oh, how greatly has the man advanced who has learned not to be his own, not to be governed by his own reason, but to surrender his mind to God!

John Calvin

A life abandoned to Christ cannot be cut short.

Sherwood Day

My Saviour, I am thine,
By everlasting bands;
My name, my heart, I would resign;
My soul is in thy hands.

Philip Doddridge

It is when God appears to have abandoned us that we must abandon ourselves most wholly to God.

François Fenelon

If so poor a worm as I
May to thy great glory live;
All my actions sanctify,
All my words and thoughts receive.
Claim me for thy service, claim
All I have and all I am.

Charles Wesley

ABORTION

If human life can be taken before birth, there is no logical reason why it cannot be taken after birth.

Francis Schaeffer

Since the Bible teaches that life in the womb is human life, one cannot accept abortion without denying the authority and truth of Scripture in practice.

Francis Schaeffer

ACTIONS

(See also: Duty; Good Deeds; Service)

All our activity is sowing; and so is our inactivity.

Words are leaves — deeds are fruit.   *Anon.*

The gospel is not a doctrine of the tongue, but of life.

John Calvin

It is not enough that our actions be good and praiseworthy, if our intentions are not pure and upright. It is to profane the good to do it with a bad end in view.

Jean Daillé

1

Behaviour is a mirror in which everyone displays his own image.

Johann Wolfgang von Goethe

No conduct of any man may be neutral. *John Hus*

Sympathy is no substitute for action.

David Livingstone

The actions of men are the best interpreters of their thoughts.

John Locke

What or whom we worship determines our behaviour.

John Murray

Affection without action is like Rachel, beautiful but barren. *John Trapp*

The actions of men form an infallible index of their character.

Geoffrey B. Wilson

ACTIVISM

(See also: Service)

There is a world of difference between activity and progress.

Velocity is no substitute for direction or purpose.

Beware of the urgent crowding out the important.

Anon.

God's service is sometimes hindered by a feverish attempt to do it. *Anon.*

What is the use of running when we are not on the right road? *Anon.*

I think the devil has made it his business to monopolize on three elements: noise, hurry, crowds ... Satan is quite aware of the power of silence. *Jim Elliot*

I am convinced that if the devil cannot make us lazy he will make us so busy here and there that the best is sacrificed for the good.

Vance Havner

The work of God cannot be done in the energy of the flesh. Too much religious activity is just old Adam in his Sunday clothes.

Vance Havner

Those dear souls who argue that the devil never takes a vacation should remember that we are not supposed to imitate the devil.

Vance Havner

Many Christians are so busy they can only hear the click and clatter of church machinery.

Walter B. Knight

The flesh loves excitement. It is always ready to jump up and run somewhere. It hurries us into action. The Holy Spirit does not. Satan rushes men. God leads them.
F. B. Meyer

One of Satan's methods today is to start so many organizations in a church that the members have no time for communion with God. *G. Campbell Morgan*

We have many irons in the fire, but none ever get hot.
Ivor Powell

There is too much working before men and too little waiting before God. There is more and more motion and less and less unction.
Alan Redpath

In an effort to get the work of the Lord done, we often lose contact with the Lord of the work. *A. W. Tozer*

We of the nervous West are victims of the philosophy of activism tragically mis-understood . . . If we are not making plans or working to carry out plans already made we feel we are failures.
A. W. Tozer

ADOPTION

The Christian is far more than a guest with God.
Donald Grey Barnhouse

Only if we walk in the beauty of God's law do we become sure of our adoption as children of the Father.
John Calvin

Adoption, as the term clearly implies, is an act of transfer from an alien family into the family of God him-self. This is surely the apex of grace and privilege.
John Murray

The spirit of prayer is the fruit and token of the Spirit of adoption. *John Newton*

God has made his children, by adoption, nearer to him-self than the angels. The angels are the friends of Christ; believers are his members. *Thomas Watson*

Since God has a Son of his own, and such a Son, how wonderful God's love in adopting us! We needed a Father, but he did not need sons. *Thomas Watson*

ADVICE

We give advice by the bucket, but take it by the grain. *W. R. Alger*

To profit from good advice requires more wisdom than to give it. *Churton Collins*

AFFECTIONS

The fundamental distinction between the godly and ungodly men consists in the object to which their affections are directed. *Anon.*

The true worth of a man is to be measured by the objects he pursues.
Marcus Aurelius

Grace comes not to take away a man's affections, but to take them up.
William Fenner

The nearer to heaven in hopes, the farther from earth in desires. *William Gurnall*

The tree will not only lie as it falls, but it will fall as it leans. What is the inclination of my soul?
J. J. Gurney

Affection is the answer to apathy. *Vance Havner*

The real test of the genuineness of any inward affection is not so much the character of the feeling as it reveals itself in our consciousness, as the course of action to which it leads. *Charles Hodge*

There is a close connection between the affections and the understanding: if we love evil, we cannot understand that which is good.
C. H. Spurgeon

Whatever is your greatest joy and treasure, that is your god. *C. H. Spurgeon*

Likeness comes from liking. We grow to be like that which we like.
Augustus H. Strong

Affection without action is like Rachel, beautiful but barren. *John Trapp*

AGNOSTICISM

Agnosticism is the philosophical, ethical and religious dry-rot of the modern world. *F. E. Abbot*

Agnosticism leads inevitably to moral indifference.
Thomas Merton

There are no agnostics in hell. *Geoffrey B. Wilson*

4

ALCOHOL
(See also: Drunkenness)

Drink has drained more blood, hung more crepe, sold more homes, armed more villains, slain more children, snapped more wedding rings, defiled more innocents, blinded more eyes, twisted more limbs, dethroned more reasons, wrecked more manhood, dishonoured more womanhood, broken more hearts, driven more to suicide than any other scourge that ever swept across the world.
Evangeline Cory Booth

Strong drink is not only the devil's way into a man, but man's way to the devil.
Adam Clarke

Every moderate drinker could abandon the intoxicating cup, if he would; every inebriate would if he could. *J. B. Gough*

I have four good reasons for being an abstainer — my head is clearer, my health is better, my heart is lighter and my purse is heavier.
Thomas Guthrie

AMBITION

Ambition is like hunger; it obeys no law but its appetite. *Josh Billings*

Seek not great things for yourself in this world, for if your garments be long they will make you stumble.
William Bridge

Ambition can creep as well as soar. *Edmund Burke*

To live happily the evils of ambition and self-love must be plucked from our hearts by the roots.
John Calvin

Ambition is the mind's immodesty.
William Davenant

Ambition is like love, impatient both of delays and rivals. *John Denham*

Most of the trouble in the world is caused by people wanting to be important.
T. S. Eliot

Nothing arouses ambition so much in the heart as the trumpet-clang of another's fame. *Baltasar Gracian*

Where ambition can cover its enterprises, even to the person himself, under the appearance of principle, it is

5

the most incurable and inflexible of passions.
David Hume

Ambition is pitiless; any merit that it cannot use it finds despicable.
Joseph Joubert

Ambition is a lust that is never quenched, but grows more inflamed and madder by enjoyment.
Thomas Otway

There are people who want to be everywhere at once and they seem to get nowhere. *Carl Sandburg*

Some climb so high that they break their necks.
George Swinnock

The itch to have the pre-eminence is one disease for which no natural cure has ever been found.
A. W. Tozer

Ambition rides without reins. *John Trapp*

AMUSEMENTS
(See also: Recreation)

Many so-called innocent amusements are but contrivances of the devil to make us forget God.
Anon.

Amusements are to virtue like breezes to the flame; gentle ones will fan it, but strong ones will put it out.
David Thomas

Is it not a strange thing and a wonder that, with the shadow of atomic destruction hanging over the world and with the coming of Christ drawing near, the professed followers of the Lord should be giving themselves up to religious amusements? *A. W. Tozer*

ANGELS

Jacob saw angels ascending and descending, but none standing still. *Anon.*

The Bible assumes, rather than asserts, the existence of angels, as it does the fact of God himself. *C. T. Cook*

Angels have a much more important place in the Bible than the devil and his demons. *Billy Graham*

We must not get so busy counting demons that we forget the holy angels.
Billy Graham

Angels are clothed with God's powers to accomplish his will in the realm of nature. *T. Hewitt*

I meditate on the blessed obedience and order of angels, without which no peace could be in heaven, and oh that it might be so on earth!   *Richard Hooker*

Angels both good and bad have a greater influence on this world than men are generally aware of.
                Increase Mather

Millions of spiritual creatures walk the earth unseen, both when we sleep and when we awake.
                John Milton

Activity is the mark of holy spirits and should be the mark of holy men.
                C. H. Spurgeon

ANGER
(See also: Hatred; Passion)

He that is inebriated with a passion is unfit for an action.
                Thomas Adams

Anger is an acid that can do more harm to the vessel in which it is stored than to anything on which it is poured.   *Anon.*

Anger is as a stone cast into a wasp's nest.   *Anon.*

He who can suppress a moment's anger may prevent a day of sorrow.
                Anon.

Angry men are blind and foolish.   *Pietro Aretino*

It is easy to fly into a passion — anybody can do that — but to be angry with the right person at the right time and with the right object and in the right way — that is not easy, and it is not everyone who can do it.
                Aristotle

Our anger and impatience often proves much more mischievous than the things about which we are angry or impatient.   *Marcus Aurelius*

The sun should not set upon our anger, neither should it rise upon our confidence.
                C. C. Colton

Anger is seldom without a reason, but seldom a good one.   *Benjamin Franklin*

A man in a passion rides a horse that runs away with him.   *Thomas Fuller*

Act nothing in a furious passion. It is putting to sea in a storm.   *Thomas Fuller*

Anger is a sin that is its own punishment.   *Matthew Henry*

7

Angry men have good memories. *Matthew Henry*

When anger was in Cain's heart, murder was not far off. *Matthew Henry*

When passion is on the throne reason is out of doors. *Matthew Henry*

Human anger never practises the things that God can approve. *D. Edmond Hiebert*

Anger at God is a symptom. The basic problem is unbelief. *Gladys Hunt*

Anger should not be destroyed but sanctified. *William Jenkyn*

When passion enters a situation, human reasoning (unassisted by grace) has as much chance of retaining its hold on truth as a snowflake in the mouth of a blast furnace. *C. S. Lewis*

Nothing makes room for Satan more than wrath. *Thomas Manton*

Anger begins in folly and ends in repentance. *Pythagoras*

The greatest remedy for anger is delay. *Seneca*

The fury of man never furthered the glory of God. *A. W. Tozer*

Anger and malice differ but in age. *John Trapp*

Anger may rush into a wise man's bosom, but should not rest there. *John Trapp*

ANNIHILATION

(See also: Death; Eternity; Judgement)

The concept of annihilationism is a doctrine of despair.

The philosophy that man will fall into oblivion, snuffed out like a candle, makes no sense of the inequalities of life. *Brian Edwards*

ANTINOMIANISM

We are not cleansed by Christ so that we can immerse ourselves continually in fresh dirt, but in order that our purity may serve the glory of God. *John Calvin*

The gospel no more excuses sin than the law does. What is repugnant to the moral

law of God is also contrary to the gospel of Christ.
Henry T. Mahan

ANXIETY
(See also: Fear; Worry)

Anxiety is the poison of human life. *Hugh Blair*

Anxiety is a word of unbelief or unreasoning dread. We have no right to allow it. Full faith in God puts it to rest. *Horace Bushnell*

Anxiety is the rust of life, destroying its brightness and weakening its power. A childlike and abiding trust in providence is its best preventative and remedy.
Tryon Edwards

Anxiety is not only a pain which we must ask God to assuage but also a weakness we must ask him to pardon — for he's told us to take no care for the morrow.
C. S. Lewis

Anxious care rests upon a basis of heathen worldly-mindedness and of heathen misunderstanding of the character of God.
Alexander Maclaren

Two things come between our souls and unshadowed

fellowship — sin and care. We must be as resolute to cast our care upon the Lord as to confess our sins to him.
F. B. Meyer

All the care in the world will not make us continue a minute beyond the time God has appointed. *J. C. Ryle*

Can we gain anything by fearing and fuming? Do we not unfit ourselves for action, and unhinge our minds for wise decision? We are sinking by our struggles when we might float by faith. *C. H. Spurgeon*

Anxious care is out of place in a heavenly Father's presence. *Kenneth Wuest*

APATHY
(See also: Complacency)

An appeaser is one who feeds a crocodile — hoping it will eat him last.
Winston Churchill

Affection is the answer to apathy. *Vance Havner*

Nothing is more dangerous to our spiritual well-being than a mild amiability that smiles at sin.
Vance Havner

Apathy

Some of us simmer all our lives and never come to the boil. *Vance Havner*

The same church members who yell like Comanche Indians at a ball game on Saturday sit like wooden Indians in church on Sunday. *Vance Havner*

We've got too many comfortable saints expanding their physical waistline instead of extending their spiritual coastline. *Vance Havner*

Spiritual indifference is always the result of losing God as the centre and source of spiritual vitality. *Festo Kivengere*

Christians are the more cold and careless in the spiritual life because they do not oftener think of heaven. *Thomas Manton*

He who aims at nothing never achieves anything else. *J. I. Packer*

Nothing is so offensive to Christ as lukewarmness in religion. *J. C. Ryle*

Our problems of spiritual coldness and apathy in the churches would quickly disappear if Christian believers generally would confess their great need for rediscovering the loveliness of Jesus Christ, their Saviour. *A. W. Tozer*

The low level of moral enthusiasm among us may have a significance far deeper than we are willing to believe. *A. W. Tozer*

No man can sit down and withhold his hands from the warfare against wrong and get peace from his acquiescence. *Woodrow Wilson*

APOSTASY

It is the creed of every sound evangelical church that those who do go back to perdition were persons who never really believed in Jesus. *A. A. Bonar*

The apostate must perish, not because the sacrifice of Christ is not of efficacy enough to expiate even his guilt, but because, continuing in his apostasy, he will have nothing to do with that sacrifice which is the only available sacrifice for sin. *John Brown*

None will have such a sad parting from Christ as those who went half-way with him and then left him. *William Gurnall*

10

To forsake Christ for the world is to leave a treasure for a trifle . . . eternity for a moment, reality for a shadow, all things for nothing. *William Jenkyn*

It is better not to have known the way of truth than not to persist in it.
John King

None prove so hopelessly wicked as those who, after experiencing strong religious convictions, have gone back again to sin and the world.
J. C. Ryle

To see a ship sink in the harbour of profession is more grievous than if it had perished in the open sea of profaneness. *William Secker*

Judas betrayed his Master with a kiss. That is how apostates do it; it is always with a kiss. *C. H. Spurgeon*

The apostate drops as a windfall into the devil's mouth. *Thomas Watson*

The root of all apostasy is the primal sin of unbelief.
Geoffrey B. Wilson

APPRECIATION

Lord, help us to glow in the other man's gift.
Tom Butler

The deepest principle in human nature is the craving to be appreciated.
William James

Next to excellence is the appreciation of it.
William Makepeace Thackeray

ART

True art is reverent imitation of God.
Tryon Edwards

Every artist writes his own autobiography.
Havelock Ellis

Art leads to a more profound concept of life, because art itself is a profound expression of feeling.
Hans Hofmann

Since I have known God in a saving manner, painting, poetry and music have had charms unknown to me before. *Henry Martyn*

The true work of art is but a shadow of the divine perfection.
Buonarroti Michaelangelo

11

Art ultimately exists for God's glory. *Robert A. Morey*

All great art is the expression of man's delight in God's work, not his own.
John Ruskin

ASSURANCE

Assurance is the cream of faith. *Anon.*

A well-grounded assurance is always attended by three fair handmaids: love, humility and holy joy.
Thomas Brooks

Assurance is *optimum maximum*, the best and greatest mercy; and therefore God will only give it to his best and dearest friends.
Thomas Brooks

Assurance makes most for your comfort but holiness makes most for God's honour. *Thomas Brooks*

Faith cannot be lost, but assurance may; therefore assurance is not faith.
Thomas Brooks

Many a Christian has his pardon sealed in the court of heaven before it is sealed in the court of his own conscience. *Thomas Brooks*

Perfect signs of grace can never spring from imperfect grace. *Thomas Brooks*

Reason's arm is too short to reach the jewel of assurance.
Thomas Brooks

Without the diligent use of means a lazy Christian has no right to expect to receive assurance. *Thomas Brooks*

Assurance does not grow like a hot-house plant, pampered in an even temperature and sheltered from every puff of wind! It is an outdoor species, meant to flourish in the ever-changing weather conditions of the world.
J. C. P. Cockerton

The gospel is the ground of the believer's assurance, while the Holy Spirit is its cause. *J. C. P. Cockerton*

Assurance is our reaction to the gift of salvation and our reflection on our trust in Christ. *Sinclair Ferguson*

Faith alone justifies, through Christ alone. Assurance is the enjoyment of that justification. *Sinclair Ferguson*

Fear to fall and assurance to stand are two sisters.
Thomas Fuller

None have assurance at all times. As in a walk that is shaded with trees and chequered with light and shadow, some tracks and paths in it are dark and others are sunshine. Such is usually the life of the most assured Christian.
Ezekiel Hopkins

Faith rests on the naked Word of God; that Word believed gives full assurance.
H. A. Ironside

None walk so evenly with God as they who are assured of the love of God.
Thomas Manton

The doctrine of assurance, biblically understood, keeps the saint on his toes.
J. A. Motyer

Where the eternal interests of the soul are concerned only a fool will give himself the benefit of the doubt.
A. W. Pink

Assurance ... enables a child of God to feel that the great business of life is a settled business, the great debt a paid debt, the great disease a healed disease and the great work 'a finished work.
J. C. Ryle

Assurance is a most delicate plant. It needs daily, hourly, watering, tending, cherishing. So watch and pray the more when you have got it.
J. C. Ryle

Assurance of faith can never come by the works of the law. It is an evangelical virtue, and can only reach us in a gospel way.
C. H. Spurgeon

Faith saves us, but assurance satisfies us. *C. H. Spurgeon*

No believer should be content with hoping and trusting, he should ask the Lord to lead him on to full assurance, so that matters of hope may become matters of certainty. *C. H. Spurgeon*

Faith will make us walk, but assurance will make us run.
Thomas Watson

The inward witness, son, the inward witness; that is proof, the strongest proof of Christianity. *Samuel Wesley*

ATHEISM
(See also: Unbelief)

Atheism is the ultimate ignorance.

An atheist is not lacking in faith – he is lacking in evidence.

It takes greater faith to be an atheist than to be a Christian.

Atheism is the main disease of the soul.   *Thomas Adams*

To be an atheist requires an infinitely greater measure of faith than to receive all the great truths which atheism would deny.
        Joseph Addison

Atheism is not an institution; it is a destitution.   *Anon.*

God never wrought miracles to convince atheism because his ordinary works convince it.   *Francis Bacon*

An atheist is a man who looks through a telescope and tries to explain what he can't see.   *O. A. Battista*

Where there is no God there is no man.
        Nicolai Berdyaev

Those who deny the existence of God are hard put to explain the existence of man.
        Harold Berry

Every atheist is a grand fool.
        Stephen Charnock

People think that when they do not believe in God they believe in nothing, but the fact is they will believe in anything.   *G. K. Chesterton*

How did the atheist get his idea of that God whom he denies?
        Samuel Taylor Coleridge

Some are atheists only in fair weather.   *Thomas Fuller*

It isn't very rational to argue that the world which is based on cause and effect is itself uncaused.
        Michael Green

No man will say, 'There is no God' till he is so hardened in sin that it has become his interest that there should be none to call him to account.
        Matthew Henry

Unless the being of God be presupposed, no tolerable account can be given of the being of any thing.
        Ezekiel Hopkins

No man is a consistent atheist.   *R. B. Kuiper*

Atheism turns out to be too simple. If the whole universe has no meaning, we should never have found out that it has no meaning: just as, if there were no light in the universe and therefore no creatures with eyes, we should never know it was dark.   *C. S. Lewis*

The footprint of the savage in the sand is sufficient to attest the presence of man to the atheist, yet he will not recognize God, whose hand is impressed upon the entire universe.   *Hugh Miller*

There are more atheists in lip than in life.
                Clark H. Pinnock

Atheists put on a false courage and alacrity in the midst of their darkness and apprehensions, like children who, when they fear to go in the dark, will sing for fear.
                Alexander Pope

The worst moment for the atheist is when he is really thankful and has nobody to thank.
                Dante Gabriel Rossetti

That God does not exist, I cannot deny. That my whole being cries out for God, I cannot forget.
                Jean-Paul Sartre

The atheist is always alone.
                Ignazio Silone

An atheist is a man who believes himself an accident.
                Francis Thompson

By night an atheist half believes in God.
                Edward Young

To see and hear an atheist die will more demonstrate that there is a God than all the learned can do by their arguments.   *Zeno*

ATONEMENT

(See also: Cross; Forgiveness by God; Jesus Christ — Death; Redemption)

The Lord Jesus took our place that we might have his peace; he took our sin that we might have his salvation.
                Anon.

When you can add brightness to the sun, beauty to the rainbow and strength to the everlasting hills, then you may try to improve the finished work of Christ.
                Anon.

The nature of the atonement settles its extent. If it merely made salvation possible, it applied to all men. If it effectively secured salvation, it had reference only to the elect.   *Loraine Boettner*

I hear the words of love,
I gaze upon the blood,
I see the mighty sacrifice,
And I have peace with God.
                Horatius Bonar

Christ hath crossed out the black lines of our sin with

15

the red lines of his own blood.   *Thomas Brooks*

Christ rose again, but our sins did not: they are buried for ever in his grave.
John Brown

Because the sinless Saviour died,
My sinful soul is counted free;
For God the Just is satisfied
To look on him, and pardon me.
Charitie Lees de Chenez

Atonement is not something contrived, as it were, behind the Father's back; it is the Father's way of making it possible for the sinful to have fellowship with him.
James Denney

'Reconciliation' in the New Testament sense is not something which we accomplish when we lay aside our enmity to God; it is something which God accomplished when in the death of Christ he put away everything that on his side meant estrangement.
James Denney

There is room enough in Christ for all comers.
Matthew Henry

Great is the gospel of our glorious God,

Where mercy met the anger of God's rod;
A penalty was paid and pardon bought,
And sinners lost at last to him were brought.
William Vernon Higham

The evidence that the death of Christ has been accepted as an expiation for sin, of infinite value and efficiency, is the fact that God has commissioned his ministers to announce to all men that God is reconciled and ready to forgive, so that whosoever will may turn to him and live.   *Charles Hodge*

To deny the necessity of atonement is to deny the existence of a real moral order.   *J. Gresham Machen.*

There is no clearer note in the Christian gospel than this: that God has put us right with himself entirely of his own free grace and at an inward cost to himself of which, in human history, Calvary is the index.
Leslie S. McCaw

Out of the wealth of his resources, God has paid debts which were no concern of his.   *J. A. Motyer*

Christ discharged the debt of sin. He bore our sins and purged them. He did not make a token payment which God accepts in place of the whole. Our debts are not cancelled; they are liquidated. *John Murray*

Those for whom Christ died are those for whom he rose again and his heavenly saving activity is of equal extent with his once-for-all redemptive accomplishments. *John Murray*

Unless we believe in the final restoration of all men we cannot have an unlimited atonement. If we universalize the extent we limit the efficacy. *John Murray*

What is offered to men in the gospel? It is not the possibility of salvation, not simply the opportunity of salvation. What is offered is salvation. *John Murray*

All peace with God is resolved into a purging atonement made for sin. *John Owen*

If Christ had not died, sin had never died in any sinner unto eternity. *John Owen*

Nothing can give perfect peace of conscience with God but what can make atonement for sin. And whoever attempt it any other way but by virtue of that

atonement will never attain it, in this world or hereafter. *John Owen*

There is no death of sin without the death of Christ. *John Owen*

The question of the extent of the atonement does not arise in evangelistic preaching; the message to be delivered is simply this — that Christ Jesus, the sovereign Lord, who died for sinners, now invites sinners freely to himself. God commands all to repent and believe; Christ promises joy and peace to all who do so. *J. I. Packer*

Nothing needs to be added to Christ's finished work, and nothing *can* be added to Christ's finished work. *Francis Schaeffer*

The atonement is not offered to an individual either as an elect man, or as a non-elect man; but as a man, and a sinner, simply. *W. G. T. Shedd*

Christ assumed both body and soul; and he offered both in our room, as was necessary to expiate guilt incurred in body and by both. *G. Smeaton*

All are not saved by Christ's death, but all which are

saved are saved by Christ's death; his death is sufficient to save all, as the sun is sufficient to lighten all.
Henry Smith

Sin mingles even with our holy things, and our best repentance, faith, prayer and thanksgiving could not be received of God were it not for the merit of the atoning sacrifice.
C. H. Spurgeon

Until God can be unjust, and demand two payments for one debt, he cannot destroy the soul for whom Jesus died. *C. H. Spurgeon*

Dear Lord, what heavenly wonders dwell
In thy atoning blood!
By this are sinners snatched from hell,
And rebels brought to God.
Anne Steele

Because Christ is man, he can make atonement for man and sympathize with man. Because Christ is God his atonement has infinite value and the union which he effects with God is complete. *Augustus H. Strong*

Christ's atonement is no passion-play. Hell cannot be cured by homoeopathy.
Augustus H. Strong

The things we have to choose between are an atonement of high value, or an atonement of wide extension. The two cannot go together.
Benjamin B. Warfield

The resurrection is the proof of our reconciliation.
Geoffrey B. Wilson

AUTHORITY

When authority goes out anarchy comes in.
Vance Havner

The overriding issue of the twentieth century is the crisis in authority.
Carl F. H. Henry

Obedience to legitimate authority is one of the fruits and evidences of Christian sincerity. *Charles Hodge*

The source of all authority is not Scripture, but Christ . . . Nowhere are we told that the Scripture of itself is able to convince a sinner or bring him to God.
Augustus H. Strong

We are finite and sinful, and we need authority.
Augustus H. Strong

18

AWE

(See also: Fear of God; Worship)

The man who cannot wonder is but a pair of spectacles behind which there is no eye.   *Thomas Carlyle*

Nothing else under the sun can be as dry, flat, tedious and exhausting as religious work without the wonder.
Vance Havner

We must rejoice in God, but still with a holy trembling.
Matthew Henry

When we have found God good, we must not forget to pronounce him great; and his kind thoughts of us must not abate our high thoughts of him.   *Matthew Henry*

The more we lose sight of the otherness of God, the more shallow our worship will be.
Alwyn Pritchard

Christ can never be known without a sense of awe and fear accompanying the knowledge . . . No one who knows him intimately can ever be flippant in his presence.   *A. W. Tozer*

BACKSLIDING

It is possible to be diligent in our religion, yet distant in our relationship.

No Christian is ever going in the right direction when he has his back to God.

If you are not as close to God as you used to be, you do not have to guess who moved.
Anon.

Withering is a slow process, barely perceptible at first either to the one who is being withered or to those who look on.
Donald Grey Barnhouse

The Christian in a declining condition . . . is as unfit to die as he is to live.
William Gurnall

To backslide in heart is more than to backslide.
William Gurnall

If you find yourself loving any pleasure more than your prayers, any book better than the Bible, any house better than the house of the Lord, any table better than the Lord's table, any persons better than Christ, or any indulgence better than the hope of heaven — be alarmed.   *Thomas Guthrie*

Taking it easy is often the prelude to backsliding. Comfort precedes collapse.
Vance Havner

God will preserve you in your ways, not in your wanderings.
William Jenkyn

Collapse in the Christian life is seldom a blowout. It is usually a slow leak.
Paul E. Little

If we know anything of true, saving religion, let us ever beware of the beginnings of backsliding. *J. C. Ryle*

It is a miserable thing to be a backslider. Of all unhappy things that can befall a man, I suppose it is the worst. A stranded ship, an eagle with a broken wing, a garden covered with weeds, a harp without strings, a church in ruins — all these are sad sights, but a backslider is a sadder sight still.
J. C. Ryle

Men fall in private long before they fall in public.
J. C. Ryle

Of all decays, the decay of goodness is the most lamentable. *Richard Sibbes*

It may be hard going forward, but it is worse going back. *C. H. Spurgeon*

BEAUTY

Beauty without virtue is a flower without perfume.
Anon.

Beauty is a gift of God.
Aristotle

Never lose an opportunity to see anything beautiful. Beauty is God's handwriting. *Charles Kingsley*

There is a beauty in holiness as well as a beauty of holiness. *George Swinnock*

BIBLE — Authority
(See also: Bible — Divine Authorship)

The Word of God is more credible than a visitor from the dead. *B. H. Carroll*

The authority of Scripture is not one that binds, but one that sets free.
William Newton Clarke

The best evidence of the Bible's being the Word of God is found between its covers. *Charles Hodge*

Never mind the scribes —
what saith the Scripture?
Martin Luther

We glory most in the fact
that Scripture so commends
itself to the conscience, and
experience so bears out the
Bible, that the gospel can go
round the world and carry
with it, in all its travel, its
own mighty credentials.
Henry Melvill

What does not agree with
Scripture does not come
from God. *Leon Morris*

It is for the Bible to form and
reform the church . . . it is
for the church to keep and
keep to the Bible.
J. I. Packer

The church no more created
the canon than Newton
created the law of gravity;
recognition is not creation.
J. I. Packer

A partially inspired Bible is
little better than no Bible at
all. *J. C. Ryle*

If the difficulties of plenary
inspiration are to be num-
bered by thousands, the
difficulties of any other view
of inspiration are to be num-
bered by tens of thousands.
J. C. Ryle

This we believe, when we
first begin to believe, that we
ought not to believe any-
thing beyond Scripture.
Tertullian

The only authoritative word
ever published is that which
comes from the Holy Scriptures. *A. W. Tozer*

Inspiration, in the full apostolic meaning of the word,
ceased when the canon of
Scripture was brought to
completion. Without such
apostolic inspiration there
can be no infallible revelation. *Geoffrey B. Wilson*

BIBLE — and Christ

The Old Testament Scrip-
tures are intelligible only
when understood as predict-
ing and prefiguring Christ.
Charles Hodge

Believing and reading Scripture means that we hear the
word from Christ's mouth.
Martin Luther

Every word in the Bible
points to Christ.
Martin Luther

Here you will find the
swaddling clothes and
manger in which Christ lies.
Martin Luther

21

I see nothing in Scripture except Christ and him crucified. *Martin Luther*

Take Christ out of the Scriptures and what will you find remaining in them? *Martin Luther*

Christ is figured in the law, foretold in the prophets and fulfilled in the gospel. *Henry Smith*

Scripture is the royal chariot in which Jesus rides. *C. H. Spurgeon*

The Scriptures are in print what Christ is in person. The inspired Word is like a faithful portrait of Christ. *A. W. Tozer*

You can be perfectly free to go to your Bible with assurance that you will find Jesus Christ everywhere in its pages. *A. W. Tozer*

BIBLE — Divine Authorship

(See also: Revelation)

A man can only deny the divine integrity of Scripture by trampling Scripture itself under his feet.

As in paradise, God walks in the Holy Scriptures, seeking man. *Ambrose*

In God's work we see his hand, but in his Word we see his face. *Anon.*

The Bible is a volume of letters from the heavenly country. *Augustine*

The fact that for fifteen centuries no attempt was made to formulate a definition of the doctrine of inspiration of the Bible testifies to the universal belief of the church that the Scriptures were the handiwork of the Holy Ghost. *George Duncan Barry*

Inspiration is the name of that all-comprehensive operation of the Holy Spirit whereby he has bestowed on the church a complete and infallible Scripture. *Abraham Kuyper*

All the words of God are weighed, counted and measured. *Martin Luther*

The Holy Scriptures did not grow on earth. *Martin Luther*

You are so to deal with the Scriptures that you bear in mind that God himself is saying this. *Martin Luther*

The Bible is God's book, not man's book.
J. Gresham Machen

Scripture is not only human witness to God, it is also divine self-testimony.
J. I. Packer

The divine Author of Scripture is not dead.
J. I. Packer

The view which I maintain is that every book, and chapter, and verse and syllable of the Bible was given by inspiration of God. *J. C. Ryle*

The Scriptures owe their origin to an activity of God the Holy Ghost and in the highest and truest sense are his creation.
Benjamin B. Warfield

What the Bible says, God says. *Benjamin B. Warfield*

Think in every line you read that God is speaking to you.
Thomas Watson

The heavens declare thy glory, Lord,
In every star thy wisdom shines;
But when our eyes behold thy Word,
We read thy name in fairer lines.
Isaac Watts

God means what he says and says what he means.
John Wilmot

BIBLE — Fulness

I have worked over the Bible, prayed over the Bible for more than sixty years, and I tell you there is no book like the Bible. It is a miracle of literature, a perennial spring of wisdom, a wonderful book of surprises, a revelation of mystery, an infallible guide of conduct, an unspeakable source of comfort.
Samuel Chadwick

The Bible . . . transcends all our categories and increasingly supplies our finite minds from its inexhaustible store of treasures.
D. Martyn Lloyd-Jones

The Word is an ocean, without bottom or banks.
Thomas Manton

We can never exhaust all the treasure and worth that is in the Word. *Thomas Manton*

There is a fulness in all Scripture far beyond our conception. *J. C. Ryle*

There is an inexhaustible fulness in Scripture.

J. C. Ryle

Nobody ever outgrows Scripture; the book widens and deepens with our years.

C. H. Spurgeon

Father of mercies, in thy Word
What endless glory shines!
For ever be thy name adored
For these celestial lines.

Anne Steele

I adore the fulness of the Scriptures. *Tertullian*

BIBLE — and the Holy Spirit

The Word is the chariot of the Spirit, the Spirit the guider of the Word.

Stephen Charnock

Revelation is the act of communicating divine knowledge by the Spirit to the mind. Inspiration is the act of the same Spirit, controlling those who make the truth known.

Charles Hodge

If God does not open and explain Holy Writ, no one can understand it; it will remain a closed book, enveloped in darkness.

Martin Luther

The Holy Ghost must be the only master to teach us, and let youth and scholar not be ashamed to learn of this tutor. *Martin Luther*

God's mind is revealed in Scripture, but we can see nothing without the spectacles of the Holy Ghost.

Thomas Manton

If you want to understand the Bible, get on your knees . . . You will learn more in one hour of prayerful communion with the Spirit than in a thousand years in all the schools of human culture.

A. T. Pierson

There is a real nutriment for the soul in Scripture brought home to the heart by the Holy Spirit.

C. H. Spurgeon

The Holy Spirit who inspired the Scriptures will expect obedience to the Scriptures, and if we do not give that obedience we will quench him. *A. W. Tozer*

BIBLE — Inerrancy

Men do not reject the Bible because they find faults in it, but because it finds faults in them.

This I have learned to do: to hold only those books which are called the Holy Scriptures in such honour that I finally believe that not one of the holy writers ever erred. *Augustine*

Scripture bears upon the face of it as clear evidence of its truth as black and white do of their colour, sweet and bitter of their taste.
John Calvin

We believe that the most scientific view, the most up-to-date and rationalistic conception, will find its fullest satisfaction in taking the Bible story literally.
Winston Churchill

Well knowing that the Scriptures are perfect as dictated (or spoken) by the Word of God, and his Spirit, a heavy punishment awaits those who add to, or take from, the Scriptures. *Irenaeus*

God's Word is such perfect truth and righteousness that it needs no patching or repair; in its course it makes a perfectly straight line, without any bends in any direction. *Martin Luther*

It is impossible that Scripture should contradict itself, only that it so appears to the senseless and obstinate hypocrites. *Martin Luther*

The Scriptures have never erred. *Martin Luther*

The Word of God is perfect; it is precious and pure; it is truth itself. *Martin Luther*

The gospel is not speculation but fact. It is truth, because it is the record of a person who is the Truth.
Alexander Maclaren

The veracity of God guarantees the trustworthiness of Scripture. *J. I. Packer*

Nothing is written by chance in the Word of God. There is a special reason for the selection of every single expression. *J. C. Ryle*

We have the truth and we need not be afraid to say so.
J. C. Ryle

The Bible is objective, absolute truth in all areas it touches upon.
Francis Schaeffer

Unless the Bible is without error, not only when it speaks of salvation matters, but also when it speaks of history and the cosmos, we have no foundation for answering questions concerning the existence of the universe and its form and the uniqueness of man.
Francis Schaeffer

25

My brethren, when you hear that a learned man has made a new discovery which contradicts the Scriptures, do not feel alarmed. Do not imagine that he is really a great man, but believe that he is just an educated idiot or a self-conceited fool.
C. H. Spurgeon

Opinions alter, but truth certified by God can no more change than the God who uttered it.
C. H. Spurgeon

We affirm that the Bible is the Word of God, and that it is not marred with human infirmities.
Christopher Wordsworth

BIBLE — Influence and Power

We must not . . . view the Bible merely as a record of what God has done but actually as a part of the saving process.
Don Garlington

Hold fast to the Bible as the sheet-anchor of our liberties; write its precepts on your hearts and practise them in your lives. To the influence of this book we are indebted for the progress made in true civilization, and to this we must look for our guide in the future. *Ulysees S. Grant*

The mightier any is in the Word, the more mighty he will be in prayer.
William Gurnall

The Bible is a disturbing book, a hammer, a fire and a sword. *Vance Havner*

The old book has been 'buried' many times, even as now men would bury God. However, the 'corpse' has a habit of coming to life in the midst of interment to outlive all the pallbearers.
Vance Havner

The Bible is alive, it speaks to me; it has feet, it runs after me; it has hands, it lays hold on me. *Martin Luther*

The Bible is not antique, or modern. It is eternal.
Martin Luther

The true Christian church is the work of the Word communicated by every available means. *Martin Luther*

The world is conquered by the Word, and by the Word the church is served and rebuilt. *Martin Luther*

The Christians who have turned the world upside down have been men and women with a vision in their hearts and the Bible in their hands.   *T. B. Maston*

The man of one book is always formidable; but when that book is the Bible he is irresistible.
William M. Taylor

Scripture is the spiritual glass to dress our souls by.
Thomas Watson

When you have read the Bible, you will know it is the Word of God, because you will have found it the key to your own heart, your own happiness and your own duty.   *Woodrow Wilson*

BIBLE — Preservation

The same God who amazingly provided the Bible has amazingly preserved it.

In his mysterious providence, God has preserved his Word. We do not have a Bible which is unreliable and glutted with error, but one that in most wondrous fashion presents the Word of God and the text of the original. · *Edward J. Young*

BIBLE — Purpose

Only one means and one way of cure has been given us and that is the teaching of the Word ... without it nothing else will avail.
Chrysostom

How precious is the Book divine,
By inspiration given!
Bright as a lamp its doctrines shine,
To guide our souls to heaven.
John Fawcett

As seed is made for soil and soil for seed, so the heart is made for God's truth and God's truth for the heart.
Richard Glover

The entire content of Scripture may be summarized under these heads: man's creation, man's fall and man's salvation.
R. B. Kuiper

At the heart of everything that the Bible says are two great truths, which belong inseparably together — the majesty of the law of God, and sin as an offence against that law.
J. Gresham Machen

Apart from the first two chapters of Genesis, which set the stage, the real subject

27

of every chapter of the Bible is what God does about our sins. *J. I. Packer*

Everything in Scripture has in view the promotion of holiness. *A. W. Pink*

God's design in all that he has revealed to us is to the purifying of our affections and the transforming of our characters. *A. W. Pink*

BIBLE — Relevance

Our inklings of the realities of God will be vague and smudged until we learn from Scripture to think correctly about the realities of which we are already aware. *John Calvin*

Unless God's Word illumine the way, the whole life of men is wrapped in darkness and mist, so that they cannot but miserably stray. *John Calvin*

All in the Bible that is vital is clear, and all that is not clear is not vital. *Guthrie Clark*

According to Christianity, the acid test of truth and goodness is scripturalness. *R. B. Kuiper*

He who rejects the Bible has nothing to live by. Neither does he have anything to die by. *R. B. Kuiper*

God has provided very wonderfully for the plain man who is not a scholar. *J. Gresham Machen*

The Bible is not a ladder but a foundation. *J. Gresham Machen*

There is no situation in which we are placed, no demand that arises, for which Scripture as the deposit of the manifold wisdom of God is not adequate and sufficient. *John Murray*

Holy Writ is to be kept not under a bushel, but under men's noses. Its message is to be held forth as diligently as it is held fast. *J. I. Packer*

Scripture is the most up-to-date and relevant reading that ever comes my way. *J. I. Packer*

I know no rule by which to judge of a man's estate but the Bible. *J. C. Ryle*

Compromising the full authority of Scripture eventually affects what it means to be a Christian theologically and

how we live in the full spectrum of human life.
Francis Schaeffer

The Bible gives not just moral limits but absolutes and truth in regard to the whole spectrum of life.
Francis Schaeffer

BIBLE — Submission to

Let us beware of being wiser than God. What he has written he has written not for our opinion but for our obedience.

We are to submit without reservation to every word of Scripture without exception.

We have no more right to tamper with Scripture than a postman has to edit our mail.

On the Day of Judgement you will not be asked, 'What did you read?' but 'What did you do?'
Thomas à Kempis

We are not to make our experience the rule of Scripture, but Scripture the rule of our experience. *Anon.*

We must surrender ourselves to the authority of Holy Scripture, for it can neither mislead nor be misled.
Augustine

As we search the Scriptures, we must allow them to search us, to sit in judgement upon our character and conduct. *Jerry Bridges*

The sum and substance of the preparation needed for a coming eternity is that you believe what the Bible tells you and do what the Bible bids you. *Thomas Chalmers*

There was never anything of false doctrine brought into the church, or anything of false worship imposed upon the church, but either it was by neglecting the Scripture, or by introducing something above the Scripture.
John Collins

Knowledge of the Scriptures does not help if it is not accompanied by a believing submission to the word of the cross, the wisdom of God. *F. W. Grosheide*

If you stand on the Word you do not stand in with the world. *Vance Havner*

Those who would have the blessings of God's testimonies must come under the bonds of his statutes.
Matthew Henry

I rest with the conviction that every word of Christ is true; and what I do not understand I commit to his grace in the hope that I shall understand it after my death.   *John Hus*

Some people are critical of everything; some embrace anything. The wise weigh all things by the Word.
                   Henry T. Mahan

We are to live under the dominion of the Word of God.   *J. A. Motyer*

It is for the Bible to form and reform the church . . . it is for the church to keep and keep to the Bible.
                   J. I. Packer

I believe that even now, when we cannot explain alleged difficulties in Holy Scripture, the wisest course is to blame the interpreter and not the text, to suspect our own ignorance to be in fault, and not any defect in God's Word.   *J. C. Ryle*

The Bible would not be the book of God if it had not deep places here and there which man has no line to fathom.   *J. C. Ryle*

What makes the difference is not how many times you have been through the Bible, but how many times and how thoroughly the Bible has been through you.
           Rodney ('Gipsy') Smith

30

Till we are above sin, we are not above Scripture.
                   Thomas Watson

BIBLE — Supremacy

No man is uneducated who knows the Bible, and no one is wise who is ignorant of its teachings.   *Samuel Chadwick*

The New Testament is the best book the world has ever known or will know.
                   Charles Dickens

I put the Scriptures above all the sayings of the fathers, angels, men and devils. Here I take my stand.
                   Martin Luther

I account the Scriptures of God the most sublime philosophy.   *Isaac Newton*

The Bible . . . the most majestic thing in our literature and . . . the most spiritually living thing we inherit.
           Arthur Quiller-Couch

BIBLE — Unity

The Bible is not simply an anthology; there is a unity which binds the whole together. An anthology is compiled by an anthologist, but

no anthologist compiled the
Bible.   *F. F. Bruce*

Thy Word is like a glorious
   choir,
And loud its anthems ring;
Though many parts and
   tongues unite,
It is one song they sing.
            Edwin Hodder

Scriptural paradoxes are
seeming, not actual, contra-
dictions. Scripture is its own
infallible interpreter and
every part of it must be
interpreted in the light of the
whole of it.   *R. B. Kuiper*

The Bible is a self-consistent
unit. What it teaches in one
place it does not contradict
elsewhere.   *R. B. Kuiper*

The Scriptures explain
themselves.   *A. W. Pink*

The Old Testament is the
Bible from the waist down
and the New Testament is
the Bible from the waist up.
            A. W. Tozer.

BIBLE STUDY

*The man who reads on the sur-
face will live on the surface – and
a superficial Christian is a
pathetic parody of the truth.*

The study of God's Word for
the purpose of discovering
God's will is the secret discipline which has formed the
greatest characters.
            James W. Alexander

It is possible to be full of
Scripture and full of car-
nality.   *Anon.*

There is no substitute for
reading the Bible; it throws a
great deal of light on the
commentaries!   *Anon.*

When the Bible is put on the
shelf the church will surely
follow it.   *Anon.*

We must study the Bible
more. We must not only lay
it up within us, but transfuse
it through the whole texture
of the soul.   *Horatius Bonar*

Reading gives us breadth,
but study gives us depth.
            Jerry Bridges

The source of all our
troubles is in not knowing
the Scriptures.   *Chrysostom*

Bible reading is not an ex-
ceptional thing for the liter-
ate Christian. It is part of his
response to God.
            Oscar Feucht

Lay hold on the Bible until
the Bible lays hold on you.
            Will H. Houghton

Faith is not an achievement, it is a gift. Yet it comes only through the hearing and study of the Word.
Martin Luther

Nothing but faith can comprehend the truth.
Martin Luther

Our first concern will be for the grammatical meaning, for this is the truly theological meaning.
Martin Luther

The Bible was written for a man with a head upon his shoulders. *Martin Luther*

To read without faith is to walk in darkness.
Martin Luther

I am tempted to say that one of the most obvious effects of the new birth should be the restoration of plain common sense in the understanding of the perfectly plain utterances of Holy Scripture.
J. Gresham Machen

I hold that the Bible is essentially a plain book. Common sense is a wonderful help in reading it.
J. Gresham Machen

We should always be chewing and sucking out the sweetness of this cud.
Thomas Manton

No verse of Scripture yields its meaning to lazy people.
A. W. Pink

Nowhere in Scripture is there any promise to the dilatory. *A. W. Pink*

Those who know most of God's testimonies desire to know more.
William S. Plumer

The Christian who is careless in Bible reading is careless in Christian living.
Max Reich

A humble and prayerful spirit will find a thousand things in the Bible which the proud, self-conceited student will utterly fail to discern.
J. C. Ryle

Ignorance of the Scriptures is the root of all error.
J. C. Ryle

We must read our Bibles like men digging for hidden treasure. *J. C. Ryle*

Neglect the Word and you neglect the Lord.
Leith Samuel

Read it to get the facts, study it to get the meaning, meditate on it to get the benefit. *David Shepherd*

Ninety-nine Christians in every hundred are merely playing at Bible study; and therefore ninety-nine Christians in every hundred are merely weaklings when they might be giants.
R. A. Torrey

It is not mere words that nourish the soul, but God himself. *A. W. Tozer*

The Bible was written in tears and to tears it will yield its best treasure. God has nothing to say to the frivolous man. *A. W. Tozer*

Whatever keeps me from my Bible is my enemy, however harmless it may appear to me. *A. W. Tozer*

BIGOTRY

A bigot is either narrow-minded in the best sense or small-minded in the worst.

Bigotry is like the pupil of the eye — the more light you pour into it, the more it contracts.
Oliver Wendell Holmes

BLASPHEMY

There is nothing worse than blasphemy. *Chrysostom*

God himself is out of the sinner's reach, and not capable of receiving any real injury; and therefore enmity to God spits at his name, and shows its ill-will.
Matthew Henry

To pray to saints is idolatry advanced to blasphemy.
Thomas Watson

CHARACTER

Character is more important than life-style.

Everything in life is a test of character.

Character is best revealed by a person's dislikes. *Anon.*

Character, like embroidery, is made stitch by stitch.
Anon.

The mark of a man is how he treats a person who can be of no possible use to him.
Anon.

The pinnacle of a man's greatness is the height of his own character. *Anon.*

33

The two great tests of character are wealth and poverty. *Anon.*

Character is better than ancestry. *Thomas Barnado*

Reputation is sometimes as wide as the horizon when character is the point of a needle. *Henry Ward Beecher*

A man is what he is, not what men say he is. His character no man can touch. His character is what he is before his God and his Judge; and only himself can damage that.
John B. Gough

Character is destiny.
Heraclitus

I have learned by experience that no man's character can be eventually injured but by his own acts. *Rowland Hill*

The test of your character is what you would do if you knew no one would ever know. *Bob Jones*

A man's heart is what he is.
R. B. Kuiper

The conduct of our lives is the true mirror of our doctrine.
Michel de Montaigne

Character tells upon others.
G. Campbell Morgan

No man can climb out beyond the limitations of his own character.
John Morley

Strive to be like a well-regulated watch, of pure gold, with open face, busy hands, and full of good works.
David C. Newquist

Thoughts, even more than overt acts, reveal character.
William S. Plumer

Man makes holy what he believes as he makes beautiful what he loves.
Ernest Renan

Character on earth will prove an everlasting possession in the world to come.
J. C. Ryle

Daylight can be seen through very small holes, so little things will illustrate a person's character.
Samuel Smiles

Not on the stage alone, in the world also, a man's real character comes out best in his asides. *Alexander Smith*

Characters that are really great are always simple.
C. H. Spurgeon

CHARITY

(See also: Generosity; Giving; Kindness)

The river of charity springs from the fountain of piety.
Thomas Adams

He that has no charity deserves no mercy. *Anon.*

In necessary things, unity; in doubtful things, liberty; in all things, charity.
Richard Baxter

We have made the slogan 'Charity begins at home' a part of our religion — although it was invented by a Roman pagan and is directly contrary to the story of the Good Samaritan. Charity begins where the need is greatest and the crisis is most dangerous.
Frank C. Laubach

Christian life consists in faith and charity. *Martin Luther*

Proportion thy charity to the strength of thy estate, lest God proportion thy estate to the weakness of thy charity.
Francis Quarles

There is nothing that the world understands and values more than true charity. *J. C. Ryle*

Charity offers honey to a bee without wings. *John Trapp*

CHASTENING

(See also: Trials)

By chastening, the Lord separates the sin that he hates from the sinner whom he loves. *Anon.*

Heaven often smites in mercy, even when the blow is severest. *Joanna Baillie*

Any chastisement that ever reaches us comes for our profit, that we might be partakers of God's holiness.
Donald Grey Barnhouse

Mercy and punishment, they flow from God, as the honey and the sting from the bee. *Thomas Brooks*

Let us learn like Christians to kiss the rod, and love it.
John Bunyan

All the judgements of God upon his own are for correction.
Lewis Sperry Chafer

God gives gifts that we may love him, and stripes that we may fear him. Yea, oftentimes he mixes frowns with his favours.
George Downame

35

The Lord does not measure out our afflictions according to our faults, but according to our strength, and looks not what we have deserved, but what we are able to bear. *George Downame*

God will go to any lengths to bring us to an acknowledgement of who he is.
Elisabeth Elliot

Fear not the knife that God wields, for his hand is sure.
François Fenelon

The very proof that God loves you is that he does not spare you, but lays upon you the cross of Jesus Christ.
François Fenelon

God dries up the channels, that you may be compelled to plunge into an infinite ocean of happiness.
Robert Hall

God's chastening originates in his love. *Vance Havner*

God delights not in the death of sinners, or the disquiet of the saints, but punishes with a kind of reluctance. *Matthew Henry*

God never afflicts us but when we give him cause to do it. He does not dispense his frowns as he does his favours, from his mere good pleasure. *Matthew Henry*

God warns before he wounds. *Matthew Henry*

Good men, even when God frowns upon them, think well of him.
Matthew Henry

When we are chastened we must pray to be taught, and look into the law as the best expositor of providence. It is not the chastening itself that does good, but the teaching that goes along with it and is the exposition of it.
Matthew Henry

He who hath heard the Word of God can bear his silences. *Ignatius*

Such is the condition of grace, that it shines the brighter for scouring, and is most glorious when it is most clouded. *William Jenkyn*

Chastening is simultaneous wrath and mercy.
R. T. Kendall

There is no chastisement in heaven, nor in hell. Not in heaven, because there is no sin; not in hell, because there is no amendment. Chastisement is a companion of them that are in the way, and of them only. *John Owen*

I thank thee more that all our joy is touched with pain;

That shadows fall on brightest hours, that thorns remain;
So that earth's bliss may be our guide, and not our chain.

For thou, who knowest, Lord, how soon our weak heart clings,
Hast given us joys, tender and true, yet all with wings;
So that we see, gleaming on high, diviner things.
Adelaide Anne Proctor

It is doubtful if God can bless a man greatly without hurting him deeply.
A. W. Tozer

We must lay our hands upon our mouths when God's hand is upon our backs.
John Trapp

The vessels of mercy are first seasoned with affliction, and then the wine of glory is poured in. *Thomas Watson*

CHRISTIAN
(See also: Christianity)

A Christian no longer has a secular life.

Jesus has always had more fans than followers.

A true Christian is both a beggar and an heir. *Anon.*

Faith makes a Christian. Life proves a Christian. Trial confirms a Christian. Death crowns a Christian.
Anon.

It is natural to be religious; it is supernatural to be Christian.
Anon.

We believers ... are the library of Christ's doings ... At present we are a poor edition, but the great Bookbinder has promised to bring out a new edition on indestructible paper and clear type with no errata, imprints of the Son of God, bound in his likeness for ever.
Donald Grey Barnhouse

Believers are not hired servants, supporting themselves by their own work, but children maintained at their Father's expense.
Horatius Bonar

The goal of the new life is that God's children exhibit melody and harmony in their conduct. What melody? The song of God's justice. What harmony? The harmony between God's righteousness and our obedience.
John Calvin

37

A Christian in this world is but gold in the ore; at death, the pure gold is smelted out and separated and the dross cast away and consumed.
John Flavel

The Christian should stand out like a sparkling diamond. *Billy Graham*

The Christian life is the only true adventure.
Wilfred Grenfell

The saints are God's jewels, highly esteemed by and dear to him; they are a royal diadem in his hand.
Matthew Henry

A Christian is one who seeks and enjoys the grace of the Lord Jesus, the love of God and the communion of the Holy Ghost. *Charles Hodge*

He is only a Christian who lives for Christ.
Charles Hodge

The Christian is a part of Christ, a member of his body. *J. B. Lightfoot*

A Christian man is a perfectly free lord of all, subject to none. A Christian man is a perfectly dutiful servant, subject to all.
Martin Luther

Christian life consists in faith and charity. *Martin Luther*

All Christians are saints and he who is not a saint is not a Christian.
Alexander Maclaren

A Christian's life is full of mysteries: poor, and yet rich; base, and yet exalted; shut out of the world, and yet admitted into the company of saints and angels; slighted, yet dear to God; the world's dirt, and God's jewels.
Thomas Manton

Every Christian is born great because he is born for heaven.
Jean Baptiste Massillon

A Christian is the world's Bible — and some of them need revising.
D. L. Moody

What God did in Christ's crucifixion and resurrection holds true of every believer. He is crucified, dead, buried, risen and ascended with Christ, and his life is hidden with Christ in God.
Klaas Runia

Saints on earth are not perfect angels, but only converted sinners. *J. C. Ryle*

The true Christian is in all countries a pilgrim and a stranger. *George Santayana*

The meaning of the word 'Christian' has been reduced to practically nothing. Surely, there is no word that has been so devalued unless it is the word 'God' itself. *Francis Schaeffer*

A Christian is not his own man. *Richard Sibbes*

A Christian is, in essence, somebody personally related to Jesus Christ. *John R. W. Stott*

Whatever makes men good Christians makes them good citizens. *Daniel Webster*

What distinguishes the Christian is not that he practises religion but that he is in Christ. *Douglas Webster*

CHRISTIANITY — Characteristics

In true Christianity, there are no short-term commitments and no escape clauses.

Christianity is not about how to escape from the difficulties of life, but about how to face them. *Brian Edwards*

It is unnatural for Christianity to be popular. *Billy Graham*

The supernatural is the native air of Christianity. *Dora Greenwell*

According to the Bible, Christianity is a matter of history, a matter of doctrine and a matter of conduct. *R. B. Kuiper*

To strip Christianity of the supernatural is to destroy Christianity. *R. B. Kuiper*

Christianity starts with repentance. *D. Martyn Lloyd-Jones*

Christianity is not engrossed by this transitory world, but measures all things by the thought of eternity. *J. Gresham Machen*

Christianity is essentially and fundamentally a sinner's religion. *Al Martin*

In Christianity, creed has always to do with Christ. *G. Campbell Morgan*

Supernatural living through supernatural empowering is at the very heart of New Testament Christianity. *J. I. Packer*

We may call the doctrine of the Christian faith exhilarating or we may call it devastating. We may call it revelation or we may call it rubbish. But if we call it dull, words simply have no meaning.   *Dorothy L. Sayers*

Christianity is summed up in the two facts: Christ *for* us and Christ *in* us.
Augustus H. Strong

A godly life is always the best advertisement for Christianity.   *Geoffrey B. Wilson*

CHRISTIANITY — Definition

Christianity can be expressed in three sentences: I deserve hell. Jesus Christ took my hell. There is nothing left for me but his heaven.   *Anon.*

Religion is man's search for God. Christianity is God's search for man.   *Anon.*

Christianity is the land of beginning again.
W. A. Criswell

Christianity is a rescue religion.   *Michael Green*

Christianity is the story of how the rightful King has landed, you might say landed in disguise, and is calling us all to take part in a great campaign of sabotage.
C. S. Lewis

Christianity is not a way of life as distinguished from a doctrine, nor a way of life expressing itself in a doctrine, but a way of life founded upon a doctrine.
J. Gresham Machen

There must be many serious-minded believers who, as they look at what is often portrayed as Christianity today, wonder if it pertains to the same God in whom we ourselves profess to believe.
John J. Murray

Christianity is not the acceptance of certain ideas. It is a personal attitude of trust and devotion to a person.   *Stephen Neill*

Christian doctrine is grace, and Christian conduct is gratitude.   *J. I. Packer*

CHRISTIANITY — Uniqueness

The glory of Christianity is to conquer by forgiveness.
William Blake

Christianity is not a mere development of the ancient world, but a new and supernatural beginning.
Jonathan Edwards

You won't get rid of your difficulties by putting away Christianity, because they will come up under philosophy. *A. A. Hodge*

Where idolatry ends, there Christianity begins; and where idolatry begins, there Christianity ends.
Friedrich H. Jacobi

Christianity has the only true God; all other gods are idols. Christianity has the only true Saviour; every other saviour so called leaves and leads men to destruction. *R. B. Kuiper*

Christianity has the only true morality; no other religion conduces to true holiness. *R. B. Kuiper*

I believe in Christianity as I believe in the sun — not only because I see it, but because by it I see everything else. *C. S. Lewis*

The life of Christianity consists in possessive pronouns.
Martin Luther

Christianity knows nothing of hopeless cases. It professes its ability to take the most crooked stick and bring it straight, to flash a new power into the blackest carbon, which will turn it into a diamond.
Alexander Maclaren

In the Christian religion all moral duties are advanced and heightened to their greatest perfection.
Thomas Manton

The uniqueness of Christianity is in Jesus Christ.
John Mbiti

The primary emphasis of biblical Christianity is the teaching that the infinite-personal God is the ultimate reality, the Creator of all else, and that an individual can come openly to the holy God upon the basis of the finished work of Christ and that alone.
Francis Schaeffer

Christianity is beyond religion. *Robert Scott*

Christianity is in its very essence a resurrection religion. The concept of resurrection lies at its heart. If you remove it, Christianity is destroyed.
John R. W. Stott

Christianity without Christ is a chest without a treasure,

a frame without a portrait, a corpse without breath.
John R. W. Stott

Union with Christ is a unique emphasis among the world's religions.
John R. W. Stott

Christianity did not begin in a school of philosophy or a mystical conception or an ideological panacea, but with a group of very ordinary men who came into vital contact with the person of Jesus Christ.
Frederick P. Wood

CHRISTLIKENESS

(See also: Godliness; Holiness)

To be much like Christ, be much with Christ. *Anon.*

We are not merely to serve Christ, we are to be like him.
Derek Copley

Even when we can cite chapter and verse for creation, corruption, predestination, election, vocation, regeneration, justification, adoption, sanctification and glorification, the test of discipleship remains incomplete; we must still deal with the crucial question of our likeness to the Master who is gentle and humble in heart.
Mariano Di Gangi

The fear of the Lord was a lovely grace in the perfect humanity of Jesus. Let it be the test of our 'predestination to be conformed to his image'. *Sinclair Ferguson*

All our salvation consists in the manifestation of the nature, life and Spirit of Jesus in our inward new man. *William Law*

To gain entire likeness to Christ, I ought to get a high esteem of the happiness of it.
Robert Murray M'Cheyne

We are never more like Christ than in prayers of intercession. *Austin Phelps*

To be like Christ in any measure is grace; to be like him in perfection is glory.
William S. Plumer

However holy or Christlike a Christian may become, he is still in the condition of 'being changed'.
John R. W. Stott

If we had to sum up in a single brief sentence what life is all about, why Jesus Christ came into this world to live and die and rise, and what God is up to in the long-drawn-out historical process both BC and AD, it would be difficult to find a more succinct explanation than this: God is making human beings more human by making them more like Christ.   *John R. W. Stott*

No Christian is where he ought to be spiritually until the beauty of the Lord Jesus Christ is being reproduced in daily Christian life.
                    A. W. Tozer

Holiness is not the laborious acquisition of virtue from without, but the expression of the Christ-life from within.   *J. W. C. Wand*

CHURCH — Attendance and Membership

No local church is perfect - but there is no way in which it can be improved by the absence of spiritually-minded Christians.

There is no place for any loose stone in God's edifice.
                    Joseph Hall

How lovely is the sanctuary in the eyes of those who are truly sanctified!
                    Matthew Henry

The church is the only institution in the world that has lower entrance requirements than those for getting on a bus.   *William Laroe*

The Christian church is the only society in the world in which membership is based upon the qualification that the candidate shall be unworthy of membership.
                    Charles Clayton Morrison

The church of Christ needs servants of all kinds, and instruments of every sort; penknives as well as swords, axes as well as hammers, chisels as well as saws, Marthas as well as Marys, Peters as well as Johns.
                    J. C. Ryle

Stating it in just about the most simple terms we know, the Christian church is the assembly of redeemed saints.
                    A. W. Tozer

There is nothing more unchristian than a solitary Christian.   *John Wesley*

No new Christian is born in a vacuum. He is delivered into the fellowship of the church. He is baptized by the one Spirit into the body of Christ. He joins the society of the saints.
                    Arthur Skevington Wood

CHURCH — Blemishes

Some churches' programmes are so full their members have no time left to be Christians.

It is a poor worship to move our hats, not our hearts.
Thomas Adams

The pastor cannot lead unless the people get behind him. *Anon.*

The idea of a church in politics can come only from that false postulate that the purpose of the church is to save the world.
Donald Grey Barnhouse

The greatest sin of the church is that she withholds the gospel from herself and the world. *Emil Brunner*

The average church is often like a congested lung with only a few cells doing the breathing. *A. J. Gordon*

From the days of Constantine to this hour Christianity fares badly when the world takes the church under its patronizing wing. I am not impressed by the smiling sponsorship of this age.
Vance Havner

It would be frightening to know how little of our church activity is the spontaneous expression of our love for Christ.
Vance Havner

Many a Christian, many a church, has everything on the showcase and nothing on the shelves. *Vance Havner*

The church can do many things after she repents, but she can do nothing else *until* she repents. *Vance Havner*

When recreation gets ahead of re-creation, then God's house has become a den of thieves. *Vance Havner*

The more exalted pomp there be of men's devising, there will be the less spiritual truth. *George Hutcheson*

Many Christians are so busy they can only hear the click and clatter of church machinery.
Walter B. Knight

If the church were strong and active, as it ought to be, the world would oppose it much more vigorously.
R. B. Kuiper

Middle-of-the-road pacifism in significant doctrinal controversy has ruined many a church. *R. B. Kuiper*

The problem of the church today is not that the gospel

has lost its power but that the church has lost its audience. *Paul Little*

Depend upon it, as long as the church is living so much like the world, we cannot expect our children to be brought into the fold.
D. L. Moody

One of Satan's methods today is to start so many organizations in a church that the members have no time for communion with God. *G. Campbell Morgan*

The church must never beg for money as if this were the secret of her strength.
Andrew Murray

The early church was not wrecked on the rocks of mere activism; nor did it sink in the quicksands of blasphemous idleness. *Stuart Olyott*

The average church knows more about promotion than prayer. *Leonard Ravenhill*

Neither a church conformed to the world, nor a church ignorant of the world can fulfil her mission in the world. *Ernst Schrupp*

That in some parts of the world the church as the new community is more a dream than a reality is a disgrace

with which sensitive Christians must never come to terms. *John R. W. Stott*

Are we just holding on to the painted mane of the painted horse, repeating a trip of very insignificant circles to a pleasing musical accompaniment? *A. W. Tozer*

Much church work and activity is thrown back upon a shaky foundation of psychology and natural talents. *A. W. Tozer*

My observations have led me to the belief that many, perhaps most, of the activities engaged in by the average church do not contribute in any way to the accomplishing of the true work of Christ on earth. I hope I am wrong, but I am afraid I am right.
A. W. Tozer

CHURCH — and Christ

The church is a community of the works and words of Jesus. *Donald English*

As the church endures hardness and humiliation as united to him who was on the cross, so she should exhibit something of supernatural energy as united with him who is on the throne.   *A. J. Gordon*

The church is taken out of dying Jesus' side, as Eve out of sleeping Adam's.
           William Gurnall

The church comes out of Christ's side in the sleep of his death.   *William Jenkyn*

The church is the fruit of the gospel.   *Hywel R. Jones*

No aspect of Christ's relationship to the church looms larger in Holy Writ than the fact that he is its Head.   *R. B. Kuiper*

The church was originated not only by Christ, but also from him, and cannot continue to exist for even a moment apart from him.
           R. B. Kuiper

The church's one foundation
Is Jesus Christ her Lord;
She is his new creation
By water and the Word;
From heaven he came and
    sought her
To be his holy bride;
With his own blood he
    bought her,
And for her life he died.
           Samuel John Stone

CHURCH — Divisions

Better a holy discord than a profane concord.
           Thomas Adams

It is better to have divisions than an evil uniformity.
           Walter Cradock

In the great things of religion, be of a mind: but when there is not a unity of sentiment, let there be a union of affections.
           Matthew Henry

Division is better than agreement in evil.
           George Hutcheson

The division of Christians is the sin of fratricide.
           J. A. Motyer

It is a fearful sin to make a rent and a hole in Christ's mystical body because there is a spot in it.
           Samuel Rutherford

CHURCH — Duties

The aim of having a church is to reach the rest of the world.   *Donald English*

The church is meant to be a working model of what God wants to do with the rest of society.   *Donald English*

The business of the church is
to demonstrate God.
Vance Havner

How blessed a constitution
were the Christian church if
all the members did their
duty! *Matthew Henry*

It is the church's task to turn
adherents to the church into
possessors of Christ.
Kenneth Kirk

God never intended his
church to be a refrigerator in
which to preserve perishable
piety. He intended it to be
an incubator in which to
hatch out converts.
F. Lincicome

If a church does not evangelize it will fossilize.
A. W. Pink

Church greatness consists in
being greatly serviceable.
J. C. Ryle

CHURCH — Fellowship

The church of Jesus Christ is
not a building where people
come together for a religious
service, but it is a gathering
of people who come together
in order to worship God and
to build each other by
mutual faith and strength.
Donald Grey Barnhouse

There are no insignificant
members in the church.
Herbert M. Carson

In public worship all should
join. The little strings go to
make up a concert, as well as
the great. *Thomas Goodwin*

As those who are grown
Christians must be willing to
hear the plainest truths
preached for the sake of the
weak, so the weak must be
willing to hear the more
difficult and mysterious
truths preached for the sake
of those who are strong.
Matthew Henry

When we take God for our
God, we take his people for
our people. *Matthew Henry*

Our Lord has many weak
children in his family, many
dull pupils in his school,
many raw soldiers in his
army, many lame sheep in
his flock. Yet he bears with
them all, and casts none
away. Happy is that Christian who has learned to do
likewise with his brethren.
J. C. Ryle

We should always regard
communion with other
believers as an eminent
means of grace. *J. C. Ryle*

The secret of good relationships in the Christian com-

munity is the recognition that Jesus Christ is Lord and that Christians live 'unto him'. *John R. W. Stott*

Christians in concert are an abridgement of heaven, shining like a firmament of bright stars.
George Swinnock

There is no room in the church for any intellectual, spiritual or social élite which separates itself from fellow-believers whom Christ has accepted.
Geoffrey B. Wilson

CHURCH — Glory

The excellence of the church does not consist in multitude but in purity. *John Calvin*

As the beauty of the human body is brought out by the variety of its parts, so the glory of the body of Christ appears in the diversity of its members. *R. B. Kuiper*

In the counsel of God the church existed even before the creation of man.
R. B. Kuiper

The Christian church is glorious in its very nature.
R. B. Kuiper

The glory of the greatest, wealthiest, most powerful and most resplendent empire of all history was as nothing, yes less than nothing, in comparison with the glory of the church of Christ.
R. B. Kuiper

The true Christian church is the work of the Word communicated by every available means. *Martin Luther*

The highest expression of the will of God in this age is the church which he purchased with his own blood.
A. W. Tozer

There are no little churches; all churches are the same size in God's sight.
A. W. Tozer

CHURCH — Oneness

The church and the churches are not the same.
Donald Grey Barnhouse

The church is not a great community made up of an accumulation of small communities, but is truly present in its wholeness in every company of believers, however small. *K. L. Schmidt*

CHURCH — Power

The one reaction the Christian church ought never to produce in the community is indifference.

The past has not exhausted the possibilities nor the demands for doing great things for God. The church that is dependent on its past history for its miracles of power and grace is a fallen church.   *E. M. Bounds*

There ought to be enough electricity in every church service to give everybody in the congregation either a charge or a shock!
Vance Havner

The church is still to be reckoned with.
A. W. Tozer

CHURCH — Security in God's purposes

When men are projecting the church's ruin God is preparing for its salvation.
Matthew Henry

The church of God is a nation without any capital on earth.
G. Campbell Morgan

The household of Abraham is the prototype of the church of God. The promise which accrued to him is the secret of the maintenance of the church.
Herman N. Ridderbos

No history ought to receive so much of our attention as the past and present history of the church of Christ. The rise and fall of worldly empires are events of comparatively small importance in the sight of God.
J. C. Ryle

CHURCH UNITY

To strive without sacrifice of truth for the visible unity of the body of Christ is to enhance its glory.
R. B. Kuiper

Unity is of the essence of the body of Christ.
R. B. Kuiper

We cannot expect the world to believe that the Father sent the Son, that Jesus' claims are true and that Christianity is true, unless the world sees some reality of the oneness of true Christians.   *Francis Schaeffer*

Unity in Christ is not something to be achieved: it is something to be recognized.
A. W. Tozer

CIRCUMSTANCES

*No Christian should feel 'under'
the circumstances, because the
circumstances are under God.*

God doesn't want to keep
changing your circum-
stances; he wants to change
you.   *J. Sidlow Baxter*

CLOTHING

Clothes are the ensigns of
our sin and covers of our
shame. To be proud of them
is as great a folly as for a
beggar to be proud of his
rags or a thief of his halter.
John Trapp

As to matters of dress, I
would recommend one
never to be first in the
fashion nor the last out of it.
John Wesley

COMMUNION WITH CHRIST

(See also: Communion with God;
Love for Christ; Meditation;
Prayer)

To be much like Christ, be
much with Christ.   *Anon.*

My soul's cry is still for more
acquaintance with the Lord
Jesus, and the Father in him.
Andrew Bonar

50

Holiness is not a merit by
which we can attain com-
munion with God, but a gift
of Christ, which enables us
to cling to him and to follow
him.   *John Calvin*

No one has any communion
with Christ but he who has
received the true knowledge
of him from the word of the
gospel.   *John Calvin*

The power to live a new life
depends upon daily com-
munion with the living
Lord.   *John Eadie*

Concentration on Christ is
not primarily a matter of the
intellect, but rather a matter
of the condition of the heart.
Sinclair Ferguson

A test of Christian devotion
is the extent to which, in
happiness as well as in
sorrow, we think of Jesus.
Frank Gabelein

It is tragic to go through our
days making Christ the subject of our study but not the
sustenance of our souls.
Vance Havner

The supreme experience is
to get past all lesser experiences to Christ himself.
Vance Havner

I thirst for the knowledge of
the Word, but most of all for

Jesus himself, the true Word.
Robert Murray M'Cheyne

It is good to be among the twelve, but it is far better to be among the three.
Robert Murray M'Cheyne

The more a person is satisfied with Christ, the more he will find his satisfaction in satisfying him.
J. A. Motyer

By union with Christ the whole complexion of time and eternity is changed and the people of God may rejoice with joy unspeakable and full of glory.
John Murray

Living is sustained by feeding. We must support the spiritual life by spiritual food, and that spiritual food is the Lord Jesus.
C. H. Spurgeon

Union with Christ is a unique emphasis among the world's religions.
John R. W. Stott

COMMUNION WITH GOD

(See also: Communion with Christ; Love for God; Meditation; Prayer)

It is impossible to be too preoccupied with God, and it is only as we fill our hearts and minds with him that we become melted out of our likeness and moulded into his.

Nothing promotes the activity of the devil more than the Christian's proximity to God.

The life rooted in God cannot be uprooted. *Anon.*

To walk with God you must walk in the direction in which God goes. *Anon.*

God is the country of the soul. *Augustine*

The Christian has to live in the world, but he must draw all his resources from outside of the world.
Donald Grey Barnhouse

The Christian must fight to be alone with God and to keep time for knowing God.
Donald Grey Barnhouse

Our ability to stay with God in our closet measures our ability to stay with God out of the closet. *E. M. Bounds*

I would rather walk with God in the dark than go alone in the light.
Mary Gardiner Brainard

We must learn to spend quality time with God.
Derek Copley

None reverence the Lord more than they who know him best.   *William Cowper*

I count all that part of my life lost which I spent not in communion with God or in doing good.   *John Donne*

How rare it is to find a soul quiet enough to hear God speak!   *François Fenelon*

Count not that thou hast lived that day in which thou hast not lived with God.
  Richard Fuller

One man with a glowing experience of God is worth a library full of arguments.
  Vance Havner

The man who lives in God is never out of season.
  Vance Havner

We must live a life of communion with God, even while our conversation is with the world.
  Matthew Henry

Whenever we enter into communion with God it becomes us to have a due sense of the vast distance and disproportion that there are between us and the holy angels, and of the infinite distance, and no proportion at all, between us and the holy God.   *Matthew Henry*

Did you ever lose by communion with God? . . . How quietly we enjoy ourselves when we have enjoyed our God!   *Thomas Manton*

Live near to God and all things will appear little to you in comparison with eternal realities.
  Robert Murray M'Cheyne

Oh for closest communion with God, till soul and body — hand, face and heart — shine with divine brilliancy! But oh for a holy ignorance of our shining!
  Robert Murray M'Cheyne

We may lay it down as an elemental principle of religion that no large growth in holiness was ever gained by one who did not take time to be often long alone with God.   *Austin Phelps*

Trees which stand on top of a cliff need to send their roots deep.   *Ivor Powell*

Dwell deep in the hidden life of God. The cedar grows more beneath the ground than above it.
  A. B. Simpson

The nearer we come to God, the more graciously will he reveal himself to us.
  C. H. Spurgeon

Communion with God is one thing; familiarity with God is quite another thing.
A. W. Tozer

God being who he is must always be sought for himself, never as a means towards something else.
A. W. Tozer

In God's presence the Christian feels overwhelmed and undone, yet there is nowhere he would rather be than in that presence.
A. W. Tozer

The Christian is strong or weak depending upon how closely he has cultivated the knowledge of God.
A. W. Tozer

The fellowship of God is delightful beyond all telling.
A. W. Tozer

The intercourse between God and the soul is known to us in conscious personal awareness. *A. W. Tozer*

We are called to an everlasting preoccupation with God.
A. W. Tozer

Talk with us, Lord, thyself reveal,
While here on earth we rove;
Speak to our hearts, and let us feel
The kindling of thy love.
Charles Wesley

The more familiar a man becomes with the meeting of God face to face the less likely he is to be deceived as to the gulf which parts him, limited, finite, defective, from the Infinite and Perfect.
Newport J. D. White

How much better I might serve God if I had cultivated a closer communion with him! *William Wilberforce*

COMMUNISM

The Communists offer one precious, fatal boon: they take away the sense of sin.
Murray Kempton

Communism is the corruption of a dream of justice.
Adlai Stevenson

COMPLACENCY
(See also: Apathy)

A Christian never falls asleep in the fire or in the water, but grows drowsy in the sunshine.
John Berridge

He that is too secure is not safe. *Thomas Fuller*

53

Complacency

He who accepts evil without protesting against it is really co-operating with it.
Martin Luther King

God's greatest curse out of hell is to allow an unsaved soul to be at peace.
Brownlow North

Keep me, Lord, from ever hardening down into the state of being just another average Christian.
A. W. Tozer

Spiritual complacency is more deadly than anything the devil can bring against us in our upward struggle.
A. W. Tozer

When I find someone who is settled down too snugly into this world and its system, I am forced to doubt whether he has ever truly been born again.
A. W. Tozer

COMPROMISE

If you are holding something back from God, then God is holding something back from you.

It is not lawful for you to make a compromise with God: to try to fulfil part of your duties, and to omit others at your own pleasure.
John Calvin

Some people want to be vaccinated with a mild dose of Christianity so as to be protected from the real thing.
William Culbertson

Compromise is but the sacrifice of one right or good in the hope of retaining another — too often ending in the loss of both.
Tryon Edwards

Conformity is the ape of harmony.
Ralph Waldo Emerson

To withhold one thing from God is theft, for everything is his.
Vance Havner

We must eternally bid defiance to that peace with men which is inconsistent with peace with God.
John Owen

Accommodation leads to accommodation — which leads to accommodation . . .
Francis Schaeffer

To accommodate to the world spirit about us in our age is nothing less than the most gross form of worldliness in the proper definition of that word.
Francis Schaeffer

You cannot compromise a proposition with God.
Billy Sunday

Anything that takes God's place is out of place.
Abe Van der Puy

CONCEIT
(See also: Pride)

The smaller the mind the greater the conceit. *Aesop*

Self-conceit is a magnifying glass through which we look at ourselves; we seem much bigger than we are. Plain window glass is better. *Anon.*

The best remedy for conceit is to sit down and make a list of all the things you don't know. *Anon.*

Conceited men are a harmless kind of creatures, who, by their overweening self-respect, relieve others from the duty of respecting them at all. *Henry Ward Beecher*

Conceit is vanity driven from all other shifts, and forced to appeal to itself for admiration. *William Hazlitt*

It is wonderful how near conceit is to insanity!
Douglas Jerrold

He who gives himself airs of importance, exhibits the credentials of impotence.
John C. Lavater

CONFESSION
(See also: Contrition; Conviction of Sin; Penitence; Repentance)

Confession must be salted with contrition. *Anon.*

The confession of evil works is the first beginning of good works. *Augustine*

Confession is the first step to repentance. *Edmund Gayton*

Little credit is to be given to confessions upon the rack.
Matthew Henry

The recognition of sin is the beginning of salvation.
Martin Luther

Wounds cannot be healed until they are revealed and sins cannot be forgiven until they are confessed.
Martin Luther

Confession is, as it were, the vomit of the soul.
Thomas Manton

Many blush to confess their faults who never blush to commit them.
William Secker

Confession is verbal humiliation. *Richard Sibbes*

You can pray till doomsday for revival, but you will never get it without repentance and confession of sin in the Christian life.

Erlo Stegan

Confession of our faults is the next thing to innocence.

Publilius Syrus

CONSCIENCE — and God

Man's conscience is the oracle of God.

George G. N. Byron

Conscience is God's deputy, and must in the exercise of this office confine itself to the orders and instructions of the sovereign Lord.

D. Clarkson

Conscience is God's sergeant. He employs it to arrest the sinner.

William Gurnall

Nothing can take off conscience from accusing but that which takes off God from threatening.

William Gurnall

A Christian's enlightened conscience is his sense of obligation to God.

William Hendriksen

There is a conscience in man, therefore there is a God in heaven.

Ezekiel Hopkins

Two things strike me with awe: the starry heavens above and the moral law within.   *Immanuel Kant*

Conscience holds us acountable to God. Drop the idea of God and the vitality of conscience is destroyed. Mere abstract ideas of 'right' and 'wrong' do not bind the conscience; the idea of God and judgement does.

R. C. H. Lenski

Conscience is not an original authority. It points to something higher than itself.

Augustus H. Strong

Conscience, the domestic chaplain.   *John Trapp*

CONSCIENCE — Importance

The glory of good men is in their conscience, and not in the mouths of men.

Thomas à Kempis

The testimony of a good conscience is the glory of a good man.

Thomas à Kempis

A quiet conscience sleeps in thunder.   *Anon.*

The best tranquillizer is a clear conscience.   *Anon.*

When a man won't listen to his conscience, it may be because he doesn't want advice from a total stranger. *Anon.*

When you have only one thing on your conscience, it is probably a silencer. *Anon.*

Conscience is the root of all true courage; if a man would be brave let him obey his conscience. *J. F. Clarke*

Religion's home is in the conscience. *T. L. Cuyler*

A quiet conscience never produced an unquiet conversation. *John Flavel*

A good conscience is the best divinity. *Thomas Fuller*

If faith be a jewel, a good conscience is the cabinet in which it is kept. *William Gurnall*

The pen with which conscience writes down our sins hath a sharp nib. *William Gurnall*

A dull conscience leads only to half-way reconciliations with God. *Ole Hallesby*

That man can never have good days that keeps an evil conscience. *Benjamin Keach*

My prison shall be my grave before I will budge a jot, for I owe my conscience to no mortal man. Right is right, even if everyone is against it; and wrong is wrong, even if everyone is for it. *William Penn*

No man's conscience is to be a judge for another. *C. H. Spurgeon*

Even when there is no law, there is conscience. *Publilius Syrus*

Conscience is that inner voice that keeps speaking within our beings — and it deserves something better from us than wisecracks and humour. *A. W. Tozer*

A pure conscience is the home of faith. *A. Paget Wilkes*

CONSCIENCE — Power

A wounded conscience is able to un-paradise paradise itself. *Thomas Fuller*

Faith and good conscience are hope's two wings. *William Gurnall*

CONSCIENCE — and Sin

Quite often when a man thinks his mind is getting broader it is only his conscience stretching. *Anon.*

A seared conscience is the sinner's heritage.
Horatius Bonar

What we call conscience is, in many instances, only a wholesome fear of the constable. *Christian Bovee*

Conscience alone has witnessed sufficiently to the moral law, so that every man is 'without excuse'.
Walter J. Chantry

Most of us follow our conscience as we follow a wheelbarrow. We push it in front of us in the direction we want to go. *Billy Graham*

No torment in the world is comparable to an accusing conscience.
William Gurnall

We must never be over-awed either by majesty or multitude to do a sinful thing and go against our consciences.
Matthew Henry

The most painful wound in the world is a stab of conscience. *John Ellis Large*

Nothing can give perfect peace of conscience with God but what can make atonement for sin. And whoever attempt it in any other way but by virtue of that atonement will never attain it, in this world or hereafter.
John Owen

Never, on any account whatever, let us do that which our conscience cannot justify. *C. H. Spurgeon*

Though consciences have to be educated, they are never to be violated, even when they are wrong.
John R. W. Stott

Some serve their consciences as David did Uriah; make it drunk that they may be rid of it. *George Swinnock*

An evil conscience is often quiet, but never secure.
Publilius Syrus

Conscience never lets you lean on someone else.
A. W. Tozer

One small drop of an evil conscience troubles a whole sea of outward comforts.
John Trapp

CONSECRATION

(See also: Abandonment; Submission; Zeal)

Rid me, good Lord, of every diverting thing.
Amy Carmichael

Consecration is not so much a step as a course, not so much an act as a position to which a course of action inseparably belongs.
Frances Ridley Havergal

If religion be worth anything it is worth everything.
Matthew Henry

Consecration isn't our giving anything to God. It is our taking our hands off what already belongs to God.
Walter B. Knight

CONTEMPT

Contempt leaves a deeper scar than anger. *Anon.*

Christ saw much in this world to weep over, and much to pray over, but he saw nothing in it to look upon with contempt.
E. H. Chaplin

CONTENTMENT

A contented spirit is a fruit of divine grace.
George Barlow

To be content with one's possessions is one of the most strongly worded exhortations in Scripture.
Jerry Bridges

Better a little fire to warm us than a great one to burn us.
Thomas Fuller

That condition of life is best for every man which is best for his soul, and keeps him most clear of the cares and snares of the world.
Matthew Henry

Contentment is natural wealth; luxury is artificial poverty. *Socrates*

CONTRITION

(See also: Confession; Conviction of Sin; Penitence; Repentance)

The only things that are improved by breaking are the hearts of sinners. *Anon.*

Sorrow for sin as long as you have sin to sorrow for.
Anon.

There is no progress possible to the man who does not see

and mourn over his defects.
George Barlow

He grieves truly that weeps without a witness.
George Swinnock

CONTROVERSY

The devil falls in when saints fall out. *Anon.*

There are some controversies prickly like brambles, and apt to scratch those that handle them, but yielding no savoury or wholesome fruit. *Isaac Barrow*

Religious contention is the devil's harvest.
Charles Fontaine

The devil's master stroke is that of dividing forces that ought to stand together.
G. Campbell Morgan

Nothing does so much harm to the cause of religion as the quarrels of Christians.
J. C. Ryle

Beware of the habits we learn in controversy.
Francis Schaeffer

Contention is sooner stirred than stinted. *John Trapp*

Divisions are Satan's powder-plot, to blow up religion.
Thomas Watson

CONVERSION
(See also: Faith — Saving; Regeneration; Repentance)

If a person claims to be converted, we are entitled to ask two questions: 'From what?' and 'Into what?'

Conversion is a deep work – a heart-work. It goes throughout the man, throughout the mind, throughout the members, throughout the entire life. *Joseph Alleine*

Conversion is no repairing of the old building; but it takes all down and erects a new structure. *Joseph Alleine*

If a man is as passionate, malicious, resentful, sullen, moody or morose after his conversion as before it, what is he converted from or to?
John Angell James

True conversion is the heart turning from Satan's control to God's, from sin to holiness, from the world to Christ. *A. W. Pink*

The surest mark of true conversion is humility.
J. C. Ryle

We are not truly converted if we are not intellectually and morally converted, and we are not intellectually and morally converted if we have not subjected our minds and our wills to the yoke of Jesus Christ.   *John R. W. Stott*

Conversion for the early New Testament Christians was not a destination; it was the beginning of a journey.
      A. W. Tozer

Before Christ, a man loves things and uses people; after Christ he loves people and uses things.   *Horace Wood*

CONVICTION OF SIN

(See also: Confession; Contrition; Penitence; Repentance)

The greater our view of Christ, the greater our view of sin.

The worst sinners are sometimes those who feel the least sinful.   *Anon.*

There is precious instruction to be got by finding we were wrong.   *Thomas Carlyle*

No man can ever enter heaven until he is first convinced he deserves hell.
      John W. Everett

Men must see sin to be sin and themselves to be sinners before they will want a Saviour.   *Vance Havner*

Christ will be sweet to us if sin be bitter.
      Matthew Henry

Conviction of sin is an indispensable prerequisite of faith in Christ.   *R. B. Kuiper*

When one is born of the Spirit one does not suddenly become perfect or even nearly so. Rather, one becomes exceedingly sinful in one's own estimation. That is to say, one comes under conviction of sin.
      R. B. Kuiper

Rightly to feel sin is the torture of all tortures.
      Martin Luther

The consciousness of sin alone leads men to turn to the Saviour from sin, and the consciousness of sin comes only when men are brought face to face with the law of God.
      J. Gresham Machen

The real prelude to a conviction of sin is the conviction of God's holiness.
      Douglas Macmillan

A full conviction of sin is a great and shaking surprisal unto a guilty soul.

John Owen

Until men know themselves better, they will care very little to know Christ at all.

John Owen

To be sensible of our corruption and abhor our own transgressions is the first symptom of spiritual health.

J. C. Ryle

We must know the depth and malignancy of our disease in order to appreciate the Great Physician.

J. C. Ryle

The very first and indispensable sign of regeneration is self-loathing and abhorrence.

Charles Simeon

They tell me I rub the fur the wrong way. I don't. Let the cat turn around!

Billy Sunday

No man shall be in heaven but he that sees himself fully qualified for hell, as a faggot that is bound up for eternal burnings unless mercy plucks the brand out of the fire.

Robert Traill

It is part of our worthiness to see our unworthiness.

Thomas Watson

COURAGE

Show when you are tempted to hide, and hide when you are tempted to show.

A. B. Bruce

One man with courage makes a majority.

Andrew Jackson

COURTESY

Courtesy is a Christian duty, fully consistent with the exercise of Christian faithfulness.

Charles Bridges

Life is short, but there is always time for courtesy.

Ralph Waldo Emerson

All doors open to courtesy.

Thomas Fuller

Sanctity is no enemy to courtesy.

John Trapp

COVENANT

The covenant is an expression of God's will, not man's, and man must listen to its terms, trust God that they are holy and just and good, and order his life accordingly.

J. Gresham Machen

As we are under the covenant of grace, we are secured against departing from the living God by the sure declaration of the covenant.
C. H. Spurgeon

Faith always sees the bow of covenant promise whenever sense sees the cloud of affliction.   *C. H. Spurgeon*

The covenant is a rocky foundation to build on for life or for death.
C. H. Spurgeon

COVETOUSNESS
(See also: Gluttony; Greed)

Wealth is the devil's stirrup whereby he gets up and rides the covetous.
Thomas Adams

Seeking empties a life; giving fills it.   *Anon.*

Covetousness is a sin that comes earliest into the human heart, and is the last and most difficult to be driven out.   *George Barlow*

Faith is the sovereign antidote to covetousness.
John Calvin

When all sins are old in us and go upon crutches, covetousness does but then lie in her cradle.   *Thomas Decker*

Riches have made more covetous men than covetousness has made rich men.
Thomas Fuller

Covetousness is commonly a master-sin and has the command of other lusts.
Matthew Henry

Covetousness is spiritual idolatry; it is the giving of that love and regard to worldly wealth which are due to God only.
Matthew Henry

Poor people are as much in danger from an inordinate desire towards the wealth of the world as rich people from an inordinate delight in it.   *Matthew Henry*

The covetous man sits hatching upon his wealth and brooding over it, till it is fledged, as the young ones under the hen, and then it is gone.   *Matthew Henry*

Covetousness swallows down any lie.   *William Jenkyn*

There are two sins which were Christ's sorest enemies, covetousness and envy. Covetousness sold Christ and envy delivered him.
Thomas Manton

We may love money without having it, just as we may

63

have money without loving it.   *J. C. Ryle*

We need not covet money, for we shall always have our God, and God is better than gold, his favour is better than fortune.
                 C. H. Spurgeon

Covetous men, though they have enough to sink them, yet have they never enough to satisfy them.
                 John Trapp

A man may be said to be given to covetousness when he takes more pains for getting earth than for getting heaven.   *Thomas Watson*

COWARDICE

Many would be cowards if they had courage enough.
                 Thomas Fuller

It is a significant fact that the Bible gives no record of a coward ever being cured of his malady.   *A. W. Tozer*

CREATION
(See also: Evolution; Nature)

Whether special creation is endorsed by every scientist in the world or rejected by all of them is
of monumental irrelevance. The Christian says God created the world because the Bible says so.

The Eternal Word stood in the same relation to the created universe as the incarnate Christ to the church.   *T. K. Abbott*

In God's works we see his hand, but in his Word we see his face.   *Anon.*

Two things strike me with awe: the starry heavens above and the moral law within.   *Immanuel Kant*

Everything above us speaks of the greatness of God, not of man.   *William S. Plumer*

Creation is the setting forth of Jesus Christ as Lord and Sovereign.   *A. W. Tozer*

The problems of origin and destiny have escaped the philosopher and the scientist, but the humblest follower of Christ knows the answer to both.
                 A. W. Tozer

We may see God's glory blazing in the sun and twinkling in the stars.
                 Thomas Watson

CRITICISM BY OTHERS

(See also: Criticism of Others)

If you are not big enough to stand criticism, you are too small to be praised. *Anon.*

Prophets of God have usually been on the receiving end of more mud than medals. *Anon.*

If you are slandered, never mind; it will all come off when it is dry.
Charles G. Finney

The most unspotted innocency and the most unparalleled excellency will not always be a fence against the reproach of tongues.
Matthew Henry

Wisdom teaches us to wink at many of the injuries that are done to us, and act as if we did not see them.
Matthew Henry

Don't defend your church or your organization against criticism. If the criticism is false it can do no harm. If it is true you need to hear it and do something about it.
A. W. Tozer

CRITICISM OF OTHERS

(See also: Criticism by Others)

Many are like barbers, that trim all men but themselves.
Thomas Adams

Criticism is often a form of self-boasting. *Anon.*

Fault-finders seldom find anything else. *Anon.*

It is a vital moment of truth when a man discovers that what he condemns most vehemently in others is that to which he is himself prone.
Anon.

It is but a short step from the critical to the hypocritical
Anon.

We do not get forward ourselves by keeping others back. *Anon.*

You have to be little to belittle. *Anon.*

We must not be busy bishops in other men's dioceses.
John Boys

It is not what we gain by detracting from others, but what we have without any comparison, that is truly praiseworthy. *John Calvin*

A blurred finger is unfit to wipe away a blot.
Jean Daillé

To speak ill of others is a dishonest way of praising ourselves. *Will Durant*

Taking to pieces is the trade of those who cannot construct.
Ralph Waldo Emerson

The unspiritual are out of court as religious critics; they are deaf men judging music. *G. G. Findlay*

It is a barren kind of criticism which tells you what a thing is not.
Rufus Wilmot Griswold

In judging and censuring our brethren we meddle with that which does not belong to us.
Matthew Henry

Pass no sentence which you cannot ask God in faith to confirm. *Matthew Henry*

No man can be severe in his judgement who feels that the mild eyes of Christ are fixed upon him. *Charles Hodge*

They only have a right to censure that have a heart to help; the rest is cruelty and injustice. *Samuel Medley*

Defamation begins and lives in the mind. *J. A. Motyer*

Nowhere does the self-centred heart of man more quickly take control than when it comes to the machinery of criticism and the promptings of self-interest. *J. A. Motyer*

The nature and end of judgement . . . must be corrective, not vindictive; for healing, not destruction.
John Owen

Never throw mud. You *may* miss your mark; but you *must* have dirty hands.
Joseph Parker

Criticism often takes from the tree caterpillars and blossoms together.
Jean Paul Richter

They are fittest to find fault in whom there is no fault to be found. *William Secker*

Reproofs should be as oils or ointments, gently rubbed in by the warm fire of love.
George Swinnock

Some men would receive blows with more patience if they were given them with more prudence.
George Swinnock

Some warmth must be in a reproof, but it must not be scalding hot.   *John Trapp*

Out of the easiest habits for any human being to acquire is the habit of criticizing others.   *Spiros Zodhiates*

CROSS

(See also Atonement; Jesus Christ — Death)

The cross of Christ is the key of paradise.   *Anon.*

The cross is the only ladder high enough to touch the threshold of heaven.
          George Boardman

Every doctrine that is not embedded in the cross of Jesus will lead astray.
          Oswald Chambers

The sufferings of our Saviour were designed to display the glory of God as the moral ruler of the universe.
          William Jay

The cross of Christ runs through the whole of Scripture.   *Martin Luther*

Among the categorical imperatives of the faith, the saving power of the cross is central and inescapable.
          G. Campbell Morgan

In the cross, sin is cursed and cancelled. In the cross, grace is victorious and available.
          G. Campbell Morgan

The glory of the cross of Christ is bound up with the effectiveness of its accomplishment.   *John Murray*

God was the master of ceremonies at the cross.
          Ernest Reisinger

As long as the world stands the cross will seem foolishness to natural man.
          J. C. Ryle

There are some sciences that may be learned by the head, but the science of Christ crucified can only be learned by the heart.
          C. H. Spurgeon

All God's justice and all God's love are focused in the cross, so that it teaches more of God and his truth than all space and time beside.
          Augustus H. Strong

The cross stands high above the opinions of men and to that cross all opinions must come at last for judgement.
          A. W. Tozer

The cross stands in bold opposition to the natural man. Its philosophy runs contrary to the processes of the unregenerate mind.

A. W. Tozer

To try to find a common ground between the message of the cross and man's fallen reason is to try the impossible, and if persisted in must result in an impaired reason, a meaningless cross and a powerless Christianity.

A. W. Tozer

We must do something about the cross, and one of two things only we can do — flee it or die upon it.

A. W. Tozer

CURIOSITY

Almost all men are affected with the disease of desiring to obtain useless knowledge.

John Calvin

It is easy to mistake curiosity for spiritual hunger.

François Fenelon

Curiosity is looking over other people's affairs, and overlooking our own.

H. L. Wayland

DEATH — Anticipation

Those who have welcomed Christ may welcome death.

Anon.

Although we must still meet death, let us nevertheless be calm and serene in living and dying, when we have Christ going before us. If anyone cannot set his mind at rest by disregarding death, that man should know that he has not yet gone far enough in the faith of Christ. *John Calvin*

If we remember that by death we are called back from exile to home, to our heavenly fatherland, shall we then not be filled with comfort? *John Calvin*

We may positively state that nobody has made any progress in the school of Christ, unless he cheerfully looks forward towards the day of his death, and towards the day of the final resurrection.

John Calvin

He who always waits upon God is ready whensoever he calls. He is a happy man who so lives that death at all times may find him at leisure to die. *Owen Feltham*

A good life fears not life nor death. *Thomas Fuller*

Let thy hope of heaven master thy fear of death. Why shouldest thou be afraid to die, who hopest to live by dying?

William Gurnall

How pleasantly does the good man speak of dying; as if it were but undressing and going to bed!

Matthew Henry

Death is never sudden to a saint; no guest comes unawares to him who keeps a constant table.

George Swinnock

DEATH — Blessings
(See also: Death — and Heaven)

All life is surrounded by a great circumference of death; but to the believer in Jesus, beyond this surrounding death is a boundless sphere of life. He only has to die once to be done with death for ever.

James Hamilton

Death will cut us down, but he shall not eternally keep us down.   *William Secker*

Death is only a grim porter to let us into a stately palace.

Richard Sibbes

Death is the waiting room where we robe ourselves for immortality.

C. H. Spurgeon

Jesus has transformed death from a dreary cavern into a passage leading to glory.

C. H. Spurgeon

The worst of a saint is past when he dies.

George Swinnock

Death will set a true saint out of gunshot and free him from sin and trouble.

Thomas Watson

The wheels of death's chariot may rattle and make a noise, but they are to carry a believer to Christ.

Thomas Watson

DEATH — Certainty

Man can defy gravity, but not the grave.

Nobody has to ask the question: 'Is there death after life?'

The two greatest facts in life are sin and death.

Men may live in crowds, but they die one by one.

Anon.

The power of mortality thrusts every generation into the graveyard.
Donald Grey Barnhouse

All human things are subject to decay,
And when fate summons, monarchs must obey.
John Dryden

You know death is strong; it is the king of terrors and the terror of kings.
William Dyer

Death takes no denial.
Euripides

Death takes no bribes.
Benjamin Franklin

Death borders on our birth, and our cradle stands in the grave.
Joseph Hall

The moment you come into this world you are beginning to go out of it.
D. Martyn Lloyd-Jones

Even Rome cannot grant us a dispensation from death.
Molière

To reckon with death is no more than sober realism, since death is life's one and only certainty.
J. I. Packer

All that is here is condemned to die — to pass away like a snowball before a summer sun.
Samuel Rutherford

All the care in the world will not make us continue a minute beyond the time God has appointed.
J. C. Ryle

We were earth, we are flesh, we shall be worm's meat.
Henry Smith

Against this arrest there is no bail.
George Swinnock

Death waits upon sin as the wages on the work.
Thomas Taylor

DEATH — and Heaven
(See also: Death — Blessings)

That to which we react with natural sorrow is something to which God reacts with supernatural joy.

Death *shortens* our way to heaven, but grace *sweetens* our way to heaven.
Anon.

Death is not a descent, but a never-ending ascent into the larger spaces and the fuller delights.
J. Ossian Davies

This world is the land of the dying; the next is the land of the living.
Tryon Edwards

Death is that delightful moment when the friendly flood heaves beneath the freed keel, and the prow is set straight and finally towards the shore of home, and the Pilot stands on board, at length seen 'face to face'. *Handley C. G. Moule*

DEATH — Indiscriminate

Death cancels everything but truth. *Anon.*

There are no pockets in a shroud. *Anon.*

Death surprises us in the midst of our hopes.
Thomas Fuller

All ages are threatened with death. *Thomas Manton*

As men, we are all equal in the presence of death.
Publilius Syrus

Death is a mighty leveller.
J. C. Ryle

DEATH — and Judgement

Death puts us all in our place.

Where death finds you, eternity binds you. *Anon.*

Death stamps the characters and conditions of men for eternity. As death finds them in this world, so will they be in the next.
Nathaniel Emmons

Damned sinners in hell shall not be allowed their light, being cast into utter darkness; and glorified saints in heaven shall not need their light, for God himself will be their everlasting light.
Matthew Henry

Death to a godly man is like a fair gale of wind to convey him to the heavenly country; but to a wicked man it is an east wind, a storm, a tempest, that hurries him away in confusion and amazement, to destruction.
Matthew Henry

If you die wrong the first time you cannot come back to die better a second time.
Robert Murray M'Cheyne

He who never thirsts for God here will thirst for him before he has been dead a minute. *Brownlow North*

With the same heart that men die, with that heart they will rise again.
J. C. Ryle

DEATH — Meaning

Death is that damp that puts out all the dim lights of vanity.　*Thomas Adams*

What men fear is not that death is annihilation but that it is not.　*Epicurus*

When death speaks, there is an instant hush in the whole house; everything else is stilled that we may listen.
Arthur John Gossip

Death by definition is something which is completely unfruitful.
D. Martyn Lloyd-Jones

Life, according to the Bible, is not just existence, but it is existence in the presence and with the favour of God; and death is not just the death of the body but it is separation from God and a doom that should fill the heart of man with a nameless dread.
J. Gresham Machen

Man is not naturally mortal; death is not the debt of nature but the wages of sin.
John Murray

All death is unnatural.
J. I. Packer

Death is only a horizon; and a horizon is nothing save the limit of our sight.
R. W. Raymond

72

Death is not a terminus but only a junction.
J. Charles Stern

DEATH — Preparation for

All living is preparation for dying.

The readiness which Christ requires of us is a personal readiness to leave the world and meet our God.
Joseph Addison Alexander

He has lived ill who knows not how to die well.
Thomas Fuller

We should be alarmed if we were not sure to live a month and yet we are careless though we are not sure to live a day.
Matthew Henry

If life be short, then moderate your worldly cares and projects; do not cumber yourselves with too much provision for a short voyage.
Thoms Manton

Live so as to be missed.
Robert Murray M'Cheyne

Plan your life, budgeting for seventy years . . . and understand that if your time proves shorter that will not

be unfair deprivation but rapid promotion.
J. I. Packer

All deaths are solemn events. Nothing in the whole history of a man is so important as his end.   *J. C. Ryle*

Death is a great fact that all acknowledge, but very few seem to realize.
J. C. Ryle

To be familiar with the grave is prudence.
C. H. Spurgeon

Let us live as people who are prepared to die, and die as people who are prepared to live.   *James S. Stewart*

DEATH — Triumph over

No philosophy that will not teach us how to master death is worth twopence to us.   *J. I. Packer*

Since Christ has made full atonement for the believer's sin and obtained remission for him, death can no more harm him than could a wasp whose venemous sting had been removed — though it might still buzz and hiss and attempt to disturb him.
A. W. Pink

Our people die well.
John Wesley

There is nothing in the fact of death, nothing in the consequences of death, which Christ has not endured for us.   *Brooke Foss Westcott*

DEMOCRACY

Democracy is not an infallible way for getting things right. The democratic vote among the Israelites in the wilderness was to go back to Egypt.

Numbers can never turn evil into good or error into truth.
F. J. Harris

Public opinion does not decide whether things are good or bad.
Cornelius Tacitus

DEPRAVITY
(See also: Guilt; Man — a Sinner; Sin; Sinful Nature)

One of the clearest proofs of the depravity of man is his implacable hatred of the only solution to his greatest problem.

The natural man is capable of natural good, but he is incapable of any spiritual good.

The Bible does not teach that there is no good in man; the doctrine of total depravity does not mean that. The Bible teaches, rather, that there is no good in man that can satisfy God.
Donald Grey Barnhouse

Man, by his fall, wounded his head and his heart; the wound in the head made him unstable in the truth, and that in his heart unsteadfast in his affections.
Stephen Charnock

Unconverted men would kill God if they could get at him.
Jonathan Edwards

Men sometimes affect to deny the depravity of our race; but it is as clearly taught in the lawyers' office and in courts of justice, as in the Bible itself. Every prison and fetter and scaffold and bolt and bar and chain is evidence that man believes in the depravity of man.
Tryon Edwards

I never say that civilization is going to the dogs. I still have some respect for dogs! Mankind without the grace of God is doing things beneath the dignity of the beasts of the field.
Vance Havner

The rejection of the gospel is as clear proof of moral depravity as inability to see the sun at noon is proof of blindness.   *Charles Hodge*

The decisive seat of evil . . . is not in social and political institutions . . . but simply in the weakness and imperfection of the human soul itself.   *George Kennan*

Depravity spells moral inability. Sin has so crippled man's moral powers that he cannot perform anything that is truly spiritual and acceptable to God.
Ernest F. Kevan

Man is totally destitute of that love to God which constitutes the very essence of holiness, and in its place he is possessed of an aversion to God which, though sometimes latent, becomes active enmity so soon as God's will comes into conflict with his own.   *Ernest F. Kevan*

The real state of human nature after the fall of man is not that one part of it has been cut off or can attain only a stunted growth, but that all of it is corrupt.
J. Gresham Machen

Man has more grandeur than the Milky Way, but how easy evil is for him, how inevitable!   *Jacques Maritain*

Nothing in man is as good as it should be. *J. I. Packer*

Since the tree of knowledge has been tasted, the key of knowledge has been rusted. *William Secker*

The sinner in his sinful nature could never have a will according to God. *J. Denham Smith*

Sinners, like water, if simply let alone, will run downhill to ruin. *Augustus H. Strong*

The root of all evil in human nature is the corruption of the will. *A. W. Tozer*

One of the products of the Fall is that we remember the things we ought to forget — and forget the things we ought to remember. *Paul Tucker*

How sad our state by nature is!
Our sin how deep it stains!
And Satan binds our captive minds
Fast in his slavish chains. *Isaac Watts*

If depravity is not preached, grace will be ignored. *Malcolm Watts*

DESIRES
(See also: Lust)

Desire without discipline breeds disappointment, but discipline without desire breeds drudgery. *Anon.*

If your desires be endless, your cares and fears will be so too. *Thomas Fuller*

Our desires must not only be offered up to God, but they must all terminate in him, desiring nothing more than God, but still more and more of him. *Matthew Henry*

Carnal desire is a gulf that is never filled up. *Thomas Manton*

DESPAIR

When there is no hope there can be no endeavour. *Samuel Johnson*

To this truth give all the Scriptures witness: that while in hell there is no place for hope, on earth there is no place for despair. *Brownlow North*

The devil would make us wade so far in the waters of repentance that we should get beyond our depth and be

75

drowned in the gulf of despair. *Thomas Watson*

DESTINY

(See also: Eternity; Heaven; Hell; Judgement)

Let it be considered that if our lives be not a journey to heaven they will be a journey to hell.
Jonathan Edwards

Destiny waits in the hand of God, not in the hands of statesmen. *T. S. Eliot*

God, his glory and his presence form the destiny of the Christian. *Sinclair Ferguson*

DIFFICULTIES

Nothing is more offensive to God than disbelief of his promise and despair of the performance of it because of some difficulties that seem to lie in the way.
Matthew Henry

Difficulties in the way to heaven serve to bring us to a despair of ourselves, not of God. *Thomas Manton*

The more terrible the storm, the more necessary the anchor. *William S. Plumer*

76

DIGNITY

The easiest way to dignity is humility. *Anon.*

I know of no case where a man added to his dignity by standing on it.
Winston Churchill

DISCIPLESHIP

As long as we live we must be scholars in Christ's school and sit at his feet; but we should aim to be head-scholars and to get into the highest form.
Matthew Henry

As the soldier follows his general, as the servant follows his master, as the scholar follows his teacher, as the sheep follows its shepherd, just so ought the professing Christian to follow Christ. *J. C. Ryle*

DISCIPLINE

Desire without discipline breeds disappointment, but discipline without desire breeds drudgery. *Anon.*

The alternative to discipline is disaster. *Vance Havner*

DISHONESTY
(See also: Lying)

Dishonesty is moral suicide, a disintegration of the moral self. *Anon.*

What a poor thing is the temporary triumph of falsehood! *C. H. Spurgeon*

DIVORCE

Divorce tells us the truth about man. It tells us nothing about marriage.
Terence Kelshaw

Divorce is always a tragedy no matter how civilized the handling of it may be. It is always a confession of human failure, even when it is the better of sorry alternatives. *Lawrence S. Kubie*

DOCTRINE
(See also: Theology)

Every doctrine that is not embedded in the cross of Jesus will lead astray.
Oswald Chambers

Biblical truth has been given to change lives, not simply to stimulate discussion.
Dick Dowsett

Doctrine is the necessary foundation of duty.
Tryon Edwards

As seed is made for soil and soil for seed, so the heart is made for God's truth and God's truth for the heart.
Richard Glover

God hath but three things dear unto him in this world, his saints, his worship and his truth; and it is hard to say which of these is dearest unto him. *Thomas Goodwin*

Doctrine is the framework of life — the skeleton of truth, to be clothed and rounded out by the living grace of a holy life. *A. J. Gordon*

He who attempts to stress Christian living by disparaging Christian doctrine is guilty of a most serious blunder. He neglects the important fact that Christian living is rooted in Christian doctrine. *R. B. Kuiper*

Middle-of-the-road pacifism in significant doctrinal controversy has ruined many a church. *R. B. Kuiper*

Nothing is to be introduced as doctrine which is not according to revelation.
Henry T. Mahan

77

The conduct of our lives is the true mirror of our doctrine.
Michel de Montaigne

In Christianity, creed has always to do with Christ.
G. Campbell Morgan

Christian doctrine is grace, and Christian conduct is gratitude. *J. I. Packer*

Miracles enable us to judge of doctrine, and doctrine enables us to judge of miracles. *Blaise Pascal*

We are far more concerned about the results of the gospel than we are about the purity of it. *A. W. Pink*

You can talk about religious experiences all you wish, but if it does not have doctrinal roots, it is like cut flowers stuck into the ground. They will soon wither and die.
J. C. Ryle

Say what men say, it is doctrine that moves the world. He who takes no position will not sway the human intellect. *W. G. T. Shedd*

A dead creed is of no use; we must have our creed baptized with the Holy Ghost.
C. H. Spurgeon

Those who do away with Christian doctrine are ... the worst enemies of Christian living. *C. H. Spurgeon*

The best theology is rather a divine life than a divine knowledge. *Jeremy Taylor*

Christianity has been watered down until the solution is so weak that if it were poison it would not hurt anyone and if it were medicine it would not cure anyone!
A. W. Tozer

The unattended garden will soon be overrun with weeds; the heart that fails to cultivate truth and root out error will shortly be a theological wilderness. *A. W. Tozer*

There is scarcely anything so dull and meaningless as Bible doctrine taught for its own sake. Truth divorced from life is not truth in its biblical sense, but something else and something less.
A. W. Tozer

Orthodoxy is my doxy; heterodoxy is another man's doxy. *William Warburton*

DOUBT

Christ distinguished between doubt and unbelief. Doubt

says, 'I can't believe.' Unbelief says, ' I won't believe.' Doubt is honest. Unbelief is obstinate. *Henry Drummond*

No alcoholic was ever more in bondage to his habit of drink than many Christians are to their habit of doubting. In fact, many Christians have settled down under their doubts as though they had contracted an incurable disease. *Billy Graham*

Doubt is brother devil to despair.
John Boyle O'Reilly

Doubt cramps energy.
F. W. Robertson

Doubt breeds distress, but trust means joy in the long run. *C. H. Spurgeon*

DRUNKENNESS
(See also: Alcohol)

The drunkard is a walking quagmire. *William Jenkyn*

Drunkenness places man as much below the level of the brutes as reason elevates him above them. *John Sinclair*

Duty is ours, events are God's. *Matthew Henry*

Our rule is not to go a step out of the way of duty, either to meet a cross or to miss one. *Matthew Henry*

Without duty, life is soft and boneless; it cannot hold itself together. *Joseph Joubert*

Duty is the sublimest word in the English language. *Robert E. Lee*

Believe in Christ and do your duty in that state of life to which God has called you. *Martin Luther*

There is nothing in the universe I fear but that I shall not know all my duty, or shall fail to do it. *Mary Lyon*

There are two things which are indispensable to true Christian life: first, a clear knowledge of duty: and, second, an obedience co-ordinate with that knowledge. *Douglas Macmillan*

Duty is the greatest liberty, and sin the greatest bondage. *Thomas Manton*

Perish discretion when it interferes with duty. *Hannah More*

The gracious operations of the Spirit were never designed to be a substitute for the Christian's discharge of duty. *A. W. Pink*

Do what you can, with what you have, where you are. *Theodore Roosevelt*

God never imposes a duty without giving time to do it. *John Ruskin*

Duties can never have too much of our diligence or too little of our confidence. *William Secker*

ELECTION — and Calling

What election means in simple terms is this: God chooses us before we choose him; God does not choose us because we deserve it; and God does not choose us to be his favourites but to be his servants. *A. M. Hunter*

When God chose certain persons unto eternal life he did not do so in order that they might be in Christ, but he viewed them from eternity as being in Christ. *R. B. Kuiper*

Better to be the elect of God than the elect of a whole nation. *C. H. Spurgeon*

We are chosen as an afflicted people and not as a prosperous people, chosen not in the palace but in the furnace. *C. H. Spurgeon*

ELECTION — and Conversion

(See also: Predestination)

Election, while it places no bar in the way of any man which would not have been there without it, resolves the salvation of the saved into mere grace. *Andrew Fuller*

Election is the holy and loving choice by God of those who are to receive his grace. *Ernest F. Kevan*

Nobody ever came to Christ because he knew he was one of the elect: he came because he needed Christ and because he wanted Christ. *Ernest F. Kevan*

Election is salvation. *R. B. Kuiper*

Let us understand that we live in a day of election, and not of universal conversion. *J. C. Ryle*

The believer who knows his own heart will ever bless God for election. *J. C. Ryle*

Election shapes everything. *C. H. Spurgeon*

It is no mean thing to be chosen of God. God's choice makes chosen men choice men. *C. H. Spurgeon*

Election and sovereignty are only sources of good. Election is not a decree to destroy, it is a decree to save. When we elect a president, we do not need to hold a second election to determine that the remaining millions shall be non-presidents. *Augustus H. Strong*

ELECTION — and Eternal Security

Our spiritual estate standeth upon a sure bottom; the beginning is from God the Father, the dispensation from the Son and the application from the Holy Ghost . . . It is free in the Father, sure in the Son, ours in the Spirit. *Thomas Manton*

Who shall the Lord's elect
  condemn?
'Tis God that justifies their
  souls,
And mercy like a mighty
  stream
O'er all their sins divinely
  rolls.
Isaac Watts

81

ELECTION — and Faith

Faith as the fruit of election is also the proof of election.
R. B. Kuiper

Christ did not die for any upon condition, if they do believe; but he died for all God's elect, that they should believe. *John Owen*

We are not elected . . . either for our faith, or according to our faith, but to our faith; that is, elected that we might believe. *William Perkins*

ELECTION — and Holiness

Election is always to sanctification. Those whom Christ chooses out of mankind, he choses not only that they may be saved, but that they may bear fruit, and fruit that can be seen. All other election beside this is a mere vain delusion, and a miserable invention of man.
J. C. Ryle

The realization that we are predestined and elected to life is one of the mightiest incentives to Christian living.
W. H. Griffith Thomas

We are not chosen because we are good; we are chosen that we may be good.
Benjamin B. Warfield

ELECTION — Mystery

In the election of man to salvation, God has the only vote.

The elect are whosoever will; the non-elect are whosoever won't.
Henry Ward Beecher

Election is a divine choice of individuals, unto salvation, made in connection with Christ the Redeemer, in eternity, based upon the mere good pleasure of God's will. *Al Martin*

Nothing gives such offence, and stirs up such bitter feeling among the wicked, as the idea of God making any distinction between man and man, and loving one person more than another.
J. C. Ryle

ELOQUENCE
(See also: Speech)

Eloquence is logic on fire.
Lyman Beecher

One of the best definitions of eloquence is 'to have something to say and to *burn* to say it'. *Henry C. Fish*

EMOTIONS

God is more concerned with the state of people's hearts than with the state of their feelings. *A. W. Tozer*

I believe that in any setting, the tendency to place personal feeling above the Scriptures is always an insult to God. *A. W. Tozer*

ENCOURAGEMENT

Nothing succeeds like encouragement. *Anon.*

The faintest whisper of support and encouragement uttered by a Christian in the ears of his fellow believer is heard in heaven.
John J. Murray

ENTHUSIASM
(See also: Zeal)

Enthusiasm is essential to the triumph of truth.
Anon.

Enthusiasm finds the opportunities and energy makes the most of them.
Henry S. Huskins

If there is any reality within the whole sphere of human experience that is by its very nature worthy to challenge the mind, charm the heart and bring the total life to a burning focus, it is the reality that revolves around the person of Christ.
A. W. Tozer

ENVY

He that looks through a green glass sees no other colour. *Thomas Adams*

Envy eats nothing but its own heart. *Anon.*

Envy never enriched any man. *Anon.*

Envy is a coal that comes hissing hot from hell.
Philip James Baily

An envious man is a squinty-eyed fool. *H. G. Bohn*

Envy is the sign of a nature that is altogether evil.
Demosthenes

Envy is the greatest of all diseases among men. *Euripides*

Envy shoots at others and wounds herself.

Thomas Fuller

If we love our neighbour we shall be so far from envying his welfare, or being displeased with it, that we shall share in it and rejoice at it.

Matthew Henry

The prosperity of those to whom we wish well can never grieve us; and the mind which is bent on doing good to all can never wish ill to any. *Matthew Henry*

Envy is its own punishment.

William Jenkyn

Too many Christians envy the sinners their pleasure and the saints their joy because they don't have either one. *Martin Luther*

Envy is a rebellion against God himself, and the liberty and pleasure of his dispensations. *Thomas Manton*

Envy is a settled, crooked malice. *Thomas Manton*

There are two sins which were Christ's sorest enemies, covetousness and envy. Covetousness sold Christ and envy delivered him.

Thomas Manton

There is not a passion so strongly rooted in the human heart as envy.

Richard Brinsley Sheridan

In spiritual things there is no envy. *Richard Sibbes*

The cure for envy lies in living under a constant sense of the divine presence, worshipping God and communing with him all the day long, however long the day may seem. *C. H. Spurgeon*

Envy does nothing with reason. *John Trapp*

Envy is a self-murder, a fretting canker.

Thomas Watson

ETERNAL SECURITY

(See also: Election and Eternal Security; Heaven — The Christian's Home)

It is possible to fall in grace, but not to fall from grace.

The Christian's place in heaven was assured before there was a single angel there to help in arranging his accommodation.

God never promises us an easy time, only a safe arrival.

Anon.

We do believe in eternal security, but we do not believe in eternal presumption. Let a man examine himself.
Donald Grey Barnhouse

The ultimate answer to the insecurity or security of the believer rests on the question of who does the work of salvation. *Lewis Sperry Chafer*

We can afford to walk in the dark now if we are assured of eternal light hereafter.
Thomas V. Moore

The perseverance of the saints reminds us very forcefully that only those who persevere to the end are truly saints. *John Murray*

He that keeps heaven for us will give us necessary graces to bring us thither.
Richard Sibbes

As we are under the covenant of grace, we are secured against departing from the living God by the sure declaration of the covenant.
C. H. Spurgeon

If God lights the candle, none can blow it out.
C. H. Spurgeon

Jesus has made the life of his people as eternal as his own.
C. H. Spurgeon

None can find out a single person whom God has forsaken after having revealed himself savingly to him.
C. H. Spurgeon

The Lord Jesus has paid too high a price for our redemption to leave us in the enemy's hand.
C. H. Spurgeon

Until God can be unjust, and demand two payments for one debt, he cannot destroy the soul for whom Jesus died. *C. H. Spurgeon*

The soul that is shaped into the image of Christ will remain for ever.
Takesaburo Uzaki

God never repents of his electing love.
Thomas Watson

God's decree is the very pillar and basis on which the saints' perseverance depends. That decree ties the knot of adoption so fast that neither sin, death nor hell can break it asunder. *Thomas Watson*

The question is not one of the retention of salvation based upon a persistence of faith, but of the possession of salvation as evidenced by a continuation of faith.
Kenneth Wuest

ETERNITY

(See also: Destiny; Heaven; Hell; Judgement)

Eternity is the lifetime of the Almighty. *Anon.*

Life, if properly viewed in any aspect, is great, but mainly great when viewed in its relation to the world to come. *Albert Barnes*

He who has no vision of eternity will never get a true hold of time.
Thomas Carlyle

The sum and substance of the preparation needed for a coming eternity is that you believe what the Bible tells you and do what the Bible bids you.
Thomas Chalmers

Whatsoever is eternal is immutable. *Stephen Charnock*

None but a theology that came out of eternity can carry you and me safely to and through eternity.
T. L. Cuyler

O God, stamp eternity on my eyeballs!
Jonathan Edwards

The crosses and comforts of this present time would not make such an impression upon us as they do if we did but believe the things of eternity as we ought.
Matthew Henry

This world is our passage not our portion.
Matthew Henry

Men that believe not another world are the ready actors of any imaginable mischiefs and tragedies in this. *John Howe*

Eternity depends upon this moment. *Thomas Manton*

Eternity is an everlasting now. *Christopher Nesse*

'For ever' is the most solemn saying in the Bible.
J. C. Ryle

One thought of eternity makes all earthly sorrows fade away. *Basilea Schlink*

Belief in the immortality of the soul and belief in the accountability of the soul are fundamental beliefs in all religion. *O. J. Smith*

Christ's resurrection is not only the best proof of immortality, but we have no certain evidence of immortality without it.
Augustus H. Strong

Science tells us that nothing in nature, not even the

tiniest particle, can disappear without a trace. Nature does not know extinction, only transformation. If God applies this fundamental principle to the most minute part of his universe, doesn't it make sense to assume that he applies it also to the soul of man?

Wernher Von Braun

Ever is a short word but it has no end.

Thomas Watson

The real value of a thing is the price it will bring in eternity. *John Wesley*

The future life only brings to fruition the seed sown here.

Geoffrey B. Wilson

Praise God for eternity to come, when the order of things shall be reversed.

Spiros Zodhiates

ETHICS

(See also: Goodness; Morality; Virtue)

The Christian must recognize that there are no degrees of right or wrong.

Donald Grey Barnhouse

Situation ethics is actually blasphemy because it pictures God as being either ignorant or stupid.

Robert A. Morey

EVANGELISM — Definition and Aim

Evangelism is the redistribution of spiritual wealth.

You can have evangelism without revival, but you cannot have revival without evangelism. *Brian Mills*

Evangelism that does not lead to purity of life and purity of doctrine is just as faulty and incomplete as an orthodoxy which does not lead to a concern for, and communication with, the lost. *Francis Schaeffer*

EVANGELISM — and Election

Election is a doctrine I am called upon to believe; evangelism is a command I am called upon to obey.

Election, so far from undermining evangelism, undergirds it, for it provides the only hope of its succeeding in its aim. *J. I. Packer*

EVANGELISM — Message

Sinners must be caught with the gospel, not with sugary morsels of worldly wisdom.
Fred A. Malone

We may boldly tell the chief of sinners that Christ loves him. Salvation is ready for the worst of men, if they will only come to Christ. If men are lost, it is not because Jesus does not love them and is not ready to save.
J. C. Ryle

EVANGELISM — Principles

The evangelist must be as bold in denouncing sin as others are in committing it.

The true glory of evangelism is rooted not in our own nervous claims to success, but in the eternal covenant of a sovereign God.

When telling thy salvation free,
Let all absorbing thoughts of thee
My heart and soul engross.
And when all hearts are bowed and stirred
Beneath the influence of thy Word
Hide me behind thy cross.
Anon.

Our Lord's first obedience was to the will of his Father, not to the needs of men; the saving of men was the natural outcome of his obedience to the Father.
Oswald Chambers

You can never give another person that which you have found, but you can make him homesick for what you have.
Oswald Chambers

Why should we fear that the arm of God should be short for others that could reach us?
Thomas Fuller

The way from God to a human heart is through a human heart.
Samuel Gordon

The person who is unconcerned about those who are perishing may well wonder whether he is a Christian.
William Hendriksen

We ought carefully to distinguish between the sinner and the sin, so as not to love the sin for the sake of the person, nor to hate the person for the sake of the sin.
Matthew Henry

Christ owes the unevangelized nothing, absolutely nothing.
A. A. Hodge

The unfinished task which lies before us is no greater than the unlimited power of God behind us.
Fred D. Jarvis

Every gospel imperative is full of the divine power of grace to effect what it demands. If it counted on even the least power in the sinner it would never secure the least effect.
R. C. H. Lenski

When we are spreading the gospel we must follow God's providential indications as to where we ought to work.
R. C. H. Lenski

Since the Lord saved *me*, I have despaired of no man living.   *Henry T. Mahan*

God has never indicated that proclamation of the gospel is to become dependent upon human performances.   *A. W. Tozer*

EVANGELISM — Responsibility for
(See also: Soul-Winning; Witnessing)

Evangelism is morally right – it is the payment of a debt.

We do not evangelize because we expect results.

We evangelize because we are sent men.   *Joe Blinco*

The gospel is not to be preserved like the Crown Jewels, locked in our ecclesiastical strong room. It is to be spread locally, and to the ends of the earth.
Herbert M. Carson

Every Christian is a postmaster for God. His duty is to pass out good news from above.   *Vance Havner*

The gospel is not a secret to be hoarded but a story to be heralded.   *Vance Havner*

Too many Christians are stuffing themselves with gospel blessings while millions have never had a taste.
Vance Havner

The greatest charity in the world is the communication of divine truth to the ignorant.   *Alexander Maclaren*

Holy Writ is to be kept not under a bushel, but under men's noses. Its message is to be held forth as diligently as it is held fast.
J. I. Packer

If a church does not evangelize it will fossilize.
A. W. Pink

89

No candle which God lights was ever meant to burn alone. *J. C. Ryle*

The highest form of selfishness is that of the man who is content to go to heaven alone. *J. C. Ryle*

The Great Commission is not an option to be considered, but a command to be obeyed.

J. Hudson Taylor

EVOLUTION

(See also: Creation; Nature)

Man is not making his way up through animism, fetishism, totemism, polytheism and monotheism to a knowledge of God. He started wth a knowledge of God and has been going the other way ever since. *Vance Havner*

Scripture answers three basic questions to which the evolutionary theory has no answer whatever. These questions concern the origin of matter, the origin of life and the origin of man as a religious being.

R. B. Kuiper

EXAMPLE

(See also: Influence)

Example is the best precept.
Æsop

The example of good men is visible philosophy. *Anon.*

If both horse and mare trot, the colt will not amble.
John Boys

Example is more forceful than precept. People look at me six days a week to see what I mean on the seventh day. *Richard Cecil*

We can do more good by being good than in any other way. *Rowland Hill*

Nothing is so infectious as example. *Charles Kingsley*

Great men's vices are more imitated than poor men's graces. *William Secker*

Man is a creature led more by patterns than by precepts. *George Swinnock*

EXCUSES

There is a vast difference between an excuse and a reason. There may be some validity in the latter, but not in the former.

Donald Grey Barnhouse

He that is good at making excuses is seldom good at anything else.
Benjamin Franklin

Bad excuses are worse than none. *Thomas Fuller*

Experience is not what happens to you; it is what you do with what happens to you.
Aldous Huxley

Experience is the great schoolmaster. *A. W. Pink*

EXPERIENCE

We are not to make our experience the rule of Scripture, but Scripture the rule of our experience. *Anon.*

The experience of Christians is not necessarily Christian experience.
Donald Grey Barnhouse

Never make a principle out of your experience; let God be as original with other people as he is with you.
Oswald Chambers

Many spiritual experiences are possible which do not in and of themselves produce maturity. Rather, it is our response to experience which will determine our progress in maturity.
Sinclair Ferguson

One man with a glowing experience of God is worth a library full of arguments.
Vance Havner

FAITH — and Deeds
(See also: Faith — Saving; Good Deeds)

Moral virtue may wash the outside, but faith washes the inside. *Thomas Adams*

Faith and works are like the light and heat of a candle; they cannot be separated.
Anon.

Faith does not set aside natural duties, but perfects and strengthens them.
J. A. Bengel

The saints of God are sealed inwardly with faith, but outwardly with good works.
John Boys

Till men have faith in Christ, their best services are but glorious sins.
Thomas Brooks

Faith justifies the person and works justify his faith.
Elisha Coles

We must come to good works by faith, and not to faith by good works.

William Gurnall

Faith must have adequate evidence, else it is mere superstition.

A. A. Hodge

Let your practice praise your creed, and your lives do honour to your heads.

William Jay

Faith is a living, restless thing. It cannot be inoperative.

Martin Luther

Good works do not make a good man, but a good man makes the works to be good.

Martin Luther

Faith is not an idle grace.

Thomas Manton

What saves is faith alone, but the faith that saves is never alone.

J. I. Packer

Obedience is the hallmark of faith.

C. H. Spurgeon

The Bible recognizes no faith that does not lead to obedience, nor does it recognize any obedience that does not spring from faith. The two are opposite sides of the same coin.

A. W. Tozer

Faith believes as if it did not work, and it works as if it did not believe.

Thomas Watson

Faith can neither be stationary nor complete.

Brooke Foss Westcott

All right believing in God is visibly reflected in right behaviour towards men.

Geoffrey B. Wilson

FAITH — Definition

(See also: Faith — Saving)

Faith is a living, daring confidence in God's grace. It is so sure and certain that a man could stake his life on it a thousand times.

Martin Luther

Faith is the instinct of the spiritual world; it is the sixth sense, the sense of the unseen.

Ian Maclaren

Faith is knowledge passing into conviction, and it is conviction passing into confidence.

John Murray

What is faith but obedience to the commands of Christ?

Salvianus

Faith is the silver thread upon which the pearls of the graces are strung.

C. H. Spurgeon

Faith is a knowledge conditioned by holy affection.
Augustus H. Strong

Faith is self-surrender to the great Physician, a leaving of our case in his hands. But it is also the taking of his prescriptions and the active following of his directions.
Augustus H. Strong

The faith that saves is not a conclusion drawn from evidence; it is a moral thing, a thing of the spirit, a supernatural infusion of confidence in Jesus Christ, a very gift of God. *A. W. Tozer*

The faith that saves reposes in the person of Christ; it leads at once to a committal of the total being to Christ, an act impossible to natural man. To believe rightly is as much a miracle as was the coming forth of dead Lazarus at the command of Christ. *A. W. Tozer*

FAITH — Essence

Faith builds a bridge from this world to the next.
Anon.

'My' is the handle of faith.
Andrew Bonar

Faith in the heart of a Christian is like the salt that was thrown into the corrupt fountain, that made the naughty waters good and the barren land fruitful.
John Bunyan

Faith ascribes all that is good to the grace of God, even its own existence.
J. C. P. Cockerton

The world will offer God almost anything but this one all-important element of belief . . . belief is too humbling. *Frank Gabelein*

Faith is the only receiving grace. *William Gurnall*

We must not confide in the armour of God, but in the God of the armour.
William Gurnall

Faith does not look at itself.
Vance Havner

Faith has no value save as it links us with God.
Vance Havner

It is the business of faith to resolve doubts.
Matthew Henry

If your faith isn't contagious it must be contaminated.
Chester Johnson

Faith is not an achievement; it is a gift. Yet it comes only through the hearing and study of the Word.
Martin Luther

Faith is the life of our lives, the soul that animates the whole body of obedience.
Thomas Manton

Learn to put your hand on all spiritual blessings in Christ and say, 'Mine'.
F. B. Meyer

The broken spirit and the contrite heart are the abiding marks of the believing soul. *John Murray*

True faith is suffused with penitence. *John Murray*

Faith is a principle of life by which the Christian lives unto God; a principle of motion, by which he walks to heaven along the highway of holiness; a principle of strength, by which he opposes the flesh, the world and the devil.
A. W. Pink

Faith always anticipates.
David C. Potter

Faith always sees the bow of covenant promise whenever sense sees the cloud of affliction. *C. H. Spurgeon*

To many, faith seems a hard thing. The truth is, it is only hard because it is easy.
C. H. Spurgeon

Faith is a gift of God to a penitent soul and has nothing whatsoever to do with the senses or the data they afford. *A. W. Tozer*

Faith is a quickening grace, the vital artery of the soul.
Thomas Watson

Repentance and faith are both humbling graces; by repentance a man abhors himself, by faith he goes out of himself. *Thomas Watson*

The steps of faith fall on the seeming void, but find the rock beneath.
John Greenleaf Whittier

FAITH — Ground

Lack of faith is such a waste of time when there is God.
Larry Burner

The true Christian should not seek proofs for his faith, but rather be firmly content with Scripture. *John Hus*

Those who need miracles are men of little faith.
John Hus

Faith rests on the naked Word of God; that Word believed gives full assurance.
H. A. Ironside

My hope is built on nothing less
Than Jesus' blood and righteousness;
I dare not trust the sweetest frame,
But wholly lean on Jesus' name.
On Christ the solid rock I stand;
All other ground is sinking sand.
Edward Mote

Faith rests upon the character of God, not upon the demonstration of laboratory or logic.   *A. W. Tozer*

for the present find comfort in him.   *Matthew Henry*

Christian life consists in faith and charity.   *Martin Luther*

Faith is the mother of obedience.   *Thomas Manton*

The Christian, like a net, must have both the lead of a godly fear and the cork of a lively faith.
George Swinnock

What we believe about God is the most important thing about us.   *A. W. Tozer*

The devil labours to put out the right eye of faith and to leave us only the left eye of reason.   *John Trapp*

FAITH — Importance

Faith in God is never out of season.   *Anon.*

I believe in order that I might understand.   *Anselm*

Of all graces faith honours Christ most; therefore of all graces Christ honours faith most.   *Matthew Henry*

We must rejoice in God when we have nothing else to rejoice in and cleave to him ... though we cannot

FAITH — Power

Faith makes things possible — it does not make them easy.   *Anon.*

Faith opens every gateway of the soul.
George Barlow

Faith is an appropriating grace.   *Thomas Brooks*

Faith does the same against the devil as unbelief does against God.
John Bunyan

95

As he that fears God fears nothing else, so, he that sees God sees nothing else.
John Donne

Faith and a good conscience are hope's two wings.
William Gurnall

The crosses and comforts of the present time would not make such an impression upon us as they do if we did but believe the things of eternity as we ought.
Matthew Henry

We look with an eye of faith farther than we can see with an eye of sense.
Matthew Henry

Faith is the life of our lives, the soul that animates the whole body of obedience.
Thomas Manton

Faith can rest in what it cannot comprehend.
John Owen

Faith, having God with her, is in a clear majority.
C. H. Spurgeon

Faith may be simple, but its effect is sublime.
J. Charles Stern

Faith is a mighty, living thing, producing wonderful results in the conscience, heart, will, mind and life of the recipient.
A. Paget Wilkes

FAITH — Rewards

Faith sees God and God sees faith. *Anon.*

Weave in faith and God will find thread. *Anon.*

Have faith in God, my heart,
Trust and be unafraid;
God will fulfil in every part
Each promise he has made.
Bryn Austin Rees

A clear faith should produce a light heart. *J. C. Ryle*

Doubt breeds distress, but trust means joy in the long run. *C. H. Spurgeon*

Upon the two hinges of faith and repentance do all the promises of the Bible hang.
George Swinnock

Every benefit flowing from the atonement of Christ comes to the individual through the gateway of faith. *A. W. Tozer*

Faith and the promise make a happy mixture, a precious confection.   *John Trapp*

FAITH — Saving

(See also: Conversion; Faith — Definition; Regeneration; Repentance)

Repentance and faith are twins.

The evidence of saving faith is not how much you believe but how well you behave.

Faith is not a distant view, but a warm embrace of Christ.   *John Calvin*

Saving faith is confidence in Jesus; a direct confidential transaction with him.
          Richard Fuller

Without faith we are not fit to desire mercy.
          William Gurnall

Faith is not a work which Christ condescends in the gospel to accept instead of perfect obedience as the ground of salvation — it is only the hand whereby we clasp the person and work of our Redeemer, which is the true ground of salvation.
          A. A. Hodge

Saving faith is not creative, but receptive. It does not

make our salvation, it takes it gratefully.
          Robert M. Horn

Conviction of sin is an indispensable prerequisite of faith in Christ.   *R. B. Kuiper*

Faith as the fruit of election is also the proof of election.
          R. B. Kuiper

Nowhere does the Bible tell us that salvation is by a faith that does not work.
          R. B. Kuiper

Salvation is only by a working faith. In short, good works are the fruit of saving faith. They are also the proof of saving faith. *R. B. Kuiper*

The only saving faith is that which casts itself on God for life or death. *Martin Luther*

Be as holy as you can, as if there were no gospel to save you. Yet ... believe in Christ as if there were no law at all to condemn you.
          Thomas Lye

Men who are dead in trespasses and sins are utterly unable to have saving faith, just as completely unable as a dead man lying in the tomb is unable to contribute the slightest bit to his resurrection.
          J. Gresham Machen

True saving faith clings to Christ and his Word, regardless of the consequences caused by that faith.
Henry T. Mahan

Faith settles the soul.
Thomas Manton

It is impossible to disentangle faith and repentance. Saving faith is permeated with repentance and repentance is permeated with faith.
John Murray

Regeneration is inseparable from its effects and one of its effects is faith.
John Murray

The embrace of Christ in faith is the first evidence of regeneration and only thus may we know that we have been regenerated.
John Murray

The faith that is unto salvation is a penitent faith and the repentance that is unto life is a believing repentance.
John Murray

Coming to Christ not only involves the abandoning of every false object of confidence, it also includes and entails the forsaking of all other competitors for my heart.   *A. W. Pink*

Saving faith is not only the heart being weaned from every other object of confidence as the ground of my acceptance before God, but it is also the heart being weaned from every other object that competes with him for my affections.
A. W. Pink

Saving faith not only historically credits the truths of God, but with the heart believes them.
William S. Plumer

If we would know whether our faith is genuine, we do well to ask ourselves how we are living.   *J. C. Ryle*

Saving faith is resting faith, the trust which relies entirely on the Saviour.
John R. W. Stott

What saves us is faith in *Christ*, not faith in our *faith*, or faith in *the* faith.
Augustus H. Strong

Faith is not a once-done act, but a continuous gaze of the heart at the triune God.
A. W. Tozer

Faith in Jesus Christ . . . in the office of justification, is neither condition nor qualification, . . . but in its very act a renouncing of all such pretences.   *Robert Traill*

Right faith is a thing wrought in us by the Holy Ghost, which changes us, turns us into a new nature, and begets us anew in God, and makes us sons of God . . . and makes us altogether new in the heart, mind, will, desire, and in all the other affections and powers of the soul — the Holy Ghost ever accompanying it and ruling the heart.   *William Tyndale*

FAITH — Supremacy

One grain of faith is more precious than a pound of knowledge.   *Joseph Hall*

Faith always shows itself in the whole personality.
    D. Martyn Lloyd-Jones

Justifying faith is that act of the soul by which a man lays hold on Christ and has peace with God.   *J. C. Ryle*

What is the life of saving faith, when once begun, but a continual leaning on an unseen Saviour's word?
    J. C. Ryle

To live by faith is a far surer and happier thing than to live by feelings or by works.
    C. H. Spurgeon

Faith is the mother-grace, the womb wherein love and all the rest of the heavenly offspring are conceived.
    John Trapp

Faith is a stooping grace.
    Thomas Watson

Faith is the master-wheel; it sets all the other graces running.   *Thomas Watson*

FAITH — Testing

Judge not the Lord by feeble sense,
But trust him for his grace;
Behind a frowning providence
He hides a smiling face.
    William Cowper

When Satan borrows sense to speak one thing, let faith borrow Scripture to speak the contrary.   *David Dickson*

Faith must be tested and it is of the essence of the testing that no escape seems possible.   *Edward Donnelly*

He who would believe, let him reconcile himself to the fact that his faith will not stay untempted.
    Martin Luther

99

FAITH — Weak

In the gospels, Jesus often rebukes weak faith, but never rejects it.

John Berridge

Waverings where faith is are like the tossings of a ship fast at anchor. *Stephen Charnock*

Faith is not always alike lively; but where it is true it is always living.

Thomas Manton

A weak hand may receive a rich jewel. *Richard Sibbes*

The promises are not made to strong faith but to true.

Thomas Watson

FAITHFULNESS

One thing you can give and still keep is your word.

Anon.

How can there be great faith where is little faithfulness?

William Gurnall

If God's goodness to us be like the morning light, which shines more and more to the perfect day, let not ours to him be like the morning cloud and the early dew that pass away.

Matthew Henry

Religion is not a matter of fits, starts and stops, but an everyday affair.

David Livingstone

FAMILY LIFE — Importance

A home with no head is a disaster; one with two is a monstrosity.

Many a fine house is something else — and less — than a home. *Anon.*

The atmosphere of a Christian home should be eloquent. *Anon.*

If family religion were duly attended to and properly discharged, I think the preaching of the Word would not be the common instrument of conversion.

Richard Baxter

Help us O Lord our homes to make
Thy Holy Spirit's dwelling place;
Our hands and hearts' devotion take
To be the servants of thy grace.

A. F. Bayley

Bringing up a family should be an adventure, not an anxious discipline in which

100

everybody is constantly graded for performance.
Milton R. Sapirstein

He that loves not his wife and children breeds a lioness at home and broods a nest of sorrows.   *Jeremy Taylor*

FAMILY LIFE — Influence on Children

Children need to be trained, not just in the facts of life, but in the ways of life.
Anon.

The best thing to spend on your children is your time.
Anon.

The child's first school is the family.   *Anon.*

The father is a debtor to his child, and owes him love, provision and nurture. The child is a debtor to his parent, and owes him honour and obedience.
William Gurnall

If a parent does not punish his sons, his sons will be sure to punish him.
Thomas Guthrie

A parent must respect the spiritual person of his child, and approach it with reverence.   *George Macdonald*

If we teach good things, it is hopeful that they will be learned. If our lives exemplify virtue, it is hopeful that they will be imitated.
Cotton Mather

The secret of home rule is self rule, first being ourselves what we want our children to be.   *Andrew Murray*

If you would train your children rightly, train them in the way they *should* go and not in the way they *would*.
J. C. Ryle

A father's holy life is a rich legacy for his sons.
C. H. Spurgeon

If we walk before the Lord in integrity, we shall do more to bless our descendants than if we bequeathed them large estates.
C. H. Spurgeon

The mistaken kindness of parents has ever proved the greatest curse to children.
David Thomas

FAMILY LIFE — a Test of Character

He that walketh not uprightly in his house is but a hypocrite at church.
William Gurnall

101

The breakfast table may call for more grace than the Lord's table. *Vance Havner*

The real test of your Christianity is not how pious you look at the Lord's table on Sunday, but how you act at the breakfast table at home.
Vance Havner

Family life is a school for character. *Martin Luther*

The easiest place in which to be spiritual is in public; the most difficult is at home.
Charles Caldwell Ryrie

FEAR
(See also: Anxiety; Worry)

God can secure us from fear, either by removing the thing feared, or by subduing the fear of the thing.
William Beveridge

No passion so effectually robs the mind of all its powers of acting and reasoning as fear. *Edmund Burke*

Those who would be fearless must keep themselves guiltless. *Matthew Henry*

We need not look upon those enemies with fear whom God looks upon with contempt. *Matthew Henry*

I know not the way he leads me, but well do I know my Guide. What have I to fear?
Martin Luther

Fear is faithlessness.
George Macdonald

A good life is a good fence against fear.
Edward Marbury

Where fear is, happiness is not. *Seneca*

This only can my fears control,
And bid my sorrows fly;
What harm can ever reach my soul
Beneath my Father's eye?
Anne Steele

Fear is of the flesh and panic is of the devil.
A. W. Tozer

FEAR OF GOD
(See also: Awe; Worship)

He who does not fear God has need to fear everything else. *Anon.*

But what is this fear of the Lord? It is that affectionate reverence, by which the child of God bends himself humbly and carefully to his Father's law.
Charles Bridges

Just as obedience to the Lord is an indication of our love for him, so is it also a proof of our fear of God.

Jerry Bridges

The fear of God is the beginning of wisdom, and they that lack the beginning have neither middle nor end.

John Bunyan

Though there is not always grace where there is fear of hell, yet, to be sure, there is no grace where there is no fear of God. *John Bunyan*

As he that fears God fears nothing else, so, he that sees God sees nothing else.

John Donne

The fear of the Lord was a lovely grace in the perfect humanity of Jesus. Let it be the test of our 'predestination to be conformed to his image'.

Sinclair Ferguson

The fear of God is the soul of godliness. *John Murray*

As faith is a grace that feeds all the rest, so fear is a grace that guards all the rest.

William Secker

He who fears God has nothing else to fear.

C. H. Spurgeon

The Christian, like a net, must have both the lead of a godly fear and the cork of a lively faith.

George Swinnock

The height of God must lay man low. *George Swinnock*

The fear of God is both a virtue and a keeper of other virtues. *John Trapp*

As the embankment keeps out the water, so the fear of the Lord keeps out uncleanness. *Thomas Watson*

FELLOWSHIP

(See also: Church — Fellowship; Friendship)

Keep such company as God keeps. *Anon.*

There is danger of losing the spiritual fellowship by thinking that our social fellowship is the climax of all fellowship. *Donald Grey Barnhouse*

Fellowship with Christians is for the sake of fellowship with God. *J. I. Packer*

The fact that we share social activities with other Christians does not of itself imply that we have fellowship with them. *J. I. Packer*

FLATTERY

Many men know how to flatter; few know how to praise. *Anon.*

Flattery is praise insincerely given for an interested purpose. *Henry Ward Beecher*

Flatterers are the very worst of sinners. *Thomas Brooks*

Whilst an ass is stroked under the belly, you may lay on his back what burden you please. *Thomas Brooks*

Flattery is a juggler, and no kin unto sincerity. *Thomas Browne*

Flattery corrupts both the receiver and giver. *Edmund Burke*

Everyone flatters himself and carries a kingdom in his breast. *John Calvin*

Flattery sits in the parlour when plain dealing is kicked out of doors. *Thomas Fuller*

Be as much troubled by unjust praises as by unjust slanders. *Philip Henry*

Spiritual flatterers are commonly more respected than spiritual fathers. *William Jenkyn*

FORGIVENESS BY GOD

(See also Atonement; Cross; Jesus Christ — Death of)

It would tire the hands of an angel to write down all the pardons God bestows upon true penitent believers. *William Bates*

Be careful to keep the old receipts which you have from God for the pardon of your sins. *William Gurnall*

The sin which is not too great to be forsaken is not too great to be forgiven. *Thomas Horton*

Forgiveness forms the church. *R. C. Lucas*

Christ comes with a blessing in each hand; forgiveness in one, holiness in the other. *A. W. Pink*

Where we went with our vicious sins, there we must go with our soiled virtues. *W. E. Sangster*

Forgiveness is a golden thread spun out of the bowels of free grace. *Thomas Watson*

As unforgiven sin presents an insuperable barrier to blessing, so the forgiveness of sins is the priceless boon

which opens the door to every other spiritual blessing.
Geoffrey B. Wilson

The magnitude of the sacrifice which our sins called forth manifests the supreme folly of looking elsewhere for their forgiveness.
Geoffrey B. Wilson

There can be no thought of 'cheap' forgiveness when we remember that our redemption cost God the life of his beloved Son.
Geoffrey B. Wilson

FORGIVENESS OF OTHERS

There is no revenge so complete as forgiveness. *Anon.*

The glory of Christianity is to conquer by forgiveness.
William Blake

Nothing causes us to so nearly resemble God as the forgiveness of injuries.
Chrysostom

There's no point in burying a hatchet if you're going to put up a marker on the site.
Sydney Harris

A Christian will find it cheaper to pardon than to resent. Forgiveness saves us the expense of anger, the cost of hatred, the waste of spirits. *Hannah More*

It is a melancholy fact that there are few Christian duties so little practised as that of forgiveness.
J. C. Ryle

No prayers can be heard which do not come from a forgiving heart.
J. C. Ryle

FORMALISM
(See also: Hypocrisy; Ritualism)

It is a poor worship to move our hats, not our hearts.
Thomas Adams

Dead devotion is a living mockery. *Anon.*

Ordinances without the Spirit are cisterns without water. *Anon.*

It is no advantage to be near the light if the eyes are closed. *Augustine*

God hates the sanctimonious hallelujah more than he hates the godless curse.
Donald Grey Barnhouse

No one can thrive spiritually on mere church member-

ship, sacraments, ritual or formality.
Donald Grey Barnhouse

God is not taken with the cabinet but the jewel.
Stephen Charnock

Many pray with their lips for that for which their hearts have no desire.
Jonathan Edwards

Many a Christian, many a church, has everything in the showcase and nothing on the shelves. *Vance Havner*

Nothing is more destructive to Christianity than placing it in modes and forms and circumstantials which eat out the essentials.
Matthew Henry

Justification is totally against formal religion. God has no room for those who persist in relying on forms or ceremonies. *Robert M. Horn*

The more exalted pomp there be of men's devising, there will be the less spiritual truth. *George Hutcheson*

Solemn prayers, rapturous devotions, are but repeated hypocrisies unless the heart and mind be conformable to them. *William Law*

Ministers are but the pole; it is to the brazen serpent you are to look.
Robert Murray M'Cheyne

External observances alone feed no consciences and sanctify no hearts. *J. C. Ryle*

It must not content us to take our bodies to church if we leave our hearts at home.
J. C. Ryle

Men have only to go on hearing without believing, listening without repenting, going to church without going to Christ, and by and by they will find themselves in hell! *J. C. Ryle*

That man must famish at last who always feeds upon the dish instead of the meat.
William Secker

Outward things will do no more good than a fair shoe to a gouty foot.
Richard Sibbes

Posture in worship is too often imposture.
Thomas Watson

FREE WILL
(See also: Will)

A dog is free to be a dog; a sinner is free to be a sinner.
Andrew Anderson

A man's choices are free in the sense that they are not just determined by external compulsion. But they are not free if by freedom is meant freedom from determination by the man's own character.
J. Gresham Machen

FRIENDSHIP
(See also: Fellowship)

The firmest friendships have been formed in mutual adversity, as iron is most strongly united by the fiercest flame. *C. C. Colton*

Every man passes his life in the search after friendship.
Ralph Waldo Emerson

It is the best and truest friend who honestly tells us the truth about ourselves even when he knows we shall not like it. False friends are the ones who hide such truth from us and do so in order to remain in our favour.
R. C. H. Lenski

In friendship there is one soul in two bodies.
Richard Sibbes

Friendship is the marriage of affections. *Thomas Watson*

FRUITFULNESS

Our Lord never thought of a relationship to him that does not issue in fruitfulness for him. *Vance Havner*

The Christian should resemble a fruit tree, not a Christmas tree.
John R. W. Stott

FUTURE
(See also: Hope)

Belief in a future life is the appetite of reason.
Walter Landor

We have come to a wretched emphasis in the Christian church, so that when we talk about the future we talk about 'eschatology' instead of heaven! *A. W. Tozer*

GENEROSITY
(See also: Charity; Giving; Kindness)

Watch lest prosperity destroy generosity.
Henry Ward Beecher

Those who give the most have most left.
George F. Burba

107

A holy life and a bounteous heart are ornaments to the gospel.   *Thomas Manton*

True liberality is the spontaneous expression of love.
     Geoffrey B. Wilson

GENTLENESS

Perhaps no grace is less prayed for or less cultivated than gentleness.
     George Bethune

Seldom do we reflect that not to be gentle is sin.
     George Bethune

Gentle words fall lightly, but they have great weight.
     Derick Bingham

Nothing is so strong as gentleness; nothing so gentle as real strength.
     François de Sales

We need power for gentleness.   *W. Graham Scroggie*

GIVING

(See also: Charity; Generosity; Kindness; Tithing)

Christian giving is not a matter of finance, it is a matter of faith.

The church treasurer counts what we give; God counts what we keep.

When we give to God we are taking the gift out of one of his hands and putting it into the other.

Give from the bottom of your heart, not from the top of your purse.   *Anon.*

He who gives only when he is asked has waited too long.
     Anon.

Seeking empties a life; giving fills it.   *Anon.*

The hand that gives gathers.
     Anon.

Nearly half the parables Jesus told have the use of money as their main subject. It is sometimes said that we should give until it hurts. But Jesus teaches that it should hurt when we cease to give!   *Ian Barclay*

They who in giving think, not how little they can give, as they would if self-enrichment were the aim, but of benefits to be conferred, will receive back on the same principle. As they do to others, so God will act to them.   *J. A. Beet*

Spirit-directed giving is depending only on the Spirit of God to direct the gifts in the case of every person, and then being willing to abide by the results of this confidence and trust.
Lewis Sperry Chafer

He who receives a benefit should never forget it; he who bestows should never remember it.
Pierre Charron

The world is composed of takers and givers. The takers *eat* better but the givers *sleep* better. *Byron Frederick*

God hates a false economy that is out to reduce a budget instead of to receive a blessing. *Vance Havner*

By practising the grace of sharing, a person is storing up treasure for himself. Gifts are investments.
William Hendriksen

Unless we feel it is an honour and a joy to give, God does not accept the offering.
Charles Hodge

God gave us riches as a means to escape wrath, by a liberal and charitable distribution of them to his glory.
Thomas Manton

The secret of true giving is the joy of the Holy Ghost.
Andrew Murray

When a man gives, the world still asks, 'What does he give?' Christ asks, 'How does he give?'
Andrew Murray

When a man dies he clutches in his hands only that which he has given away in his lifetime.
Jean-Jacques Rousseau

A giving Saviour should have giving disciples.
J. C. Ryle

As you have done unto others, so will the Lord do unto you. Empty your pockets! *C. H. Spurgeon*

Faith's way of gaining is giving. *C. H. Spurgeon*

Giving is true having.
C. H. Spurgeon

I may expect that as much of prosperity as will be good for me will come to me as a gracious reward for a liberal course of action.
C. H. Spurgeon

We are to give to the poor out of pity. Not to be seen and applauded, much less to get influence over them; but out of pure sympathy and compassion we must give them help.   *C. H. Spurgeon*

All believers are taught to give — but there is such a thing as a special gift of giving.   *A. W. Tozer*

Mercy is not miserly; charity is no churl.   *John Trapp*

Arrogant giving can turn the best of gifts to ashes.
   Kenneth L. Wilson

GLUTTONY
(See also: Covetousness; Greed)

Gluttony kills more than the sword.   *Anon.*

Gluttony is the sepulchre of the living, and a kind of spiritual drowning of a man.
   William Jenkyn

GOD — Eternity

God is not the great 'I WAS'; he is the great 'I AM'.
   Eric Alexander

Eternity is the lifetime of the Almighty.   *Anon.*

Time writes no wrinkle on the brow of the Eternal.
   Anon.

God doesn't rush men; he owns time.   *John Hercus*

God's duration is without succession.   *George Swinnock*

Whatever God is he is infinitely.   *A. W. Tozer*

Unlike mortal man, God is incorruptible and so immortal.   *Geoffrey B. Wilson*

GOD — Existence

A dead God is the creation of men; a living God is the Creator of men.   *Anon.*

The being of a God is the guard of the world.
   Stephen Charnock

If every gnat that flies were an archangel, all that could but tell me that there is a God; and the poorest worm that creeps tells me that.
   John Donne

Let us weigh the gain and the loss in wagering that God is. If you win, you win all; if you lose, you lose nothing. Do not hesitate, then, to wager that he is.
   Blaise Pascal

What we believe about God is the most important thing about us.   *A. W. Tozer*

110

If God did not exist, he would have to be invented.
Voltaire

GOD — Glory

A concern for the glory of God is the ultimate motive for Christian living. *Anon.*

God's greatest glory is his grace.
Donald Grey Barnhouse

My God, how wonderful thou art!
Thy majesty how bright!
How beautiful thy mercy-seat,
In depths of burning light!
Frederick W. Faber

We cannot make God greater or higher than he is; but if we adore him as infinitely great, and higher than the highest, he is pleased to reckon this magnifying and exalting him.
Matthew Henry

The ultimate end of all things that come to pass, including the ultimate end of the great drama of redemption, is found in the glory of the eternal God.
J. Gresham Machen

God cannot allow another to be partaker of honours due to him without denying himself. It is as much his prerogative to be God alone as to be God at all.
William S. Plumer

God, and all that he has made, is not more than God without anything that he has made. *William Secker*

God will get glory out of every human life. Man may glorify God voluntarily by love and obedience, but if he will not do this he will be compelled to glorify God by his rejection and punishment. *Augustus H. Strong*

God's glory is that which makes him glorious.
Augustus H. Strong

His own glory is the only end which consists with God's independence and sovereignty.
Augustus H. Strong

If the universe were God, theology would be the only science.
Augustus H. Strong

God is transcendent above all his works even while he is immanent within them. He is here and the whole universe is alive with his life!
A. W. Tozer

A sight of God's glory humbles. The stars vanish when the sun appears.
Thomas Watson

Glory is the sparkling of the Deity. *Thomas Watson*

We may see God's glory blazing in the sun and twinkling in the stars.
Thomas Watson

The Lord Jehovah reigns;
His throne is built on high,
The garments he assumes
Are light and majesty:
His glories shine with beams so bright,
No mortal eye can bear the sight.
Isaac Watts

GOD — Goodness

God's riches are never lessened by his generosity.

Nothing good comes except from God and nothing except good comes from God.

God's giving deserves our thanksgiving. *Anon.*

God's goodness is the pre-eminent expression of his glory. *Jerry Bridges*

God has two sheepdogs: Goodness and Mercy. He sends them to us from his throne of grace; sometimes to bark at us, to badger us; sometimes to woo us by persuading us that his will is good and perfect for our lives. *Sinclair Ferguson*

He who feeds his birds will not starve his babes.
Matthew Henry

Times are bad; God is good.
Richard Sibbes

God never tires of giving.
William Still

It is not enough that we acknowledge God's infinite resources; we must believe also that he is infinitely generous to bestow them.
A. W. Tozer

High in the heavens, eternal God,
Thy goodness in full glory shines;
Thy truth shall break through every cloud
That veils and darkens thy designs.
Isaac Watts

GOD — Immutability

God may change our circumstances, but our circumstances can never change God.

God never 'becomes'; God is.

God is where he was.
Anon.

To deny the immutability of God is to deny that he is God. *R. B. Kuiper*

God is the most obligated being that there is. He is obligated by his own nature. He is infinite in his wisdom; therefore he can never do anything that is unwise. He is infinite in his justice; therefore he can never do anything that is unjust. He is infinite in his goodness; therefore he can never do anything that is not good. He is infinite in his truth; therefore it is impossible that he should lie.
J. Gresham Machen

Nothing created can ever alter the Creator.
Stuart Olyott

Human unbelief cannot alter the character of God.
A. W. Tozer

The immutability of God appears in its most perfect beauty when viewed against the mutability of men. In God no change is possible; in men change is impossible to escape. *A. W. Tozer*

Still restless nature dies and grows,
From change to change the creatures run:
Thy being no succession knows,
And all thy vast designs are one.

Isaac Watts

GOD — Independence

Being self-existent, God cannot but be self-sufficient, and therefore all-sufficient, and the inexhaustible fountain of being and bliss.
Matthew Henry

God does not stop to consult us. *D. Martyn Lloyd-Jones*

God is a law unto himself, and . . . he is under no obligation to give an account of his matters to any.
A. W. Pink

GOD — Inscrutability

The Christian who is truly spiritual revels as much in his ignorance of God as in his knowledge of him.

Were the works of God really understandable by human reason, they would

be neither wonderful nor unspeakable.
Thomas à Kempis

God's decrees, impossible to
be resisted, and leaving us in
the dark as to what may
come next, are calculated to
fill the mind with holy awe.
Albert Barnes

A cockle-fish may as soon
crowd the ocean into its
narrow shell as vain man
ever comprehend the decrees
of God. *William Beveridge*

God, to keep us sober, speaks
sparingly of his essence.
John Calvin

It is visible *that* God is; it is
invisible *what* he is.
Stephen Charnock

We better understand what
God is *not* than what he *is*.
Stephen Charnock

Were I fully able to describe
God, I should be God my-
self, or God must cease to be
what he is. *Epictetus*

It is part of God's wise providence that he will not be
apprehended by intellectual
speculation. *T. S. Evans*

God's works are never above
right, though often above
reason. *Thomas Fuller*

We cannot know all about
God for the obvious reason
that the finite cannot comprehend the infinite.
R. B. Kuiper

Instinctively we know that
we cannot box God up in
any conceptual framework
of our own devising, and
that if we think we have suc-
ceeded in doing so, then
what we have in our box is
not God. *John R. W. Stott*

There is in the awful and
mysterious depths of the
triune God neither limit nor
end. *A. W. Tozer*

God is beyond human
examination and can be
known only by those to
whom he chooses to reveal
himself. *Geoffrey B. Wilson*

GOD — Jealousy

*God is jealous for the good of his
redeemed people – but he can
never be jealous of anything or
anyone.*

God, as a jealous God, is
filled with a burning desire
for our holiness, for our
righteousness, for our goodness. *Donald Grey Barnhouse*

GOD — Love

God looks over us but never overlooks us.

God loves his people when he strikes them as well as when he strokes them.
Anon.

The true measure of God's love is that he loves without measure. *Anon.*

O love of God, how strong
and true!
Eternal and yet ever new;
Uncomprehended and un-
bought,
Beyond all knowledge and
all thought.
Horatius Bonar

God's love is a free love, having no motive or foundation but within itself.
Thomas Brooks

Divine love is no abstract theory; it is a living Person.
Harry Foster

The point . . . is not that the world is so big that it takes a great deal of love to embrace it, but that the world is so bad that it takes an exceedingly great kind of love to love it at all. *R. B. Kuiper*

God does not love us because we are valuable, but we are valuable because God loves us. *Martin Luther*

God smothers repenting sinners in forgiving and redemptive love.
Al Martin

I know of no truth in the whole Bible that ought to come home to us with such power and tenderness as that of the love of God.
D. L. Moody

God is far more willing to save sinners than sinners are to be saved. *J. C. Ryle*

There is an infinite willingness in God to save man, if man is only willing to be saved. *J. C. Ryle*

Lord, send us such a flood-tide of thy love that we shall be washed beyond the mire of doubt and fear.
C. H. Spurgeon

God's favourite word is — come! *Robert L. Sterner*

God never repents of his electing love.
Thomas Watson

Our total welfare is the constant concern of God's loving heart.
W. J. C. White

Immortal love, for ever full,
For ever flowing free,
For ever shared, for ever
  whole,
A never-ebbing sea!
                    John Greenleaf Whittier

GOD — Name

The titles of God are virtually promises.
                    David Clarkson

God's name, as it is set out in the Word, is both a glorious name, full of majesty; and also a gracious name, full of mercy.   *William Gouge*

That God should be kindly disposed to a world that hates, so as to bring the gospel of good news to them all is gracious, and that he should go further and actually apply that gospel in such away as to rescue men and transform them is marvellous.   *Erroll Hulse*

The name Jehovah carries majesty in it; the name Father carries mercy in it.
                    Thomas Watson

GOD — Omnipotence

What is impossible to God? Not that which is difficult to his power, but that which is contrary to his nature.
                    Ambrose

We should never tire of the thought of God's power.
                    Donald Grey Barnhouse

God hath in himself all power to defend you, all wisdom to direct you, all mercy to pardon you, all grace to enrich you, all righteousness to clothe you, all goodness to supply you, and all happiness to crown you.
                    Thomas Brooks

We are not to think that, where we see no possibility, God sees none. *Marcus Dods*

We must learn to cease from measuring the power of God by our own, and reasoning from one to the other.
                    Marcus Dods

When God is about to do something great, he starts with a difficulty. When he is about to do something truly magnificent, he starts with an impossibility.
                    Armin Gesswein

God is not waiting to show us strong in his behalf, but himself strong in our behalf. That makes a lot of difference. He is not out to demonstrate what we can do but what he can do.
                    Vance Havner

Man's extremity is God's opportunity of helping and saving.   *Matthew Henry*

God can do without any exception what he wills to do.
R. B. Kuiper

The power of God is not diminished when it is said that he cannot die and cannot sin; for if he could do these things, his power would be less.
R. B. Kuiper

God is not wasted by bestowing.   *Thomas Manton*

God works without labour.
William S. Plumer

The presence of God in the flood is better than a ferry-boat.   *C. H. Spurgeon*

God raises the level of the impossible.   *Corrie ten Boom*

In the New Testament it is not believers who tremble at the power of Satan, but demons who tremble at the power of God.
Stephen Travis

God's riches are imparted, not impaired.
Thomas Watson

GOD — Omnipresence

Nature is too thin a screen; the glory of the omnipresent God bursts through everywhere.
Ralph Waldo Emerson

The notion that there is a God but that he is comfortably far away is not embodied in the doctrinal statement of any Christian church.   *A. W. Tozer*

GOD — Omniscience

If one thing lies at the basis of the whole biblical teaching about God it is that God knows all things.
J. Gresham Machen

Is it not clear that God foreknows what will be because he has decreed what shall be? God's foreknowledge is not the cause of events, rather are events the effects of his eternal purpose.
A. W. Pink

God looks most where man looks least.
William Secker

Because God knows all things perfectly, he knows no thing better than any other thing, but all things equally well. He never discovers

117

anything, he is never surprised, never amazed.
                    A. W. Tozer

GOD — Patience

Many have been reprieved that were never forgiven.
                    Stephen Charnock

Though the patience of God be lasting, yet it is not everlasting.   William Secker

God's forbearance is no acquittance.   *John Trapp*

GOD — Perfection

God's attributes coincide with his being.
                    Herman Bavinck

Doubting any perfection of God is tantamount to robbing him of his glory.
                    William S. Plumer

GOD — Purposes

God's purposes are sometimes delayed but they are never abandoned.

If it pleases God's purposes, he can bring a millionaire to the breadline and set up a pauper in a palace.

Any attempt to justify God's ways is arrogant and childish. Any attempt to seize on what we regard as evidence that he was right after all is fatuous.   *Elisabeth Elliot*

The most crooked tree will make timber for the temple, if God be pleased to hew it.
                    Thomas Fuller

Nothing whatever surprises God; all things that happen are absolutely certain from all eternity because they are all embraced in God's eternal plan.
                    J. Gresham Machen

The many decrees all constitute just one purpose or one plan. They are not without relation to one another, but form a mighty unity as God himself is one.
                    J. Gresham Machen

God is his own motive.
                    Alexander Maclaren

God is working out his eternal purpose, not only in spite of human and satanic opposition, but by means of them.   *A. W. Pink*

What God is and has, he is and has for all his people's good.   *William S. Plumer*

God's whole purpose, conceived in past eternity, being

worked out for and in his people in history, to be completed in the glory to come, may be encapsulated in this single concept: God intends to make us like Christ.
John R. W. Stott

If we had to sum up in a single brief sentence what life is all about, why Jesus Christ came into this world to live and die and rise, and what God is up to in the long-drawn-out historical process both BC and AD, it would be difficult to find a more succinct explanation than this: God is making human beings more human by making them more like Christ. *John R. W. Stott*

To suppose that God has a multitude of plans, and that he changes his plan with the exigencies of the situation, is to make him infinitely dependent upon the varying wills of his creatures, and to deny him one necessary element of perfection, namely, immutability.
Augustus H. Strong

God has no problems, only plans. *Corrie ten Boom*

GOD — Sovereignty

The devil's way of extinguishing goodness is God's way of advancing it.
George Barlow

The conclave of hell can do nothing without a commission from heaven.
Thomas Brooks

God is the world's Sovereign, but a good man's Father. He rules heaven and earth, but he loves his holy ones. Other things are the objects of his providence, and a good man is the end of it.
Stephen Charnock

There can be but one Infinite. *Elisha Coles*

God's ways are behind the scenes, but he moves all the scenes which he is behind.
John Nelson Darby

Appearances can be deceptive. The fact that we cannot see what God is doing does not mean that he is doing nothing. *Sinclair Ferguson*

The title deed to this world does not belong to dictators, to Communism, nor to the devil, but to God.
Vance Havner

Whatever point of compass the wind is in, it is fulfilling God's word, and turns about by his counsel.

Matthew Henry

God is a totalitarian Ruler who demands full allegiance from his subjects.

R. B. Kuiper

If God were less than sovereign, man would be less than responsible. Since God is absolutely sovereign, man is wholly responsible to him.

R. B. Kuiper

The sovereignty of God may be defined as his absolute right to govern and dispose of all his creatures according to his good pleasure.

R. B. Kuiper

Let God be God!

Martin Luther

All nature, including the nature of man, is a wondrous instrument of many strings, delicately tuned to work God's will and upon which he plays with a master hand.

J. Gresham Machen

Even the wicked actions of men serve God's purposes and it is by his works of providence that he permits those wicked actions to be done.

J. Gresham Machen

Wicked men may not think they are serving God's purposes; but they are serving his purposes all the same, even by the most wicked of their acts.

J. Gresham Machen

The man who measures things by the circumstances of the hour is filled with fear; the man who sees Jehovah enthroned and governing has no panic.

G. Campbell Morgan

God is too great to be knocked off course by the malpractice of wicked men.

J. A. Motyer

The Christ who rules us rules all things for us.

J. I. Packer

The world belongs to God and he wants it back.

David Pawson

Alternatives confront us, and between them we are obliged to choose; either God governs, or he is governed; either God rules, or he is ruled; either God has his way, or men have theirs. And is our choice between these alternatives hard to make?

A. W. Pink

God is working out his eternal purpose, not only in spite of human and satanic opposition, but by means of them. *A. W. Pink*

If then we see the sovereignty of God displayed throughout all creation why should it be thought a strange thing if we behold it operating in the midst of the human family? *A. W. Pink*

Sovereignty characterizes the whole being of God. He is sovereign in all his attributes. *A. W. Pink*

We read the Scriptures in vain if we fail to discover that the actions of men, evil men as well as good, are governed by the Lord God. *A. W. Pink*

Where the sovereignty of God is denied there will be no holy awe of him. *A. W. Pink*

God is choice in keeping the keys of time at his own girdle. *Matthew Poole*

In the saving of individuals, as well as in the calling of nations, God acts as a sovereign, and gives no account of his matters. *J. C. Ryle*

Of all the doctrines of the Bible none is so offensive to human nature as the doctrine of God's sovereignty. *J. C. Ryle*

The hands of the wicked cannot stir one moment before God allows them to begin, and cannot stir one moment after God commands them to stop. *J. C. Ryle*

The wickedest enemies of God are only axes and saws and hammers in his hands, and are ignorantly his instruments for doing his work in the world. *J. C. Ryle*

God can never be outmanoeuvred, taken by surprise, or caught at a disadvantage. He is a God who knows no crisis . . . Before an emergency arises, God in his providence has made adequately and perfectly timed provision to meet it. *J. Oswald Sanders*

If God lights the candle, none can blow it out. *C. H. Spurgeon*

If the Lord will not suffer it, neither men nor devils can do it. *C. H. Spurgeon*

The devices of the wicked are overruled for their defeat. *C. H. Spurgeon*

We must believe in the grace of sovereignty as well as the sovereignty of grace. *Augustus H. Strong*

121

God does not do many things that he can, but he does all things that he will.
George Swinnock

God's plan will continue on God's schedule.
A. W. Tozer

Whatever God did and was able to do and willing to do at any time, God is able and willing to do again, within the framework of his will.
A. W. Tozer

Absolutely nothing lies outside the scope of God's sovereignty.
Geoffrey B. Wilson

Satan's malice is always frustrated by God and made to minister a blessing *to his people*. The 'all things' of Romans 8:28 admits of no exceptions.
Geoffrey B. Wilson

The work of Satan is overruled so that it assists in bringing to pass the divine purpose, though Satan on his part uses his utmost powers to thwart that purpose.
Geoffrey B. Wilson

GOD — Wrath

No cloud can ever hang over a Christian's life that is darker than a cloud of anger on the face of God.

The real horror of being outside of Christ is that there is no shelter from the wrath of God.
Eric Alexander

There is terror in the Bible as well as comfort.
Donald Grey Barnhouse

Though the Lord should damn us eternally, he should do us no wrong, but only that which our nature deserveth.
Daniel Cawdray

The doctrine of the wrath of God is not a popular doctrine, but there is no doctrine that is more utterly pervasive in the Bible.
J. Gresham Machen

The fact is that the subject of divine wrath has become taboo in modern society, and Christians by and large have accepted the taboo and conditioned themselves never to raise the matter.
J. I. Packer

Every wrathful judgement of God in the history of the world has been a holy act of preservation.
A. W. Tozer

God is as faithful in his menaces as in his promises.
John Trapp

Sinners may oppose God's ways, but not his wrath.
Thomas Watson

GODHEAD

(See also: God)

The Trinity is (not *are*) God the Father, God the Son, God the Holy Spirit.
Donald Grey Barnhouse

The word 'Trinity' is not found in the Bible, but the truth of this doctrine is in every part of the book.
Donald Grey Barnhouse

The doctrine of the Trinity is basic to the Christian religion. It is no exaggeration to assert that the whole of Christianity stands or falls with it.   *R. B. Kuiper*

Our sincerest effort to grasp the incomprehensible mystery of the Trinity must remain for ever futile, and only by deepest reverence can it be saved from actual presumption.
A. W. Tozer

GODLINESS

(See also: Christlikeness; Holiness)

Godliness . . . is devotion to God which results in a life that is pleasing to him.
Jerry Bridges

The words 'godly' and 'godliness' actually appear only a few times in the New Testament; yet the entire book is a book on godliness.
Jerry Bridges

Godliness separates us from the pollutions of the world, and by true holiness unites us to God.   *John Calvin*

True godliness is that which breeds the quarrel between God's children and the wicked.   *John Dod*

We are transformed into the image of the Lord by beholding it, not by reflecting it.   *Charles Hodge*

Godliness is living to the glory of the Lord from the heart out of gratitude.
R. T. Kendall

He who attempts to stress Christian living by disparaging Christian doctrine is guilty of a most serious blunder. He neglects the important fact that Christian living is rooted in Christian doctrine.   *R. B. Kuiper*

Sincerity is of the essence of the life of godliness.
Iain H. Murray

The fear of God is the soul of godliness.   *John Murray*

Godliness is the constitution of a real Christian.
George Swinnock

A godly life is always the best advertisement for Christianity.   *Geoffrey B. Wilson*

GOOD DEEDS

(See also: Faith — and Deeds; Fruitfulness; Holiness — and Justification)

Justification never results from good deeds; justification always results in good deeds.

Good deeds are such things that no man is saved for them nor without them.
    Thomas Adams

Duties may be good crutches to go upon, but they are bad christs to lean upon.
    Anon.

Our good deeds are to be scattered upon all men, Christian and non-Christian.   *Jerry Bridges*

The gospel teaches us that while believers are not rewarded on account of their works, they are rewarded according to their works.
    R. L. Dabney

While our works are naught as a ground of merit for justification, they are all-important as evidences that we are justified.   *R. L. Dabney*

I have taken my good deeds and bad deeds and thrown them together in a heap and fled from them both to Christ, and in him I have peace.   *David Dickson*

I count all that part of my life lost which I spent not in communion with God or in doing good.   *John Donne*

If there be ground for you to trust in your own righteousness, then all that Christ did to purchase salvation, and all that God did to prepare the way for it, is in vain.
    Jonathan Edwards

The luxury of doing good surpasses every other personal enjoyment.
    John Gay

We are not justified by doing good works, but being justified we then do good.
    William Jenkyn

Even if I knew the world would be destroyed tomorrow I would plant a tree today.   *Martin Luther*

I believe that the root of almost every schism and heresy from which the Christian church has ever suffered has been the effort of men to earn, rather than to receive, their salvation.
    John Ruskin

Our best works before we are justified are little better than splendid sins.

J. C. Ryle

If you be found in your own righteousness you will be lost in your own righteousness.

William Secker

It is our bounden duty to live *in* obedience, but it would prove our utter ruin to live *on* obedience.

William Secker

I would not give much for your religion unless it can be seen. Lamps do not talk, but they do shine.

C. H. Spurgeon

GOODNESS

(See also: Ethics; Morality; Virtue)

A man is only as good as what he loves. *Saul Bellow*

The best practical definition of goodness is given in the life and character of Jesus Christ: 'Jesus of Nazareth, who went about doing good'. *George Bethune*

When you are alone, think of good things; and when you are in company, speak of good things.

William Bridge

Goodness that preaches undoes itself.

Ralph Waldo Emerson

A good life fears not life nor death. *Thomas Fuller*

We can circumvent a lot of our worries by giving our attention to the good. Most of our ailments will die from neglect. *Vance Havner*

We can do more good by being good than in any other way. *Rowland Hill*

No man knows how bad he is until he has tried to be good. *C. S. Lewis*

Every man has far more knowledge of good than he uses. *Alexander Maclaren*

A good life is a good fence against fear.

Edward Marbury

A musician is commended not that he played so long, but that he played so well. And thus it is not the days of our life, but the goodness of our life . . . that is acceptable unto God Almighty.

Josias Shute

When the mists have cleared away and all things appear in their proper light I think it will be revealed that goodness and greatness are synonymous. I do not see how it could be otherwise in a moral world.   *A. W. Tozer*

GOSPEL

(See also: Evangelism; Soul-Winning)

The gospel is a glorious declaration of the mighty acts of God when he invaded this earth in the person of his eternal Son, the Lord Jesus Christ.

The gospel is not a human plan for reaching up to God, but a divine plan for reaching down to man.

The gospel is who Jesus is and what Jesus did.

The blindness of unbelievers in no way detracts from the clarity of the gospel; the sun is no less bright because blind men do not perceive its light.   *John Calvin*

The gospel is not a doctrine of the tongue, but of life.
    John Calvin

The gospel is the ground of the believer's assurance, while the Holy Spirit is its cause.   *J. C. P. Cockerton*

The gospel cannot stand in part and fall in part.
    Cyprian

As there is only one God, so there can be only one gospel.
    James Denney

The law was for the *condemnation* of sinners; the gospel was for the *saving* of sinners and the ministration of forgiveness.   *C. J. Ellicott*

The gospel is the gospel of a happy God, because he now has an ever-growing family of those who by faith share the perfect life of his perfect Son.   *Harry Foster*

God will not allow the light of his truth to be covered up indefinitely.
    David E. Gardner

The success of the gospel exasperates its enemies.
    Matthew Henry

The rejection of the gospel is as clear proof of moral depravity as inability to see the sun at noon is proof of blindness.   *Charles Hodge*

That God should be kindly disposed to a world that hates him so as to bring the gospel of good news to them all is gracious, and that he should go further and actually apply that gospel in such a way as to rescue men and transform them is marvellous.   *Erroll Hulse*

The church is the fruit of the gospel.   *Hywel R. Jones*

The vitality of the heavenly seed is not dependent upon the feelings of the sower, but upon the perpetual energy of the Spirit of truth.
G. H. Lang

The gospel is not so much a miracle as a marvel, and every line is suffused with wonder.   *Martin Luther*

The gospel is not speculation but fact. It is truth, because it is the record of a person who is the Truth.
Alexander Maclaren

Apart from the bright hope of the gospel everything would be meaningless.
Poul Madsen

The gospel no more excuses sin than the law does. What is repugnant to the moral law of God is also contrary to the gospel of Christ.
Henry T. Mahan

God and his truth cannot be changed; the gospel is not negotiable.   *John Marshall*

The gospel will never be fashionable at any period of history or in any country.
Jules-Marcel Nicole

We are far more concerned about the results of the gospel than we are about the purity of it.   *A. W. Pink*

The annals of the world tell us not of one instance where a sinner was converted, sanctified, filled with pious hopes, made willing to suffer in the cause of God and enabled mightily to triumph over the world, the flesh and the devil, over fears, temptations and death itself, except by the gospel of Christ.   *William S. Plumer*

The gospel is neither a discussion nor a debate. It is an announcement.
Paul S. Rees

The light which men got from Moses and the law was at best only starlight compared to noonday.
J. C. Ryle

There are no incurable cases under the gospel. Any sinner may be healed if he will only come to Christ.   *J. C. Ryle*

We have an unchanging gospel, which is not today green grass and tomorrow dry hay; but always the abiding truth of the immutable Jehovah.
C. H. Spurgeon

The gospel is a declaration, not a debate.

James S. Stewart

There are two things to do about the gospel — believe it and behave it.

Susannah Wesley

The ethical demand for holy living is inseparable from what is freely given in the gospel. *Geoffrey B. Wilson*

GOSSIP

(See also: Rumour; Slander; Speech)

Gossip is the art of confessing other people's sins. *Anon.*

There would not be so many open mouths if there were not so many open ears.

Joseph Hall

GRACE — The Christian's indebtedness to

He who is graceless in the day of grace will be speechless in the Day of Judgement.

Anon.

There is no reason for grace but grace. *Anon.*

Every day we are objects of the grace of God.

Donald Grey Barnhouse

Perfection demands perfection; that is why salvation must be by grace, and why works are not sufficient.

Donald Grey Barnhouse

All that I was, my sin, my guilt,
My death, was all my own;
All that I am I owe to thee,
My gracious God, alone.

Horatius Bonar

True grace always produces vigilance rather than complacency; it always produces perseverance rather than indolence. *Jerry Bridges*

Grace, 'tis a charming sound,
Harmonious to my ear;
Heaven with the echo shall resound
And all the earth shall hear.

Philip Doddridge

A supply of grace is in store for believers against all exigencies; but they are only supplied with it as the need arises. *A. R. Fausset*

There is a greater gulf between grace and no grace than between weak grace and strong.

William Gurnall

God's grace is not only amazing grace, it is abounding grace.   *Vance Havner*

Knowledge is but folly unless it is guided by grace.
George Herbert

It takes grace to accept grace.   *Robert M. Horn*

Nature without grace is as Samson without his guide when his eyes were out.
John King

In all the Word of God there is no doctrine which, if properly applied, is more conducive to godly living than is the doctrine of salvation by grace, and by grace alone.   *R. B. Kuiper*

Whatever contribution men make to their salvation they make by the grace of God. And that makes salvation the work of grace a hundred per cent.   *R. B. Kuiper*

Every gospel imperative is full of the divine power of grace to effect what it demands. If it counted on even the least power in the sinner it would never secure the least effect.
R. C. H. Lenski

Always distinguish between the words 'attain' and 'obtain'. We can never

attain or earn God's gracious help by prayer or service, but we can obtain, appropriate and take it.
F. B. Meyer

There is no grace unless God bestows it, and there is no real peace unless it flows forth from God's reconciliation with sinful man.
J. J. Muller

If there is to be in our celestial garment but one stitch of our own making we are all of us lost.
C. H. Spurgeon

God does not owe you salvation. You deserve damnation, but he provides salvation.   *Billy Sunday*

Behold, what wondrous grace
The Father hath bestowed
On sinners of a mortal race,
To call them sons of God.
Isaac Watts

GRACE — Common Grace

God, by the seasonable weeping of the heaven, has caused the plentiful laughter of the earth.
Thomas Fuller

The common grace of God enables us to interpret world history.   *Erroll Hulse*

may not give gain, but he will give grace.
                    C. H. Spurgeon

GRACE — Daily

They travel lightly whom God's grace carries.
                    Thomas à Kempis

God's grace is sufficient for us anywhere his providence places us.   *Anon.*

Yesterday's hits won't win today's game.   *Anon.*

A man can no more take in a supply of grace for the future than he can eat enough for the next six months or take sufficient air into his lungs at one time to sustain life for a week. We must draw upon God's boundless store of grace from day to day as we need it.
                    D. L. Moody

The sanctifying grace of God is appropriated by the obedient and unrelenting activity of the regenerate man.   *J. A. Motyer*

Grace is stronger than circumstances.   *J. C. Ryle*

The Lord may not give gold, but he will give grace; he

GRACE — Essence

Grace is incapable of explanation.

Grace has long arms.

Grace is the free favour of God; peace is the condition which results from its reception.   *H. L. Goudge*

From what the Bible says it seems to me that we shall not know the full explanation of grace, even in heaven.
                    Robert M. Horn

Grace is nothing but an introduction of the virtues of God into the soul.
                    Thomas Manton

Grace is love in action.
                    G. Campbell Morgan

Grace in God is his compassion on the unworthy.
                    Andrew Murray

Grace in the New Testament is not . . . an impersonal energy automatically switched on by prayer and sacraments, but the heart and hand of the living almighty God.   *J. I. Packer*

God's grace cannot stand with man's merit.
William Perkins

We cannot seek grace through gadgets.
J. B. Priestley

Grace and nature can no more amalgamate than oil and water. *J. C. Ryle*

Grace that cannot be seen, like light, and tasted, like salt, is not grace but hypocrisy. *J. C. Ryle*

Grace is the oil of gladness; and the more of this oil, the more of gladness.
George Swinnock

Grace is both a grace and a vessel to receive grace.
John Trapp

True grace is operative and will not lie dormant.
John Trapp

GRACE — and Heaven

Death *shortens* our way to heaven, but grace *sweetens* our way to heaven.
Anon.

The least grace is a better security for heaven than the greatest gifts or privileges whatsoever. *John Owen*

Grace shall always lead to glory. *J. C. Ryle*

There are many who are barely Christians and have scarcely enough grace to float them into heaven, the keel of their vessel grating on the gravel all the way.
C. H. Spurgeon

Grace is glory inchoate; glory is grace consummate.
George Swinnock

GRACE — and Salvation

Grace is not a reward for faith; faith is the result of grace.

Grace is what all need, what none can merit and what God alone can give.
George Barlow

Saving grace makes a man as willing to leave his lusts as a slave is willing to leave his galley, or a prisoner his dungeon, or a thief his bolts, or a beggar his rags.
Thomas Brooks

Grace comes not to take away a man's affections, but to take them up.
William Fenner

The first step to grace is to see they have no grace; the

131

first degree of grace is the desire of grace.

William Fenner

We are born with our backs upon God and heaven, and our faces upon sin and hell, till grace comes and that converts — turns us.

Philip Henry

Efficacious grace is invincible.

Ernest F. Kevan

They have no grace that can be content with a little grace.

Thomas Manton

It is a sure mark of grace to desire more.

Robert Murray M'Cheyne

It is grace, not place, which makes people believers.

J. C. Ryle

Sovereign grace can make strangers into sons.

C. H. Spurgeon

It is a greater work of God to bring men to grace than, being in the state of grace, to bring them to glory; because sin is far more distant from grace than grace is from glory.

John Trapp

Grace is power. It does not instruct, it energizes; and what dead men need is energizing, such energizing as raises the dead.

Benjamin B. Warfield

My God, how excellent thy grace,
Whence all our hope and comfort spring!
The sons of Adam in distress
Fly to the shadow of thy wing

Isaac Watts

GRACE — Supremacy

God's greatest glory is in his grace.

Donald Grey Barnhouse

As heat is opposed to cold, and light to darkness, so grace is opposed to sin. Fire and water may as well agree in the same vessel as grace and sin in the same heart.

Thomas Brooks

The life of grace is the death of sin, and the growth of grace the decay of sin.

Thomas Brooks

Grace is the most important word in the Protestant vocabulary.

Robert Macafee Brown

Grace is as large in renewing us as sin was in defacing.

Stephen Charnock

The ocean will hold a boat or a battleship, and God's grace will stand any weight you put on it.

Vance Havner

The stream of grace and righteousness is deeper and broader than the stream of guilt. *Matthew Henry*

The word 'grace' is unquestionably the most significant single word in the Bible.
Ilion T. Jones

God's grace can never break down. *Ernest F. Kevan*

The grace of God ... is a much higher thing than the grace of a king to his dutiful subjects; it has its inspiration not in the worthiness of those to whom it is shown but entirely in the heart of God himself. *Ernest F. Kevan*

There is no chemistry like to that of grace.
Thomas Manton

Grace is what the New Testament is about.
J. I. Packer

Where grace exists it reigns; it is the dominant factor in the situation. *J. I. Packer*

Grace is above all conditions. *Richard Sibbes*

GRACES

The richest pearl in the Christian's crown of graces is humility. *John Mason Good*

The strength of every grace lies in the *sincerity* of it.
A. W. Pink

Some graces grow best in winter. *Samuel Rutherford*

No grace is stronger than humility. *Richard Sibbes*

GRATITUDE
(See also: Thanksgiving)

He who receives a benefit should never forget it; he who bestows should never remember it.
Pierre Charron

Gratitude is the most exquisite form of courtesy.
Jacques Maritain

Gratitude to God makes even a temporal blessing a taste of heaven.
William Romaine

A grateful mind is both a great and happy mind.
William Secker

The man who forgets to be grateful has fallen asleep in life. *Robert Louis Stevenson*

GREED
(See also: Covetousness; Gluttony)

Big mouthfuls often choke.
Anon.

The lack of faith is the source of greed.
John Calvin

Greed is a bottomless pit which exhausts the person in an endless effort to satisfy the need without ever reaching satisfaction.
Erich Fromm

If your desires be endless, your cares and fears will be so too. *Thomas Fuller*

Riches have made more covetousness than covetousness has made rich men.
Thomas Fuller

Avarice is as destitute of what it has as poverty of what it has not.
Publilius Syrus

GROWTH

The soul of all improvement is the improvement of the soul. *Anon.*

You may not be the best judge of the distance you have travelled, but you ought to have a good idea of the direction in which you are travelling. *Anon.*

There is no progress possible to the man who does not see and mourn over his defects.
George Barlow

Let us not cease to do the utmost, that we may incessantly go forward in the way of the Lord; and let us not despair because of the smallness of our accomplishments.
John Calvin

If I cease becoming better, I shall soon cease to be good.
Oliver Cromwell

Progress towards maturity is not to be measured by victory over the sins we are aware of, but by hatred of the sins which we had overlooked and which we now see all too clearly.
Arthur C. Custance

Many spiritual experiences are possible which do not in and of themselves produce maturity. Rather, it is our response to experiences which will determine our progress in maturity.
Sinclair Ferguson

We discern the growth of grace as the growth of plants, which we perceive rather to have grown than to grow. *John Flavel*

The business of life is to go forward.   *Samuel Johnson*

Spiritual maturity comes not by erudition, but by compliance with the known will of God.   *D. W. Lambert*

We grow in proportion as we know.   *J. A. Motyer*

If I have observed anything by experience it is this: a man may take the measure of his growth and decay in grace according to his thoughts and meditations upon the person of Christ and the glory of Christ's kingdom and of his love.
John Owen

In this life we never ascend to a plateau above and beyond which there is no further ground to gain.
Charles Caldwell Ryrie

There is a state of grace which *can* be enjoyed by Christians demonstrably higher than that which *is* commonly enjoyed.
W. E. Sangster

However holy or Christlike a Christian may become, he is still in the condition of 'being changed'.
John R. W. Stott

The growth of grace is the best evidence of the truth of it; things that have no life will not grow.
Thomas Watson

Progress is the only alternative to falling. We must advance or we shall decline. To prevent decay we must grow.   *John Wilmot*

GUIDANCE
(See also: Will of God)

Listen to no man who fails to listen to God.   *Anon.*

God leads his people out of sin by faith; through the world by hope; into heaven by love.   *Michael Ayguan*

I dare not choose my lot;
I would not if I might;
Choose thou for me, my God,
So shall I walk aright.
Horatius Bonar

Unless God's Word illumine the way, the whole life of men is wrapped in darkness and mist, so that they cannot but miserably stray.
John Calvin

While providence supports,
Let saints securely dwell;
That hand which bears all nature up
Shall guide his children well.
Philip Doddridge

135

Guidance is not normally ecstatic or mystical. It is always ethical and intensely practical. *Sinclair Ferguson*

Guidance, knowing God's will for our lives, is much more a matter of thinking than of feeling.
Sinclair Ferguson

Very often when young people say they are having problems about guidance, what they are really faced with is a problem about obedience.
Sinclair Ferguson

Where God guides he provides. He is responsible for our upkeep if we follow his directions. He is not responsible for expenses not on his schedule. *Vance Havner*

Men give advice; God gives guidance. *Leonard Ravenhill*

If disappointment, trouble, frustration or failure have influenced our decision, we should be doubly careful before acting on it. Had Paul and Silas allowed their reception in Philippi to sway them in their guidance Europe might still have been without the gospel.
J. Oswald Sanders

In some ways I find guidance, if anything, gets harder rather than easier the longer I am a Christian. Perhaps God allows this so that we have to go on relying on him and not on ourselves.
David Watson

GUILT

(See also: Depravity; Man — a Sinner; Sin; Sinful Nature)

Worry, like guilt, is a reflection of our human privilege as made in God's image. We are able to feel guilty because we have been given moral responsibility by God. We are able to feel anxiety because we have been given creative imagination by God. *Roy Clements*

The burden of sin is the wrath of God.
Edward Marbury

HABIT

Habit is a shirt made of iron.
Anon.

Habits, like fish-hooks, are lots easier to get caught than uncaught. *Frank A. Clark*

We first make our habits, then our habits make us.
John Dryden

The chains of habit are generally too small to be felt until they are too strong to be broken.   *Samuel Johnson*

Custom of sinning takes away the sense of it; the course of the world takes away the shame of it.
John Owen

Beware of the habits we learn in controversy.
Francis Schaeffer

The best way to break a bad habit is to drop it.
D. S. Yoder

HAPPINESS

(See also: Humour; Joy)

Happiness is the art of making a bouquet of those flowers within reach.
Anon.

To seek God is to desire happiness; to find him *is* that happiness.   *Augustine*

When our holiness is perfect, our happiness shall be perfect; and if this were attainable on earth, there would be but little reason for men to long to be in heaven.
Thomas Brooks

To live happily the evils of ambition and self-love must be plucked from our hearts by the roots.   *John Calvin*

Happiness can be built only on virtue, and must of necessity have truth for its foundation.
Samuel Taylor Coleridge

God did not save us to make us happy but to make us holy.   *Vance Havner*

The world's happiness should be spelled 'happenness', because it depends on what happens.
Vance Havner

A man should look after a happiness that will last as long as his soul lasts.
Thomas Manton

God has linked together holiness and happiness; and what God has joined together we must not think to put asunder.   *J. C. Ryle*

Never was there a greater mistake than to suppose that vital Christianity interferes with human happiness.
J. C. Ryle

Those who fancy that true religion has any tendency to make men unhappy are greatly mistaken. It is the absence of it that does this, not the presence.
J. C. Ryle

We must love our happiness no further than we can have it with God's leave and liking.   *Richard Sibbes*

There can be no happiness if the things we believe in are different from the things we do.   *Treya Stark*

Happiness is nothing but the sabbath of our thoughts.
George Swinnock

Christians have every right to be the happiest people in the world. We do not have to look to other sources — for we look to the Word of God and discover how we can know the faithful God above and draw from his resources.
A. W. Tozer

The reason we have to search for so many things to cheer us up is the fact that we are not really joyful and contentedly happy within.
A. W. Tozer

HATRED

(See also: Anger)

Hatred is self-punishment.
Hosea Ballou

The price of hating other human beings is loving one-self less.   *Eldridge Cleaver*

HEART

(See also: Soul)

No man is conquered until his heart is conquered.
George Barlow

The keeping and right managing of the heart in every condition is the great business of the Christian's life.   *John Flavel*

As seed is made for soil and soil for seed, so the heart is made for God's truth and God's truth for the heart.
Richard Glover

Our hearts are slippery commodities.   *Thomas Goodwin*

A man's heart is what he is.
R. B. Kuiper

If you would have the life holy before men, let the heart be pure before God.
Thomas Manton

There is nothing in the life but what was first in the heart.   *Thomas Manton*

Rather look to the cleansing of thine heart than to the cleansing of thy well; rather look to the feeding of thine heart than to the feeding of thy flock; rather look to the defending of thine heart than to the defending of thine house; rather look to the keeping of thine heart than to the keeping of thy money. *Peter Moffat*

The heart in the Scriptures is variously used; sometimes for the mind and understanding, sometimes for the will, sometimes for the affection, sometimes for the conscience ... *Generally*, it denotes the whole soul of man and all the faculties of it. *John Owen*

If the keeping of the heart be the great work of the Christian, then how few *real* Christians are there in the world! *A. W. Pink*

The heart is the warehouse, the hand and tongue are but the shops; what is in *these* is from *thence* — the heart contrives and the members execute. *A. W. Pink*

Sin and the devil will always find helpers in our hearts. *J. C. Ryle*

The seeds of every wickedness lie hidden in our hearts. They only need the convenient season to spring forth into a mischievous vitality. *J. C. Ryle*

There is far more wickedness in all our hearts than we know. *J. C. Ryle*

There is a concert of all the members when the heart is in tune. *Henry Smith*

The heart is the metal of the bell, the tongue but the clapper. *George Swinnock*

God is more concerned with the state of people's hearts than with the state of their feelings. *A. W. Tozer*

The heart of man is like a musical instrument and may be played upon by the Holy Spirit, by an evil spirit or by the spirit of man himself. *A. W. Tozer*

HEAVEN — The Christian's Eternal Home
(See also: Destiny; Eternal Security; Eternity)

We were born on the earth, we live on the earth, we cling to the earth as long as we can – yet as Christians we do not actually belong here at all. Our legal domicile is in heaven.

Christ is preparing saints for heaven and heaven for saints. *Anon.*

Everyone will get to heaven who could live there. *Anon.*

Saints are never far from home. *Anon.*

The saint's enduring riches are in the future, locked up in the heavenly casket.

George Barlow

Heaven would be no heaven were there any strangers there.   *Thomas Brooks*

If we look around us, a moment can seem a long time, but when we lift up our hearts heavenwards, a thousand years begin to be like a moment.

John Calvin

Heaven's number of glorified saints is made up of justified sinners.

William Gurnall

The Christian's heaven is to be with Christ, for we shall be like him when we see him as he is.   *Charles Hodge*

It is the gospel alone which connects us with the era to come.   *R. C. H. Lenski*

You must not only *seek* heaven; you must also *think* heaven.   *J. B. Lightfoot*

Heaven will not fully be heaven to Christ till he has all his redeemed with himself.   *A. W. Pink*

As surely as God is eternal, so surely is heaven an endless day without night and hell an endless night without day.   *J. C. Ryle*

Grace shall always lead to glory.   *J. C. Ryle*

They that enter heaven will find that they are neither unknown nor unexpected.

J. C. Ryle

Heaven is not a lease which soon expires, but an inheritance.   *Thomas Watson*

HEAVEN — Glory

I would not give one moment of heaven for all the joy and riches of the world, even if it lasted for thousands and thousands of years.

Martin Luther

There is a land of pure
   delight,
Where saints immortal
   reign;
Infinite day excludes the
   night,
And pleasures banish pain.

Isaac Watts

All here are but shadows; all above is substance.

Andrew Welwood

HEAVEN — God's Presence

Would you know what makes heaven heaven? It is communion with God. And would you know what makes hell hell? It is to be forsaken of God.   *R. B. Kuiper*

Without God, heaven would be no heaven.
                    William S. Plumer

HEAVEN — Perfection

Heaven's riches are moth-proof, rust-proof and burglar-proof.

Nothing that has ruined man's life on earth will be allowed to do so in heaven.

No line in Scripture indicates any sorrow or grief in heaven.
          Donald Grey Barnhouse

In heaven is no warfare but all well-fare.   *John Boys*

Heaven is reserved for heaven.   *James Janeway*

Heaven will mean the realization of all the things for which man was made and the satisfaction of all the outreachings of his heart.
          Ernest F. Kevan

I would not give one moment of heaven for all the joys and riches of the world, even if it lasted for thousands and thousands of years.
          Martin Luther

Earth has no sorrow that heaven cannot heal.
          Thomas Moore

The road is not to be complained of, as it leads to such a home.   *John Newton*

There will be no sin in heaven, for those who are in heaven will not have it in them to sin any more.
          J. I. Packer

If contentment were here, heaven were not heaven.
          Samuel Rutherford

Nothing but glory will make tight and fast our leaking and rifty vessels.
          Samuel Rutherford

Heaven makes amends for all.   *J. C. Ryle*

Heaven is a kingdom where there are no perils to brave, no loneliness to face, no wants to suffer, no crosses to bear.   *Basilea Schlink*

The Lamb's wedding is a time for boundless pleasure, and tears would be out of place.   *C. H. Spurgeon*

141

Heaven is the proper place for comfort, earth for grace.
George Swinnock

Here, joy begins to enter into us; there, we enter into joy.
Thomas Watson

HEAVEN — Preparation for

Christ brings the heart to heaven first, and then the person.
Richard Baxter

All the way to heaven is heaven.
Catherine of Siena

Those who have the new Jerusalem in their eye must have the ways that lead to it in their heart.
Matthew Henry

Christians are the more cold and careless in the spiritual life because they do not oftener think of heaven.
Thomas Manton

There is a difference between being willing to go to heaven and wanting to stay on earth — and wanting to go to heaven while being willing to stay on earth.
David Pawson

The highway of holiness is the only path which leads to heaven.
A. W. Pink

Heaven itself would be no heaven if we entered it with an unsanctified character.
J. C. Ryle

Our hearts must be in tune for heaven if we are to enjoy it.
J. C. Ryle

We must be saints on earth if we ever mean to be saints in heaven.
J. C. Ryle

Heaven must be in thee before thou canst be in heaven.
George Swinnock

HEDONISM
(See also: Pleasures)

The best cure for hedonism is the attempt to practise it.
John MacMurray

Pleasure-seeking, as we learn from experience, is a barren business; happiness is never found till we have the grace to stop looking for it and to give our attention to persons and matters external to ourselves.
J. I. Packer

HELL
(See also: Destiny; Eternity; Judgement; Satan)

At the end of the day, hell is anywhere outside of heaven.

In hell, even the gospel is bad news.

It is never true to say that something 'hurts like hell'. Nothing hurts like hell.

To believe in heaven but not in hell is to declare that there were times when Jesus was telling the truth and times when he was lying.

The most awful fact in the world is the fact of hell and that some of our dearest relations and friends with whom we have lived, worked and worshipped will spend an eternity of anguish, away from God, eternally unforgiven, eternally doomed.
Isaac H. A. Ababio

He shall have hell as a debt who will not have heaven as a gift. *Anon.*

'Too late' is written on the gates of hell. *Anon.*

Eternity of eternity is the hell of hell.
Thomas Brooks

God has but one hell, and that is for those to whom sin has been commonly a heaven in this world.
Thomas Brooks

The damned in hell may weep their eyes out of their heads, but they can never weep sin out of their souls.
Thomas Brooks

The greatest and the hottest fires that ever were on earth are but ice in comparison of the fire of hell.
Thomas Brooks

The truth is, were there the least real joy in sin, there could be no perfect hell, where men shall most perfectly sin, and be most perfectly tormented with their sin. *Thomas Brooks*

Sure I am, that if hell can be disproved in any way that is solid and true, and consistent with God's honour and man's good, there is not a trembling sinner in this land that would hail the demonstration with more joy than I would.
Robert L. Dabney

Vain are the dreams of infatuated mortals who suppose that the only punishment to be endured for sin is in the present life.
J. L. Dagg

There is many a learned head in hell. *John Flavel*

Were the fire out as to positive torments, yet a hell would be left in the dismal darkness which the soul

would sit under for want of God's presence.
William Gurnall

If I am afraid of sin I need not be afraid of hell.
Rowland Hill

Would you know what makes heaven heaven? It is communion with God. And would you know what makes hell hell? It is to be forsaken of God. *R. B. Kuiper*

Men are not in hell because God is angry with them: they are in wrath and darkness because they have done to the light, which infinitely flows forth from God, as that man does to the light who puts out his own eyes.
William Law

Exit is not a word found in the vocabulary of hell.
Robert G. Lee

The safest road to hell is the gradual one — the gentle slope, soft underfoot, without sudden turnings, without milestones, without signposts. *C. S. Lewis*

Let not anyone who thinks that fear of hell should be put out of the mind of unregenerate men ever suppose that he has the slightest understanding of what Jesus

came into the world to say and do. *J. Gresham Machen*

When the world dissolves, all places will be hell that are not heaven.
Christopher Marlowe

If you are still unconverted, thank God that you are still not in hell. *Andrew Murray*

You will be a believer some day. If you never believe on earth, you will believe in hell. *Brownlow North*

An endless hell can no more be removed from the New Testament than an endless heaven can. *J. I. Packer*

As surely as God is eternal, so surely is heaven an endless day without night and hell an endless night without day. *J. C. Ryle*

Hell itself would be endurable if after millions of ages there was a hope of freedom and of heaven. But universal salvation will find no foothold in Scripture.
J. C. Ryle

Once let the old doctrine about hell be overthrown and the whole system of Christianity is unsettled, unscrewed, unpinned and thrown into disorder.
J. C. Ryle

The darkness endured by our blessed Surety on the cross was only for three hours. The chains of darkness which shall bind all who reject his atonement and die in sin shall be for evermore.

J. C. Ryle

The saddest road to hell is that which runs under the pulpit, past the Bible and through the midst of warnings and invitations.

J. C. Ryle

The existing demoralization in society and politics . . . is due, mainly, to a disbelief of the doctrine of endless punishment.

W. G. T. Shedd

Hell will be seen to be hell all the way through.

A. W. Tozer

Hell is an abiding place, but no resting place.

Thomas Watson

Many a man goes to hell in the sweat of his brow.

Thomas Watson

The wicked in hell shall be always dying but never dead. *Thomas Watson*

There are no agnostics in hell. *Geoffrey B. Wilson*

Hell is the penitentiary of the moral universe.

J. S. Wrightnour

HERESY

The most dangerous of all false doctrine is the one seasoned with a little truth.

Anon.

The wind of error does not blow long in the same direction. *Anon.*

They that will give God a new tongue shall feel his old hand. *Thomas Adams*

Heresy flourishes when those who know the truth fail to maintain it resolutely.

Brian Beevers

When a half truth is presented as a whole truth it becomes an untruth.

Walter J. Chantry

Unless your vision of Christ is as large as it can possibly be, you will always be in danger of heresy.

Donald English

False doctrine always uses a plausible gimmick to get its foot in the door — and it is always the back door!

Vance Havner

145

One error is a bridge to another. *William Jenkyn*

Whom God intends to destroy, he gives them leave to play with Scripture.
Martin Luther

Truth lives in the cellar, error on the doorstep.
Austin O'Malley

We constantly flirt with heresies that are not new but old. *Roger C. Palms*

I believe that the root of almost every schism and heresy from which the Christian church has ever suffered has been the effort of men to earn, rather than to receive, their salvation.
John Ruskin

Ignorance of the Scriptures is the root of all error.
J. C. Ryle

There is no mercy in keeping back from men the subject of hell. *J. C. Ryle*

Fellowship with known and vital error is participation in sin. *C. H. Spurgeon*

The faculty of inventing false doctrine is ruinous.
C. H. Spurgeon

No heresy is ever entertained with impunity.
A. W. Tozer

The human heart is heretical by nature.
A. W. Tozer

Orthodoxy is my doxy; heterodoxy is another man's doxy. *William Warburton*

Error damns as well as vice.
Thomas Watson

Anyone who burdens the church with false teaching shall not escape being burdened with a crushing judgement.
Geoffrey B. Wilson

A truncated Christology forms the foundation of all false teaching.
Geoffrey B. Wilson

False teaching not only poisons the mind, but also demoralizes the life.
Geoffrey B. Wilson

HISTORY

History as men see it is a Punch and Judy show manipulated by unseen hands behind the scenes . . . but God will dispose of both manikins and manipulators one of these days.
Vance Havner

If you know how to read between the lines of secular

history, you will see that God is writing another history, and some people who are very important in secular history are only incidental in God's history. If they have any importance at all, it depends on how they relate to Jesus Christ.
Vance Havner

God is in the facts of history as truly as he is in the march of the seasons, the revolutions of the planets, or the architecture of the worlds.
John Lanahan

Pondering the past is often the best way of providing for the future.
Thomas V. Moore

God orders history for the good of the elect.
Robert A. Morey

Jesus Christ is the one to whom the whole alphabet of history points.
Lesslie Newbigin

Learning from history and basking in nostalgia are two different things.
Roger C. Palms

No history ought to receive so much of our attention as the past and future history of the church of Christ. The rise and fall of worldly empires are events of com-

paratively small importance in the sight of God.
J. C. Ryle

HOLINESS — Definition
(See also: Christlikeness; Godliness)

Holiness is that perspective through which we must see God. *Thomas Adams*

God's will is the rule of righteousness, and his righteousness is the rule of his will. *Elisha Coles*

Holiness in us is the copy or transcript of the holiness that is in Christ.
Philip Henry

Righteousness is obedience to law, observance of duty and fidelity to conscience.
J. P. Hopps

We in Christ = justification; Christ in us = sanctification.
Martin Luther

What is holiness except Christlikeness?
John R. W. Stott

HOLINESS — Essence

A holy heart is always attended with a holy life.
Thomas Brooks

A man that is really holy will be holy among the holy and he will be holy among the unholy. *Thomas Brooks*

True holiness makes a man divinely covetous.
Thomas Brooks

Holiness is not a merit by which we can attain communion with God, but a gift of Christ which enables us to cling to him and to follow him. *John Calvin*

Perfect holiness is the *aim* of the saints on earth and it is the *reward* of the saints in heaven. *Joseph Caryl*

What health is to the heart, that holiness is to the soul.
John Flavel

There is nothing destroyed by sanctification but that which would destroy us.
William Jenkyn

To be holy is to be like Jesus.
C. H. McIntosh

The Christian life is not applied like make-up to the outside of our personalities, but is an outgrowth from an inner transformation.
J. A. Motyer

The life of sanctification is the life of obedience.
J. A. Motyer

Holiness is exemplified in obedience to the commandments of God.
John Murray

Sanctification is the immediate work of the Spirit of God upon our whole nature, by which we are being changed into Christ's likeness. *Ernest C. Reisinger*

The first rule in holy living is 'Don't lie to God'.
Jeremy Taylor

I am the little servant of an illustrious Master.
J. Hudson Taylor

HOLINESS — God's Work

God does not expect any good in us but what he has wrought in us. *Anon.*

Holiness is offered to every believer.
Donald Grey Barnhouse

Whatever good we do, God does in us. *A. R. Fausset*

As God makes use of all the seasons of the year for the harvest — the frost and cold of the winter, as well as the heat of the summer — so doth he, of fair and foul, pleasing and unpleasing providences, for promoting holiness.   *William Gurnall*

This is the great design of God, to have his people holy. It runs like a silver thread through all God's other designs.
William Gurnall

What God requires of us he himself works in us, or it is not done.   *Matthew Henry*

Holiness is not something we do or attain; it is the communication of the divine life, the inbreathing of the divine nature; the power of the divine presence resting on us.   *Andrew Murray*

We may lay it down as an elemental principle of religion that no large growth in holiness was ever gained by one who did not take time to be often long alone with God.   *Austin Phelps*

Christ comes with a blessing in each hand; forgiveness in one, holiness in the other.
A. W. Pink

The regenerate have a spiritual nature within that fits them for holy action, otherwise there would be no difference between them and the unregenerate.
A. W. Pink

Sanctification, in Scripture, is always something that God does.
Kenneth F. W. Prior

HOLINESS — Importance

A holy God calls his people to holy living. It is inconceivable that it should be otherwise.

Live so that the preacher can tell the truth at your funeral.   *Anon.*

There was nothing of any importance to me but holiness of heart and life and the conversion of the Indians to God.   *David Brainerd*

Assurance makes most for your comfort, but holiness makes most for God's honour.   *Thomas Brooks*

A baptism of holiness, a demonstration of godly living, is the crying need of our day.   *Duncan Campbell*

There is no detour to holiness. Jesus came to the resurrection through the cross, not around it.
Leighton Ford

A sanctified heart is better than a silver tongue.
Thomas Goodwin

149

The beauty of holiness needs no paint. *Matthew Henry*

Christianity has the only true morality; no other religion conduces to true holiness. *R. B. Kuiper*

Fully aware that he will not reach the goal of moral perfection in this life, the Christian must yet press on with might and main towards that very mark. *R. B. Kuiper*

A redeemed flock should live in redemption's pastures. *Henry Law*

A holy life and a bounteous heart are ornaments to the gospel. *Thomas Manton*

Holiness is a Christian's ornament, and peaceableness is the ornament of holiness. *Thomas Manton*

I feel there are two things it is impossible to desire with sufficient ardour — personal holiness and the honour of Christ in the salvation of souls. *Robert Murray M'Cheyne*

There is no argument like a holy life. *Robert Murray M'Cheyne*

A holy life will produce the deepest impression. Lighthouses blow no horns; they only shine. *D. L. Moody*

All through the New Testament, when God's work in human lives is spoken of, the ethical takes priority over the charismatic. *J. I. Packer*

Scriptural holiness is in fact the most positive, potent and often passionate quality of life that is ever seen. *J. I .Packer*

The New Testament does not say that Christians must lead holy lives in order to become saints; instead, it tells Christians that, because they are saints, they must henceforth lead holy lives! *J. I. Packer*

The serene beauty of a holy life is the most powerful influence in the world next to the power of God. *Blaise Pascal*

Everything in Scripture has in view the promotion of holiness. *A. W. Pink*

The highway of holiness is the only path which leads to heaven. *A. W. Pink*

God has linked together holiness and happiness; and what God has joined together we must not think to put asunder. *J. C. Ryle*

The names and number of the elect are a secret thing, no doubt ... But if there is one thing clearly and plainly laid down about election, it is this — that elect men and women may be known and distinguished by holy lives.
J. C. Ryle

We must be saints on earth if ever we mean to be saints in heaven. *J. C. Ryle*

Those that look to be happy must first look to be holy.
Richard Sibbes

Holiness is the best sabbath dress — but it is equally suitable for everyday wear.
C. H. Spurgeon

Only sanctified souls are satisfied souls.
C. H. Spurgeon

Regeneration is a change which is known and felt: known by works of holiness and felt by a gracious experience. *C. H. Spurgeon*

The best theology is rather a divine life than a divine knowledge. *Jeremy Taylor*

The true Christian ideal is not to be happy but to be holy. *A. W. Tozer*

We can never know that we are elected of God to eternal life except by manifesting in our lives the fruits of election.
Benjamin B. Warfield

HOLINESS — and Justification

While our works are naught as a ground of merit for justification, they are all-important as evidences that we are justified.
R. L. Dabney.

God did not save us to make us happy but to make us holy.
Vance Havner

We in Christ = justification; Christ in us = sanctification.
Martin Luther

Be as holy as you can, as if there were no gospel to save you. Yet ... believe in Christ as if there were no law at all to condemn you.
Thomas Lye

While justification and sanctification are to be sharply distinguished they must not be divorced. *A. W. Pink*

There are none justified who are not sanctified and there are none sanctified who are not justified. *J. C. Ryle*

By grace we are what we are in justification, and work what we work in sanctification.   *Richard Sibbes*

When God declares a man righteous he instantly sets about to make him righteous.   *A. W. Tozer*

Those who are unwilling to cleanse themselves from every stain of sin only show that they have not been cleansed from the guilt of sin. The unsanctified are the unjustified.   *Geoffrey B. Wilson*

HOLINESS — Man's Part

The best way to prepare for tomorrow is to seek God's kingdom and righteousness first today.

The renewed heart has within it the desire to glorify God by presenting a moral life.   *Donald Grey Barnhouse*

There is no true holiness without humility.   *Thomas Fuller*

The sanctifying grace of God is appropriated by the obedient and unrelenting activity of the regenerate man.   *J. A. Motyer*

Holiness is no more by faith without effort than it is by effort without faith.   *J. I. Packer*

I am convinced that the first step towards attaining a higher standard of holiness is to realize more fully the amazing sinfulness of sin.   *J. C. Ryle*

The grace of God will do very little for us if we resolve to do nothing for ourselves. God calls us to co-operate with him in the perfecting of character.   *W. Graham Scroggie*

Brethren, we can be much more holy than we are. Let us attain first to that holiness about which there is no controversy.   *C. H. Spurgeon*

The secret of clean living is clear thinking.   *John R. W. Stott*

So let our lips and lives express
The holy gospel we profess;
So let our works and virtues shine,
To prove the doctrine all divine.

Isaac Watts

HOLINESS — Motive

The thought of the great nobility God has conferred upon us ought to whet our desire for holiness and purity.   *John Calvin*

The ethical demand for holy living is inseparable from what is freely given in the gospel.   *Geoffrey B. Wilson*

HOLINESS — Rewards

Holiness in the seed shall have happiness in the harvest.   *Thomas Adams*

When our holiness is perfect, our happiness shall be perfect; and if this were attainable on earth, there would be but little reason for men to long to be in heaven.
     Thomas Brooks

Nothing can make a man truly great but being truly good and partaking of God's holiness.   *Matthew Henry*

It is the tendency of righteousness to produce blessings, as it is the tendency of evil to produce misery.
     Charles Hodge

The way of uprightness is the way of heavenly wealth.
     C. H. Spurgeon

The Lord has two heavens to dwell in, and the holy heart is one of them.
     Thomas Watson

HOLY SPIRIT
(See also: Godhead)

The fruit of the Spirit is active, not just academic.

Before Pentecost, the disciples were like rabbits; after Pentecost, they were like ferrets!   *Anon.*

The Holy Ghost does not flow through methods but through men. He does not come on machinery but on men. He does not anoint plans but men — men of prayer.   *E. M. Bounds*

The first work of the Spirit is to make a man look upon sin as an enemy and to deal with sin as an enemy, to hate it as an enemy, to loathe it as an enemy and to arm against it as an enemy.
     Thomas Brooks

The Spirit never loosens where the Word binds; the Spirit never justifies where the Word condemns; the Spirit never approves where the Word disapproves; the Spirit never blesses where the Word curses.
     Thomas Brooks

153

What the Spirit does is exactly what the Lord does; the Spirit's work is not an additional or special work *beyond* the Lord's; the Spirit is the Lord at work.
F. D. Bruner

As the soul does not live idly in the body, but gives motion and vigour to every member and part, so the Spirit of God cannot dwell in us without manifesting himself by the outward effects.   *John Calvin*

The gospel is the ground of the believer's assurance, while the Holy Spirit is its cause.   *J. C. P. Cockerton*

Unless there is that which is above us, we shall soon yield to that which is about us.
P. T. Forsyth

The Spirit of God knows the things of God because he is one with God.
Matthew Henry

The Holy Spirit may be had for the asking.   *R. B. Kuiper*

Come, Holy Spirit, God and Lord!
Be all thy graces now out-poured
On the believer's mind and soul,
To strengthen, save, and make us whole.
Martin Luther

God's mind is revealed in Scripture, but we can see nothing without the spectacles of the Holy Ghost.
Thomas Manton

Remember, we may grieve the Spirit as truly by not joyfully acknowledging his wonders as by not praying to him.
Robert Murray M'Cheyne

The Holy Spirit is the great beautifier of souls.
John Owen

The gracious operations of the Spirit were never designed to be a substitute for the Christian's discharge of duty.   *A. W. Pink*

The gift of the Holy Spirit made the apostles at home with the miraculous.
Adolph Schlatter

A dead creed is of no use; we must have our creed baptized with the Holy Ghost.
C. H. Spurgeon

He is your credentials as a Christian: he is your life as a believer.   *C. H. Spurgeon*

I do not believe in a repetition of Pentecost, but I do believe in a perpetuation of Pentecost — and there is a vast difference between the two.   *A. W. Tozer*

154

The filling of the Holy Spirit brings a sharp separation between the believer and the world.   *A. W. Tozer*

The gospel is light but only the Spirit can give sight.
A. W. Tozer

To possess a Spirit-indwelt mind is the Christian's privilege under grace.
A. W. Tozer

We have a Celebrity in our midst.   *A. W. Tozer*

Why should the children of a King
Go mourning all their days?
Great Comforter, descend, and bring
Some tokens of thy grace.
Isaac Watts

HONESTY

(See also: Truth)

No honest man ever repented of his honesty.   *Anon.*

No man is really honest; none of us is above the influence of gain.   *Aristophanes*

The more honesty a man has, the less he affects the air of a saint.   *J. C. Lavater*

A straight line is shortest in morals as well as in geometry.   *I. Rahel*

Honesty that can be trusted and respected is a very fragrant flower in the life of the Christian.   *A. W. Tozer*

HOPE

(See also: Eternal Security; Future; Heaven)

Christ is our hope of glory and the glory of our hope.
Anon.

Our hope lies not in the man we put on the moon, but in the man we put on the cross.
Don Basham

A man full of hope will be full of action.   *Thomas Brooks*

We are refugees from the sinking ship of this present world order, so soon to disappear; our hope is fixed in the eternal order, where the promises of God are made good to his people in perpetuity.   *F. F. Bruce*

The word 'hope' I take for faith; and indeed hope is nothing else but the constancy of faith.
John Calvin

When you stop hoping you are on the vestibule of hell, for there is no hope there.
A. J. Cronin

155

Hope is the only tie which keeps the heart from breaking. *Thomas Fuller*

If it were not for hopes, the heart would break. *Thomas Fuller*

Faith and a good conscience are hope's two wings. *William Gurnall*

The nearer to heaven in hopes, the farther from earth in desires. *William Gurnall*

The Christian's hope is like a rainbow. It is essentially one, yet made up of the most glorious colours which, though they merge together to form an exquisite whole, may each be admired individually. *Graham Heaps*

The ground of our hope is Christ in the world, but the evidence of our hope is Christ in the heart. *Matthew Henry*

Like faith, New Testament hope carries unconditional certainty within itself. *E. Hoffmann*

The Christian hope is the hope of a time when even the possibility of our sinning will be over. It is not the hope then of a return to the condition of Adam before the Fall but the hope of an entrance into a far higher condition. *J. Gresham Machen*

Apart from the bright hope of the gospel everything would be meaningless. *Poul Madsen*

What an excellent ground of hope and confidence we have when we reflect upon these three things in prayer — the Father's love, the Son's merit and the Spirit's power! *Thomas Manton*

From Christ's death flow all our hopes. *J. C. Ryle*

As God is the author of our salvation, so Christ is the embodiment of our hope. *Geoffrey B. Wilson*

Our risen and glorified Lord is himself our hope, because his triumph over sin and death provides the objective pledge of our final redemption. *Geoffrey B. Wilson*

HUMANISM

The most a thoroughgoing humanist can do is to express his own opinion about what is 'good' and 'right' and there may be a hundred different views about that! *J. B. Phillips*

The weakness of nice people without faith is that they have nothing to offer the 'not nice people'.

J. B. Phillips

Humanism is the defiant denial of the God who is there, with man defiantly set up in the place of God as the measure of all things.

Francis Schaeffer

Naturalistic humanism leads to a diminishing of man and eventually to a zeroing of man. *Francis Schaeffer*

The concept that the final reality is energy which has existed forever in some form and takes its present form by chance has totally destructive consequences for life.

Francis Schaeffer

When one accepts the secular world view that the final reality is only material or energy shaped by chance, then human life is lowered to the level of animal existence.

Francis Schaeffer

If you mix humanism with Christian truths, the basic message of Christianity is destroyed.

John W. Whitehead

HUMILITY — Blessings

God thinks most of the man who thinks himself least.

The easiest way to dignity is humility. *Anon.*

The lowliest Christian is the loveliest Christian. *Anon.*

If you lay yourself at Christ's feet he will take you into his arms. *William Bridge*

He that is down needs fear no fall;
He that is low, no pride.
He that is humble ever shall
Have God to be his Guide.
John Bunyan

Nothing sets a person so much out of the devil's reach as humility.

Jonathan Edwards

When God intends to fill a soul, he first makes it empty. When he intends to enrich a soul, he first makes it poor. When he intends to exalt a soul, he first makes it sensible to its own miseries, wants and nothingness.

John Flavel

God can only fill valleys, not mountains. *Roy Hession*

God's choice acquaintances
are humble men.
Robert Leighton

The way to rise is to fall.
Thomas Manton

Humble hearts lie in the
valleys where streams of
grace are flowing, and hence
they drink of them.
C. H. Spurgeon

The more we are humbled
in grace, the more we shall
be exalted in glory.
C. H. Spurgeon

HUMILITY — Characteristics

A humble spirit loves a low
seat. *William Gurnall*

The Christian is like the
ripening corn; the riper he
grows, the more lowly bends
his head. *Thomas Guthrie*

Humility is not only a
clothing, but an ornament.
Thomas Manton

Men frequently admire me;
but I abhor the pleasure that
I feel. *Henry Martyn*

True humility makes way for
Christ and throws the soul at
his feet. *J. Mason*

The fullest and best ears of
corn hang lowest towards
the ground.
Edward Reynolds

Of all garments, none is so
graceful, none wears so well,
and none is so rare, as
humility. *J. C. Ryle*

Lord, give me humility or I
perish. *George Whitefield*

Think as little as possible
about yourself. Turn your
eyes resolutely from any
view of your influence, your
success, your following.
Above all speak as little as
possible about yourself.
Samuel Wilberforce

HUMILITY — Essence

Great men never think they
are great — small men never
think they are small.
Anon.

The true way to be humble
is not to stoop until you are
smaller than yourself, but to
stand at your real height
against some higher nature
that will show you what the
real smallness of your greatness is. *Phillips Brooks*

By humility I mean not the
abjectness of a base mind;
but a prudent care not to

over-value ourselves upon any account.
Obadiah Grew

Humility is the grace which lies prostrate at God's footstool, self-abasing and self-disparaging, amazed at God's mercy and abhorring its own vileness.
James Hamilton

The best of God's people have abhorred themselves. Like the spire of a steeple, we are least at the highest.
Thomas Manton

Humility is not diffidence. Humility is that disposition of honest recognition: He is God, I am but a creature.
Al Martin

The true secret of spiritual strength is self-distrust and deep humility. *J. C. Ryle*

Pride is a sinner's torment, but humility is a saint's ornament. *William Secker*

Let my name be forgotten, let me be trodden under the feet of all men, if Jesus may thereby be glorified.
George Whitefield

O heavenly Father, for thy dear Son's sake, keep me from climbing.
George Whitefield

HUMILITY — False

He who brags of his humility loses it. *John Boys*

To see a man humble under prosperity is one of the greatest rarities in the world.
John Flavel

You can have no greater sign of a confirmed pride than when you think you are humble enough.
William Law

If our humility is not unconscious it is exhibitionism.
D. Martyn Lloyd-Jones

We can be proud of our humility, indeed I think we always are if we try to give the impression of humility.
D. Martyn Lloyd-Jones

HUMILITY — Importance

He who knows himself best esteems himself least.
Henry G. Bohn

Humility in every area of life, in every relationship with other people, begins with a right concept of God as the one who is infinite and eternal in his majesty and holiness. *Jerry Bridges*

Show when you are tempted to hide, and hide when you are tempted to show.
A. B. Bruce

How easy it is to reason out man's humility, but how hard to reason man into it.
Stephen Charnock

Christ demands a humility which is foolishness to the world. *J. N. Figgis*

The greatest men are those who are humble before God. The tallest men are those who bend before God.
Richard Halverson

God grant us the beatitude of the background, that only he may be seen!
Vance Havner

Those whom God will employ are first struck with a sense of their unworthiness to be employed.
Matthew Henry

No garment is more becoming to a child of God than the cloak of humility.
Cyril M. Jackson

Until a man is nothing God can make nothing of him.
Martin Luther

The great secret of a right waiting upon God is to be brought down to utter impotence. *Andrew Murray*

There walks not this earth a man who is too humble in the sight of God.
William S. Plumer

I believe the first test of a truly great man is his humility. *John Ruskin*

Humility is the very first letter in the alphabet of Christianity. *J. C. Ryle*

The surest mark of true conversion is humility.
J. C. Ryle

If God has made us men, let us not make ourselves gods.
Richard Sibbes

Let us be humble that we may not need to be humbled, but may be exalted by the grace of God.
C. H. Spurgeon

Humility neither falls far, nor heavily. *Publilius Syrus*

Knowledge without humility is vanity. *A. W. Tozer*

HUMOUR
(See also: Happiness; Joy)

If you want to know whether a man's life is made up of frivolous or serious things, watch what he laughs at.
Anon.

160

There ain't much fun in medicine, but there's a good deal of medicine in fun.
Josh Billings

Genuine laughing is the vent of the soul, the nostrils of the heart, and it is just as necessary for health and happiness as spring water is for a trout. *Josh Billings*

Nothing shows a man's character more than what he laughs at.
Johann Wolfgang von Goethe

I have never understood why it should be considered derogatory to the Creator to suppose that he has a sense of humour.
William Ralph Inge

Nothing is so insipid as indiscriminate good humour.
J. Gresham Machen

Few things are as useful in the Christian life as a gentle sense of humour and few things are as deadly as a sense of humour out of control. *A. W. Tozer*

There's plenty to laugh at in the world — but be sure you don't laugh at something that God takes seriously.
A. W. Tozer

We should all be aware by this time that one way the devil has of getting rid of something is to make jokes about it. *A. W. Tozer*

Whenever humour takes a holy thing as its object that humour is devilish at once.
A. W. Tozer

HYPOCRISY
(See also: Formalism; Ritualism)

What you are in public will never blind God to what you are in private.

Hypocrites are like pictures on canvas: they show fairest at farthest. *Thomas Adams*

The hypocrite fries in words, freezes in works.
Thomas Adams

The hypocrite has much angel without, more devil within. *Thomas Adams*

The hypocrite is like Hosea's dough-baked cake, only hot on the visible side.
Thomas Adams

The hypocrite desires holiness only as a bridge to heaven. *Joseph Alleine*

Many wear God's livery but are not his servants.
Anon.

161

The hypocrite's bellows blow out the candle under pretence of kindling the fire.
Richard Baxter

A man who hides behind the hypocrite is smaller than the hypocrite. *W. E. Biederwolf*

If the world despises a hypocrite, what must they think of him in heaven?
Josh Billings

A man who does not practise what he preaches destroys what he builds.
Bonaventura

An apple, if it be rotten at the core, though it have a fair and shining outside, yet rottenness will not stay long, but will taint the outside also ... hypocrisy will discover itself in the end. *John Bond*

The hypocrite is a cloud without rain, a blossoming tree without fruit, a star without light, a shell without a kernel. *Thomas Brooks*

There is not more counterfeit coin this day in the world than there is counterfeit holiness in the world.
Thomas Brooks

Do not seek to cover up your sins with the varnish of hypocrisy, the fine gloss that pleases men.
William C. Burns

A hypocrite may well be termed a religious atheist, an atheist masked with religion.
Stephen Charnock

Hypocrisy is a lie with a fair cover over it.
William Gurnall

Hypocrisy is too thin a veil to blind the eyes of the Almighty. *William Gurnall*

We must not spread our sails of profession in a calm and furl them up when the wind rises. *William Gurnall*

Many a Christian, many a church, has everything in the showcase and nothing on the shelves. *Vance Havner*

There is no use singing of milk and honey, figs and pomegranates, if all we have to show is crab apples!
Vance Havner

Hypocrites and betrayers of Christ are no better than devils. *Matthew Henry*

Hypocrites do the devil's drudgery in Christ's livery.
Matthew Henry

The day is coming when hypocrites will be stripped of their fig-leaves.
Matthew Henry

Where the hypocrite's work ends, there the true Christian's work begins.
Matthew Henry

A good name upon an unchanged nature is but white feathers upon a black skin.
William Jenkyn

Hereafter all paint must fall off which is not laid in the oil of sincerity.
William Jenkyn

There are many who are lip-servants but not life-servants. *William Jenkyn*

There are over many who have much knowledge and little virtue, and who often speak of God while rarely speaking to him. *Malaval*

The hypocrite will have the lowest place in hell.
J. C. Ryle

Whatever we are in our religion, let us resolve never to wear a cloak. Let us by all means be honest and real.
J. C. Ryle

No hypocrite can bear the cross. *Henry Smith*

When hypocrites ran up against Jesus it was like a cat running into a mowing machine. *A. W. Tozer*

We must not think to dance with the devil all day and sup with Christ at night.
John Trapp

IDOLATRY

Inordinate affections bring extraordinary affliction.
Anon.

Idolatry is everywhere represented in Scripture as the greatest insult the creature can offer the Creator.
Charles Hodge

Where idolatry ends, there Christianity begins; and where idolatry begins, there Christianity ends.
Friedrich H. Jacobi

All idols are the product of human imagination.
R. B. Kuiper

Ever since man ruined the image of God in which he had been created he has been fashioning gods in his own image.
R. B. Kuiper

Ultimately, all idolatry amounts to worship by the idolator of himself.
R. B. Kuiper

We easily fall into idolatry, for we are inclined to it by

163

nature; and coming to us by inheritance, it seems pleasant.
Martin Luther

All idolatry is stupid, though not all equally indecent.
William S. Plumer

Whatever a man seeks, honours, or exalts more than God, this is the god of idolatry. *William Ullathorne*

An idol may be defined as any person or thing that has usurped in the heart the place of pre-eminence that belongs to the Lord.
Arthur Wallis

An image lover is a God hater. *Thomas Watson*

In his natural state, every man born into the world is a rank idolator. *John Wesley*

Man in his rebellion against the Creator remains incurably religious, and he seeks to satisfy this instinct by making his own deities. He much prefers these lifeless puppets to the one true living God, because they allow him to pull the strings.
Geoffrey B. Wilson

IGNORANCE

Atheism is the ultimate ignorance.

164

It is unlikely in the foreseeable future that there will be a serious shortage of ignorance. *Anon.*

Passion does not compensate for ignorance.
Samuel Chadwick

He that knows nothing will believe anything.
Thomas Fuller

There is nothing more frightful than ignorance in action.
Johann Wolfgang von Goethe

The opposite of ignorance in the spiritual realm is not knowledge but obedience.
Howard Hendricks

Nothing in the world is more dangerous than sincere ignorance and conscientious stupidity.
Martin Luther King

The ultimate proof of the sinner is that he does not know his own sin.
Martin Luther

There is nothing so costly as ignorance. *Horace Mann*

He who would be cured of ignorance must confess it.
Michel de Montaigne

The worst ignorance in the world is not to know ourselves. *J. C. Ryle*

To feel that we are ignorant is the first beginning of all saving knowledge.

J. C. Ryle

Because of our ignorance we are not fully aware of our sins of ignorance.

C. H. Spurgeon

Ignorance is not the mother of religion, but of irreligion.

Benjamin B. Warfield

IMPATIENCE

Our anger and impatience often proves much more mischievous than the things about which we are angry or impatient.

Marcus Aurelius

The cure for impatience with the fulfilment of God's timetable is to believe his promises, obey his will and leave the results to him.

Jerry Bridges

I have not so great a struggle with my vices, great and numerous as they are, as I have with my impatience. My efforts are not absolutely useless; yet I have never been able to conquer this ferocious wild beast.

John Calvin

We must suffer patiently, because impatience is rebellion against the justice of God.

John Calvin

Impatience dries the blood sooner than age or sorrow.

Cleon

Our impatience only learns patience through the thorn of delay and darkness.

J. Charles Stern

IMPENITENCE

There are no impenitent people in the kingdom of heaven.

J. C. Ryle

The impenitent heart will find the Bible but a skeleton of facts without flesh or life or breath.

A. W. Tozer

INCARNATION —
Jesus Christ

In the creation, the Lord made man like himself; but in the redemption he made himself like man.

John Boys

The earth wondered, at Christ's nativity, to see a new star in heaven; but heaven might rather wonder to see a new sun on earth.

Richard Clerke

165

Jesus Christ is perennial and he who makes his boast in him stays fresh for ever.
Vance Havner

He took the form of a servant while he retained the form of God! It is exactly that which makes our salvation possible and achieves it. *William Hendriksen*

It was to *save* sinners that Christ Jesus came into the world. He did not come to help them to save themselves, nor to induce them to save themselves, nor even to enable them to save themselves. He came to *save* them!
William Hendriksen

The early Christians did not say in dismay, 'Look what the world has come to,' but in delight, 'Look what has come to the world!'
Carl F. H. Henry

To the human mind there is something almost illogical in the assertion that God became a man. It is like speaking about a square circle. Yet this is what Christmas says — and we take refuge from our bewilderment not in explanation but in adoration.
Ralph P. Martin

The Son of God . . . came to seek us where we are in order that he might bring us to be with him where he is.
J. I. Packer

Let earth and heaven combine,
Angels and men agree,
To praise in songs divine,
The incarnate Deity,
Our God contracted to a span,
Incomprehensibly made man.
Charles Wesley

INCONSISTENCY

No seal can be set on running water. *Thomas Adams*

The damage of the sin of inconsistency in the life of the Christian is that it sours even our worship of God.
J. A. Motyer

The natural man cannot be expected to love the gospel, but let us not disgust him by inconsistency. *J. C. Ryle*

The glaring disparity between theology and practice among professing Christians is a more destructive evil in its effect upon the Christian religion than Communism, Romanism and liberalism combined. *A. W. Tozer*

How many by the wind of popular breath have been blown to hell!

Thomas Watson

INDOLENCE

All our activity is sowing; and so is our inactivity.

Wasting time is a kind of unarmed robbery.

Between the great things we cannot do and the little things we will not do, we are in danger of doing nothing.

Anon.

Footprints on the sands of time are never made by sitting down.

Anon.

Idleness is the nest in which mischief lays its eggs.

Anon.

Rust wastes more than use.

Anon.

Satan selects his disciples when they are idle; but Christ chose his when they were busy at their work, either mending their nets, or casting them into the sea.

Anon.

The devil does most when men are doing least. *Anon.*

The devil tempts all, but the idle man tempts the devil.

Anon.

The way to be nothing is to do nothing. *Anon.*

A lazy Christian will always lack four things: comfort, content, confidence and assurance. *Thomas Brooks*

Idleness is the very source of sin. *Thomas Brooks*

The only thing necessary to the triumph of evil is for good men to do nothing.

Edmund Burke

No temptation is more frequently before us than that of easing up. *Sinclair Ferguson*

The man who does things makes many mistakes, but he never makes the biggest mistake of all — doing nothing. *Benjamin Franklin*

Whom God sends he employs, for he sends none to be idle. *Matthew Henry*

Not to serve God is to serve Satan. *Charles Hodge*

The man who tries to do something and fails is infinitely better than the man who tries to do nothing and succeeds.

D. Martyn Lloyd-Jones

167

When the hands are idle, the tongue is usually very active.
Henry T. Mahan

Activity may lead to evil, but inactivity cannot lead to good. *Hannah More*

There has never yet been a man in our history who led a life of ease whose name is worth remembering.
Theodore Roosevelt

Idleness is the key of beggary. *C. H. Spurgeon*

Some temptations come to the industrious, but all temptations attack the idle.
C. H. Spurgeon

Idleness is the burial of our persons, and negligence is the burial of our actions.
George Swinnock

The idle man may call the prodigal brother.
George Swinnock

Idleness is a kind of business. *John Trapp*

Not to do what we ought to do is as bad as doing what we ought not to do.
George W. Truett

The great God never sealed any warrants for idleness.
Thomas Watson

Satan finds some mischief still for idle hands to do.
Isaac Watts

INFLUENCE
(See also: Example)

Every life is a profession of faith, and exercises an inevitable and silent influence.
Henri Amiel

Every hair makes its shadow on the ground. *Anon.*

We are called to be thermostats, not thermometers — affecting our environment, not reflecting it.
Charles R. Hembree

A holy life will produce the deepest impression. Lighthouses blow no horns; they only shine. *D. L. Moody*

The serene beauty of a holy life is the most powerful influence in the world next to the power of God.
Blaise Pascal

No one is a light unto himself, not even the sun.
Antonio Porchia

One live coal may set a whole stack on fire.
John Trapp

INGRATITUDE

The vast majority of mankind never gives a thought of gratitude towards God for all his care and blessings.
Donald Grey Barnhouse

Unthankfulness is the devil's text.   *John Boys*

Thankless men are like swine feeding on acorns, which, though they fall upon their heads, never make them look up to the tree from which they come.
Jean Daillé

I believe that the best definition of man is the ungrateful biped.
Feodor Dostoevsky

Ingratitude is not only the basest and meanest of sins, but it is the most frequent.
Wilton Merle Smith

INSECURITY

There is nothing so characteristic of our world as its instability and uncertainty.
D. Martyn Lloyd-Jones

This age is a gadget-filled paradise suspended in a hell of insecurity. *Foy Valentine*

INTOLERANCE

God is the only being in the world who has a right to be intolerant.
Donald Grey Barnhouse

Nothing dies so hard or rallies so often as intolerance. *Henry Ward Beecher*

Intolerance has been the curse of every age and state.
Samuel Davies

The devil loves nothing better than the intolerance of reformers, and dreads nothing so much as their charity and patience.
J. R. Lowell

JESUS CHRIST —
Ascension

When Jesus went back to heaven his desk was clear.

Since Christ, our Head, has ascended to heaven, we should leave our carnal desires behind and lift our hearts upward to him.
John Calvin

If Christ had not ascended he could not have interceded, as he now does in heaven for us. And do but take away Christ's intercession and you starve the hope of the saints.

John Flavel

The head that once was
crowned with thorns
Is crowned with glory now;
A royal diadem adorns
The mighty Victor's brow.

Thomas Kelly

JESUS CHRIST — Death

(See also: Atonement; Cross; Forgiveness by God)

The death of Christ not only demonstrates something, it demands everything.

That tiny hill in that tiny land is the centre of all history, not only of this world, but of all the countless galaxies and island universes of outer space from eternity to eternity.

Paul E. Billheimer

Jesus did not die just to give us peace and a purpose in life; he died to save us from the wrath of God.

Jerry Bridges

There is a fountain filled with blood
Drawn from Immanuel's veins;
And sinners plunged beneath that flood
Lose all their guilty stains.

William Cowper

170

It does not follow that because the death of Christ has a special application to the elect that it has no reference to the whole world. It is the ground on which salvation is offered to all who hear. The merit of Christ's death is immeasurable.

E. F. Kevan

He humbled himself to the accursed death of the cross. There were no lower depths possible, for the cross bespeaks the whole curse of God upon sin. It is humiliation inimitable, unrepeated, unrepeatable.

John Murray

From Christ's death flow all our hopes. *J. C. Ryle*

The blood of Christ is the seal of the testament.

Henry Smith

The magnitude of the sacrifice which our sins called forth manifests the supreme folly of looking elsewhere for their forgiveness.

Geoffrey B. Wilson

JESUS CHRIST — Deity and Humanity

He who made man was made man. *Anon.*

He who sees the Son sees the Father in the face of Christ. The Son exactly represents and reflects the Father.
J. A. Bengel

If Jesus Christ is not true God, how could he *help* us? If he is not true man, how could he help *us*?
Dietrich Bonhoeffer

Jesus is the human form of the original Word through whom the worlds were brought into being.
Donald English

Jesus is God spelling himself out in a language that man can understand.
S. D. Gordon

It was great condescension that he who was God should be made in the likeness of flesh; but much greater that he who was holy should be made in the likeness of sinful flesh! *Matthew Henry*

Jesus did not cease to be the Son of God when he became man. He did not drop his deity, which is an impossible thought. He remained what he was and added what he had not had, namely a human nature, derived out of a woman, a human mother. He became the God-man. *R. C. H. Lenski*

Anything that one imagines of God apart from Christ is only useless thinking and vain idolatry.
Martin Luther

I have had so many experiences of Christ's divinity, that I must say: either there is no God, or he is God. *Martin Luther*

If Christ is only man, then I am an idolator. If he is very God, then the man who denies it is a blasphemer. There can be no union between those who hold his deity and those who deny it.
G. Campbell Morgan

In becoming man Christ took upon him a nature that was *capable* of dying. This the angels were not; and in this respect he was, for a season, made lower than they.
A. W. Pink

The Saviour of sinners knows what it is to be poor.
J. C. Ryle

Unless our Lord Jesus is very God of very God, there is an end of his mediation, his atonement, his advocacy, his priesthood, his whole work of redemption. *J. C. Ryle*

Christ stands ... solitary and alone among all the heroes of history and pre-

171

sents to us an unsolvable problem, unless we admit him to be more than man, even the eternal Son of God.
Philip Schaff

Christ assumed both body and soul; and he offered both in our room, as was necessary to expiate guilt incurred in both and by both.
G. Smeaton

Let us come to Jesus — the person of Christ is the centre of theology. *H. B. Smith*

All that man can know of God and his love in this life is revealed in Jesus Christ.
A. W. Tozer

Christ's consciousness of deity was not suspended during his earthly life.
Marvin R. Vincent

He was like a king who temporarily puts on the garments of a peasant while at the same time remaining king. *John F. Walvoord*

He who was the Son *by nature* willingly took the form of a servant so that we who were by nature the servants of sin might become sons by the adoption of *grace!*
Geoffrey B. Wilson

JESUS CHRIST — Glory

Christ is our hope of glory and the glory of our hope.
Anon.

Christ contains in himself the totality of divine powers and excellencies.
George Barlow

If Socrates would enter the room, we should rise and do him honour. But if Jesus Christ came into the room, we should fall down on our knees and worship him.
Napoleon Bonaparte

The name of Christ excludes all merit of our own.
John Calvin

Unless your vision of Christ is as large as it can possibly be, you will always be in danger of heresy.
Donald English

When the sun is up, the moon seems to have no light.
George Estey

The excellencies of Christ are perfectly exclusive of all their opposites.
John Flavel

In his life Christ is an example, showing us how to live; in his death he is a sacrifice, satisfying for our sin;

in his resurrection, a conqueror; in his ascension, a king; in his intercession, a high priest. *Martin Luther*

The Jesus of the New Testament has at least one advantage over the Jesus of modern reconstruction — he is real. *J. Gresham Machen*

Without the miracles, you would have in Jesus a teacher and an example; but with the miracles you have a Saviour from your sins.
J. Gresham Machen

Jesus Christ is the one to whom the whole alphabet of history points.
Lesslie Newbigin

Jesus Christ is the centre of everything and the object of everything, and he who does not know him knows nothing of the order of nature and nothing of himself. *Blaise Pascal*

Jesus is the cornerstone of humanity. If he were taken away, it would shake the world to its foundations.
Ernest Renan

They lose nothing who gain Christ. *Samuel Rutherford*

No man ever errs on the side of giving too much honour to God the Son.
J. C. Ryle

No man ever thought too much of Christ.
J. C. Ryle

There is an infinite fulness in Jesus Christ. *J. C. Ryle*

No physician like the Lord, no tonic like his promise, no wine like his love.
C. H. Spurgeon

The glory of Jesus and of the Father are so wrapped up together that the grace which magnifies the one magnifies the other.
C. H. Spurgeon

We have much more to receive, but God has no more to give than he has given in Jesus Christ.
John R. W. Stott

Join all the glorious names
Of wisdom, love and power,
That ever mortals knew,
That angels ever bore;
All are too mean to speak his
    worth,
Too mean to set my Saviour
    forth.
Isaac Watts

Christ is the fulfiller and fulfilment of all the promises of God because he is the sum and substance of them.
Geoffrey B. Wilson

173

JESUS CHRIST — Holiness

The Lord Jesus Christ would have the whole world to know that though he pardons sin he will not protect it.   *Joseph Alleine*

Jesus was never guarding himself, but always invading the lives of others with his holiness.   *Phillips Brooks*

JESUS CHRIST — Intercession

Where high the heavenly temple stands,
The house of God not made with hands,
A great High Priest our nature wears,
The Saviour of mankind appears.
      Michael Bruce

Faith asks no signal from the skies
To show that prayers accepted rise;
Our Priest is in the holy place
And answers from the throne of grace.
      Josiah Conder

Before the throne of God above
I have a strong, a perfect plea,
A great High Priest, whose name is love,
Who ever lives and pleads for me.
      Charitie Lees de Chenez

JESUS CHRIST — Life and Influence

Christ's actions are our patterns.   *Anon.*

The example of Christ is supreme in its authority.
      George Barlow

The sublimest virtue according to philosophy is to live the life of nature, but Scripture points us to the perfect Christ as our example.
      John Calvin

The fear of the Lord was a lovely grace in the perfect humanity of Jesus. Let it be the test of our 'predestination to be conformed to his image'.
      Sinclair Ferguson

We must not heed what others did who were before us, but what Christ did who was before all.
      Thomas Fuller

Jesus was the most disturbing person in history.
      Vance Havner

I cannot think of even one lonely passage in the New Testament which speaks of Christ's revelation, manifestation, appearing or coming that is not directly linked with moral conduct, faith and spiritual holiness.

A. W. Tozer

If there is any reality within the whole sphere of human experience that is by its very nature worthy to challenge the mind, charm the heart and bring the total life to a burning focus, it is the reality that revolves around the person of Christ.

A. W. Tozer

Jesus Christ left us an example for our daily conduct and from it there can be no appeal.

A. W. Tozer

My dear Redeemer and my
   Lord,
I read my duty in thy Word;
But in thy life the law
   appears
Drawn out in living characters.

Isaac Watts

JESUS CHRIST —
Lordship

The lordship of Christ is neither optional nor negotiable.

There is never a day when the Lord could love his people more - or less.

Christ will either be a whole Saviour or none at all.

John Berridge

Certainly if we are to believe what our eyes see, then the kingdom of Christ seems to be on the verge of ruin. But [the] promise that Christ will never be dragged from his throne but that rather he will lay low all his enemies banishes from us all fear.

John Calvin

The beginning of self-mastery is to be mastered by Christ, to yield to his lordship. *D. G. Kehl*

How divinely supreme is our Lord above all others!

D. Martyn Lloyd-Jones

Where Christ does not rule, sin does.

J. I. Packer

JESUS CHRIST —
Perfection

Christ was made sin, but never a sinner. Sinner means one who is personally affected by sin; Christ's person never was. He never had any fellowship with sin

other than that of love and compassion, to bear it as our High Priest and Substitute.
A. Kuiper

While always in contact with sin, Christ continued sinless, for the infection never spread to him.
G. Smeaton

There was not a particle of evil in any one of the Redeemer's tears. Salt there may have been, but not fault.
C. H. Spurgeon

The heavenly perfection of Jesus discloses to us the greatness of our own possible being, while at the same time it reveals our infinite shortcoming and the source from which all restoration must come.
Augustus H. Strong

JESUS CHRIST — Power

Christ himself is the dynamic of all his demands.

The power of Christ manifests to the full its irresistible energy and attains its highest results by performing works of power with powerless instruments.
J. A. Beet

Jesus Christ is no security against life's storms, but he is perfect security in life's storms.
Wendell Loveless

There is no pit so deep that Jesus is not deeper still.
Corrie Ten Boom

JESUS CHRIST — Uniqueness

Jesus Christ is light to the eye, honey to the taste, music to the ear, joy to the heart.
Anon.

Religion without Christ is a lamp without oil.
Anon.

Christ is wisdom for your ignorance, strength for your weakness, righteousness for your guilt, sanctification for your corruption, redemption from all the thraldom of your apostasy.
Richard Fuller

Christ is not only the Saviour but the salvation itself.
Matthew Henry

All is loss that comes between us and Christ.
George Macdonald

He who thinks he hath no need of Christ hath too high thoughts of himself. He who thinks Christ cannot help him hath too low thoughts of Christ.   *J. M. Mason*

Everything that is really worth while in the morality of today has come to the world through Christ. Dismiss his standards of right and wrong and try to draw up your own ethical code, and see where you will be!
G. Campbell Morgan

When God spoke to humanity in Jesus, he said the last thing he has to say.
G. Campbell Morgan

Christ is the meeting-point between the Trinity and the sinner's soul.   *J. C. Ryle*

JOY

(See also: Happiness; Humour)

We are meant to enjoy our salvation, not endure it.

A cheerful countenance has a lot of face value.   *Anon.*

Joys are our wings; sorrows are our spurs.   *Anon.*

Nothing will stop your song quicker than your sin.   *Anon.*

Keep company with the more cheerful sort of the godly; there is no mirth like the mirth of believers.
Richard Baxter

Lord, take away from me all joy which does not come directly from the Lord Jesus.
Oswald Chambers

The joy that Jesus gives is the result of our disposition being at one with his own disposition.
Oswald Chambers

Only in obedience can we discover the great joy of the will of God.
Sinclair Ferguson

There are more believers who have peace than have joy, because there are more whose evidences are dark and weak — and it is their own fault.   *Philip Henry*

Sorrows and joys alike are temporary. In a moment all may be changed. Therefore to one who judges rightly, earthly grief is not over grievous and earthly joy not over joyous.
J. B. Lightfoot

Joy ceases to be joy when it ceases to be 'in the Lord'.
J. A. Motyer

It is an unrealistic concept of spirituality to think that joy and heaviness cannot go together. Indeed, it is unbiblical.
Charles Caldwell Ryrie

Carnal joy is always outward, and easy to express.
Richard Sibbes

People really full of joy do not usually talk much.
C. H. Spurgeon

Joy is a great therapeutic for the mind. *A. W. Tozer*

Here, joy begins to enter into us; there, we enter into joy. *Thomas Watson*

JUDGEMENT

(See also: Destiny; Eternity; Eternal Life; Heaven; Hell)

No one is redeemed except through unmerited mercy, and no one is condemned except through merited judgement. *Augustine*

Condemnation will always be in exact proportion to guilt; and guilt is in proportion to abused light and privileges. *Albert Barnes*

All men's secret sins are printed in heaven, and God will at last read them aloud in the ears of all the world.
Thomas Brooks

Mortal man, however, however inimical he may be, cannot carry his enmity beyond death, but the power

of God is not confined to such narrow limits. We often escape from men; we cannot escape the judgement of God. *John Calvin*

Let me ask every day what reference it has to the Day of Judgement and cultivate a disposition to be reminded of that day. *Richard Cecil*

The gospel teaches us that while believers are not rewarded on account of their works, they are rewarded according to their works.
R. L. Dabney

The hours which come fresh to you out of the mercy of your heavenly Father will carry for ever the imprint which your life leaves on them, until all accounts are closed at his Last Assize.
Sinclair Ferguson

Those that will not hear the comfortable voice of God's Word shall be made to hear the dreadful voice of his rod.
Matthew Henry

Those who will not observe the judgements of God's mouth shall not escape the judgements of his hand.
Matthew Henry

Those who hated God here will hate him there; the morally careless in daily life will be morally careless still; the defiant will continue defiant, and the unclean will remain uncleansed and un-repentant.   *J. A. Motyer*

Human tribunals deal with crime; they have punish-ments but no rewards. The divine tribunal has both.
A. Plummer

It is character rather than separate acts that will be rewarded or punished.
A. Plummer

The judgement seat of Christ lends a seriousness to all life.
William Childs Robinson

We shall have to render an account of every privilege that was granted to us and of every ray of light that we enjoyed.   *J. C. Ryle*

The instinct of retribution is the strongest instinct of the human heart.
Augustus H. Strong

Sin is the weight on the clock which makes the hammer to strike.   *George Swinnock*

The resurrection and the judgement will demonstrate before all worlds who won and who lost. We can wait!
A. W. Tozer

Two stimuli are necessary to make man endeavour to conform with accepted moral standards: belief in an ultimate judgement and belief in the immortality of the soul. *Wernher von Braun*

In this liberal age we tend naturally to avoid any thought of God's judgement.
David Watson

JUSTICE

Let justice be done though the world perish. *Augustine*

Justice always makes mercy dumb when sin has made the sinner deaf.
Thomas Brooks

The world is a ring, and justice is the diamond in that ring; the world is a body, and justice is the soul in that body.   *Thomas Brooks*

Indeed, I tremble for my country when I reflect that God is just.
Thomas Jefferson

A God who could pardon without justice might one day pardon without reason.
C. H. Spurgeon

JUSTIFICATION

(See also: Faith — and Deeds;
Holiness — and Justification)

*Justification does mean that we
are right with God, but it does
not imply that we are equal with
him.*

If there be ground for you to
trust in your own righteousness, then all that Christ did
to purchase salvation, and
all that God did to prepare
the way for it, is in vain.
Jonathan Edwards

Faith alone justifies, through
Christ alone. Assurance is
the enjoyment of that justification. *Sinclair Ferguson*

The stream of grace and
righteousness is deeper and
broader than the stream of
guilt. *Matthew Henry*

In every period when God
has awakened his people, the
gospel of justification has
come to the fore.
Robert M. Horn

Justification is totally against
formal religion. God has no
room for those who persist in
relying on forms or cere-
monies. *Robert M. Horn*

Remove justification and the
church begins to crumble.
Robert M. Horn

We need to get such a hold
on justification that in the
dark day we shall find it
holding us.
Robert M. Horn

When we lack the peace *of*
God, we should turn to our
peace *with* God.
Robert M. Horn

Justification does not *make*
the sinner any different: it
declares him just in the eyes of
the law. *Ernest F. Kevan*

Justification has to do not
with our *state*, but with our
standing: it refers to our
position before God.
Ernest F. Kevan

Justification supplies the
only efficient motive to
obedience.
Ernest F. Kevan

Justification is still the
article of the standing or falling church. *John Murray*

I had rather learn what
some men really judge about
their own justification from
their *prayers* than their
writings. *John Owen*

Justification is God's act of
remitting the sins of guilty
men, and accounting them
righteous, freely, by his
grace, through faith in
Christ, on the ground, not of

their own works, but of the representative law-keeping and redemptive blood-shedding of the Lord Jesus Christ on their behalf.
J. I. Packer

No amount of good deeds can make us good persons. We must be good before we can do good.
Chester A. Pennington

There is a double degree of justification: one in our conscience now, another at the Day of Judgement.
Richard Sibbes

Christ hides our unrighteousness with his righteousness, he covers our disobedience with his obedience, he shadows our death with his death, that the wrath of God cannot find us.
Henry Smith

The real reason why the doctrine of justification by grace alone through faith alone is unpopular is that it is grievously wounding to our pride.
John R. W. Stott

The doctrine of justification by faith . . . is a blessed relief from sterile legalism and unavailing self-effort.
A. W. Tozer

Justification is through faith, not on account of faith.
Benjamin B. Warfield

God does not justify us because we are worthy, but justifying makes us worthy.
Thomas Watson

KINDNESS
(See also: Love for Others; Mercy to Others)

If we are not very kind we are not very holy. *Anon.*

Kindness is the truest revealer of a person's greatness. *Anon.*

Kindness has converted more sinners than zeal, eloquence or learning.
Frederick W. Faber

The disposition to give a cup of cold water to a disciple is a far nobler property than the finest intellect.
William Dean Howells

Kindness always brings its own reward. The kind person will seldom be without friends. *J. C. Ryle*

Kindness is a grace that all can understand.
J. C. Ryle

Fidelity to God does not require any to act uncharitably to his servants.
C. H. Spurgeon

You can accomplish by kindness what you cannot do by force. *Publilius Syrus*

KNOWLEDGE
(See also: Mind; Reason)

He who is proud of his knowledge ... has gout in the wrong end.
Thomas Adams

All men naturally desire to know, but what doth knowledge avail without the fear of God? *Thomas à Kempis*

Knowledge humbles the great man, astonishes the common man, puffs up the little man. *Anon.*

Knowledge is folly, except grace guide it. *Anon.*

Zeal without knowledge is the sister of folly. *Anon.*

Wisdom has never made a bigot, but learning has.
John Billings

There is no fear of knowing too much, but there is much fear of practising too little.
Thomas Brooks

We can never hear too often that we can never learn too well. *Thomas Brooks*

Almost all men are infected with the disease of desiring to obtain useless knowledge.
John Calvin

A man may be theologically knowing and spiritually ignorant. *Stephen Charnock*

Knowledge is the foundation of wisdom.
Stephen Charnock

If you have knowledge, let others light their candles at it. *Thomas Fuller*

Knowledge is to be the usher of grace; information in the understanding must go before reformation in the will and affections.
Thomas Fuller

One grain of faith is more precious than a pound of knowledge. *Joseph Hall*

Seldom was ever any knowledge given to keep, but to impart. *Joseph Hall*

You can have a head full of Scripture and a heart full of sin. *Vance Havner*

Every man has far more knowledge of good than he uses. *Alexander Maclaren*

Let me always remember that it is not the amount of religious knowledge which I have, but the amount which I use, that determines my religious position and character.

Alexander Maclaren

There are over many who have much knowledge and little virtue, and who often speak of God while rarely speaking to him. *Malaval*

The devil has more knowledge than any of us, and yet is no better for it.

J. C. Ryle

Since the tree of knowledge has been tasted, the key of knowledge has been rusted.

William Secker

What a lamentable condition is that man in whose knowledge is only sufficient to damn his own soul!

Richard Sibbes

There may be a clear head without a clean heart.

George Swinnock

Knowledge without humility is vanity. *A. W. Tozer*

What is a knowing head without a fruitful heart?

Thomas Watson

KNOWLEDGE OF GOD

(See also: Revelation)

The Christian who is truly spiritual revels as much in his ignorance of God as in his knowledge of him.

Nearly all the wisdom we possess, that is to say, true and sound wisdom, consists of two parts: the knowledge of God and of ourselves.

John Calvin

Man is not making his way up through animism, fetishism, totemism, polytheism and monotheism to a knowledge of God. He started with a knowledge of God and has been going the other way ever since. *Vance Havner*

'To know' is not a mere exercise of the head. Nothing is 'known' until it has also passed over into obedience.

J. A. Motyer

We grow in proportion as we know. *J. A. Motyer*

If ever man is to come to a knowledge of God ... two veils must be taken away: that which hides God's mind and that which clouds our heart. God in his mercy removes both. Thus our knowledge of God, first to last, is his gracious gift. *J. I. Packer*

To affirm, as some do, that man can discover and know God without God speaking to him is really to deny that God is personal.

J. I. Packer

The knowledge of God is very far from the love of him. *Blaise Pascal*

The fact beats ceaselessly into my brain these days that there is a world of difference between knowing the Word of God and knowing the God of the Word.

Leonard Ravenhill

To feel that we are ignorant is the first beginning of all saving knowledge.

J. C. Ryle

We cannot seek God till we have found him.

George Swinnock

LAW OF GOD

God forbids sin not to prevent us enjoying ourselves, but to prevent us destroying ourselves.

The law of God is like a mirror; it can reveal flaws, but not remove them.

Not only does God's law open my eyes to my guilt, it shuts my mouth when I try to excuse myself.

The man who does not set himself under the law of God sets himself above it.

The law may *express* sin but it cannot *suppress* sin.

Thomas Adams

The law, though it has no power to condemn us, has power to command us.

Thomas Adams

Man everywhere is under law, written or unwritten; and he is morally obligated to obey it. *George Barlow*

The law sends us to the gospel for our justification; the gospel sends us to the law to frame our way of life ... Christ has freed us from the *manner* of our obedience, but not from the *matter* of our obedience. *Samuel Bolton*

Just as the moon and the stars, though they are themselves bright and spread their light over all the earth, yet vanish before the greater brightness of the sun, so the law, however glorious in itself, has no glory in face of the gospel's grandeur.

John Calvin

Only if we walk in the beauty of God's law do we become sure of our adoption as children of the Father.

John Calvin

Moral law imposes no heavy bondage. It points to the glorious liberty of love, joy and peace. All its ways are good for a man.

Walter J. Chantry

No man can break any of the Ten Commandments; he can only break himself against them.

G. K. Chesterton

The law was for the *condemnation* of sinners, the gospel was for the *saving* of sinners and the ministration of forgiveness. *C. J. Ellicott*

The law sends us to Christ to be justified, and Christ sends us to the law to be regulated.

John Flavel

Actually you cannot break the law of God. If you jump off a skyscraper you do not break the law of gravitation, you break your neck.

Vance Havner

One might as well attack Gibraltar with a popgun as to attack the moral law of the universe and the God who reigns in righteousness.

Vance Havner

There is a universe of moral law, whether we like it or not, and when we disregard it we pull down the house on ourselves and our generation. *Vance Havner*

The strongest inducement for a Christian to obey the divine law is the fact that he has been graciously pardoned for having broken it.

Ernest F. Kevan

A low view of law leads to legalism in religion; a high view makes man a seeker after grace.

J. Gresham Machen

At the heart of everything that the Bible says are two great truths, which belong inseparably together — the majesty of the law of God, and sin as an offence against that law.

J. Gresham Machen

The consciousness of sin alone leads men to turn to the Saviour from sin, and the consciousness of sin comes only when men are brought face to face with the law of God.

J. Gresham Machen

In the Ten Commandments we have a transcript of the moral constitution of Deity.

Douglas Macmillan

The law reflects the nature and character of God just as surely as does the gospel.

Douglas Macmillan

The gospel no more excuses sin than the law does. What

is repugnant to the moral law of God is also contrary to the gospel of Christ.
Henry T. Mahan

God's law was once impressed upon our natures, and we are obliged to all that was written upon Adam's heart.
Thomas Manton

The Christian must remember that he is called not only to believe revealed doctrine but to obey revealed law.
J. A. Motyer

Avoid as you would a deadly snake any man who denies the law of God is the Christian's rule of life.
A. W. Pink

The light which men got from Moses and the law was at best only starlight compared to noonday.
J. C. Ryle

The law by which God rules us is as dear to him as the gospel by which he saves us.
William Secker

The law of God will not take ninety-nine for a hundred.
William Secker

The law is not opposed to grace by preparing for it; it is only opposed to it if we stay in it after grace has come.
A. Lukyn Williams

It is the function of the law to convict men of their sin and drive them to faith in the promise. Consequently even the Old Testament saints were saved by their faith in the promise, and not by their obedience to the law.
Geoffrey B. Wilson

LEGALISM

Christian morality differs radically from legalism. Legalism is obedience to the letter of the law to the neglect of the spirit; Christian morality is obedience to the spirit of the law as well as the letter.
R. B. Kuiper

What is legalism? It is a wrong attitude towards the code of laws under which a person lives ... Thus legalism may be defined as 'a fleshly attitude which conforms to a code for the purpose of exalting self'.
Charles Caldwell Ryrie

LIBERALISM

Modernism is politically a volcano and theologically a windbag.
Carl F. H. Henry

Modernism is not a brand of Christianity, but a denial of it.   *R. B. Kuiper*

Theological liberalism, in spite of all its clamour for ecumenism and church union, is working more effectively towards the disruption of the church of Christ than is any other force.   *R. B. Kuiper*

A cardinal doctrine of modern liberalism is that the world's evil may be overcome by the world's good; no help is thought to be needed from outside the world.   *J. Gresham Machen*

Liberalism is totally different from Christianity, for the foundation is different. Christianity is founded upon the Bible ... liberalism on the other hand is founded upon the shifting emotions of sinful men.
J. Gresham Machen

The grace of God is rejected by modern liberalism. And the result is slavery — the slavery of the law, the wretched bondage by which man undertakes the impossible task of establishing his own righteousness as a ground of acceptance with God.   *J. Gresham Machen*

Liberalism ... is unfaithfulness; it is spiritual adultery towards the divine Bridegroom.   *Francis Schaeffer*

The real difference between liberalism and biblical Christianity is not a matter of scholarship but of presuppositions.   *Francis Schaeffer*

LIBERTY

Better starve free than be a fat slave.   *Aesop*

There is no true liberty except the liberty of the happy who cleave to the eternal law.   *Augustine*

The Bible ... presupposes that only in so far as a man is free *for* God can he be truly free *from* all those things which would prevent him from being his best.
J. C. P. Cockerton

He is the freeman whom the truth makes free, and all are slaves beside.
William Cowper

True liberty consists only in the power of doing what we ought to will, and in not being constrained to do what we ought not to will.
Jonathan Edwards

Liberty unregulated by law degenerates into anarchy.
Lowell Fillmore

What then is the nature of true liberty? Not being free to do anything you want to do, but in coming to the place where you delight in the performance of what you ought to do. *Al Martin*

Happy is the man who can use Christian liberty without abusing it. *J. C. Ryle*

We have been born under a monarchy; to obey God is freedom. *Seneca*

The freedom of the Christian is freedom *in* the law.
Augustus H. Strong

We need to be delivered from the freedom which is absolute bondage into the bondage which is perfect freedom. *William Temple*

Where we go when we are free to go where we will is a near-infallible index of character.
A. W. Tozer

Our real freedom from sin and the bondage to sin is found in our enslavement, both body and soul, to Christ, the Lord of all.
Spiros Zodhiates

LIFE

All living is preparation for dying.

Everything in life is a test of character.

Life ought not merely to contain acts of worship, it should be an act of worship.

The two greatest facts in life are sin and death.

Every life without Christ is a mission field; every life with Christ is a missionary. *Anon.*

It is not how long but how well we live that matters.
Anon.

Life is measured by its depth, not its duration.
Anon.

Life is not a solo but a chorus. We live in relationships from cradle to grave.
Anon.

Life is worth living better than most men live it.
Anon.

Live your best, and act your best, and think your best each day, for there may be no tomorrows. *Anon.*

Live your own life, and you will die your own death.
Anon.

Today is the first day of the rest of your life.   *Anon.*

Life, if properly viewed in any aspect, is great, but mainly great when viewed in its relation to the world to come.   *Albert Barnes*

A person who really wishes to learn to know how to live more successfully must first know whether he has life to live, or whether he possesses nothing more than mere existence.
Donald Grey Barnhouse

Life is too short to be small.
Benjamin Disraeli

Life with its joys and griefs, business, the use of the world, must be carried on as under notice to quit, by men prepared to cast loose from the shores of time.
G. G. Findlay

Every man's life is his opportunity of doing that which will make for him in eternity.   *Matthew Henry*

This world is our passage not our portion.
Matthew Henry

Life in worldly pleasure is only life in appearance.
H. J. Holtzmann

The great use of life is to spend it for something that outlasts it.   *William James*

Life, according to the Bible, is not just existence, but it is existence in the presence and with the favour of God; and death is not just the death of the body but it is separation from God and a doom that should fill the heart of man with a nameless dread.
J. Gresham Machen

If life be short, then moderate your worldly cares and projects; do not cumber yourseves with too much provision for a short voyage.
Thomas Manton

Live so as to be missed.
Robert Murray M'Cheyne

Life in itself is neither good nor evil; it is the scene of good or evil, as you make it.
Michel de Montaigne

Life must be filled with life.
Andrew Murray

Plan your life, budgeting for seventy years . . . and understand that if your time proves shorter that will not be unfair deprivation but rapid promotion.
J. I. Packer

Between us and heaven or hell there is only life, which

is the frailest thing in the world. *Blaise Pascal*

All the care in the world will not make us continue a minute beyond the time God has appointed. *J. C. Ryle*

We are not so to live as if we had nothing but a body. *J. C. Ryle*

Man, made in the image of God, has a purpose — to be in relationship to God, who is there. Man forgets his purpose and thus he forgets who he is and what life means. *Francis Schaeffer*

The primary test of life is not service but love, both for man and for God. *William Still*

The secret of life is theological and the key to heaven as well. *A. W. Tozer*

Life can only be enjoyed as one acquires a true perspective of life and death and of the real purpose of life. *Spiros Zodhiates*

LITERATURE

Literature can be our most effective medium of mass communication of the gospel.

In terms of the price paid for it, the number of people reached and the fact that the message can be read over and over again until it is understood, there is no other method than can compare with literature. *Harold Cook*

If the crowns of all the kingdoms were laid down at my feet in exchange for my books and my love of reading, I would spurn them all. *François Fenelon*

I read for eternity. *John C. Ryland*

LORD'S DAY

Sunday is the summer of the week. *Anon.*

Use your sabbaths as steps to glory. *Richard Baxter*

I never knew one man or woman who steadily avoided the house of prayer and public worship on the Lord's day, who did not come to grief, and bring other people to grief. *Henry Whitney Bellows*

The sabbath is God's special present to the working man, and one of its chief objects is to prolong his life, and

preserve efficient his working tone. The savings bank of human existence is the weekly sabbath.
William G. Blaikie

Sunday should strike the keynote for the week.
J. Wilbur Chapman

Sunday is the core of our civilization, dedicated to thought and reverence. It invites to the noblest solitude and to the noblest society.
Ralph Waldo Emerson

Make not that wearisome that should always be welcome. *Thomas Fuller*

The sabbath is not only a blessing and privilege for those who keep it. In an increasingly despairing and restless world, its observance is a sign and witness of the hope God's people have.
Richard B. Gaffin

It would be as difficult to take an inventory of the benefits the world receives from the sunshine as to enumerate the blessings we derive from the Christian sabbath.
Hervey Doddridge Ganse

When a nation remembers Sunday as the Lord's day and keeps it holy unto him this is both pleasing to God

and beneficial to the country. *W. R. Mohon*

I never knew a man escape failures in either mind or body who worked seven days a week. *Robert Peel*

Holiness is the best sabbath dress — but it is equally suitable for everyday wear.
C. H. Spurgeon

The Jews' seventh day was buried in Christ's grave.
George Swinnock

Break down Sunday, close the churches, open the bars and the theatres on that day, and where would values be? What was real estate worth in Sodom?
H. L. Wayland

Oh, what a blessing is Sunday, interposed between the waves of worldly business like the divine path of the Israelites through Jordan! There is nothing in which I would advise you to be more strictly conscientious than in keeping the sabbath day holy.
William Wilberforce

191

LOVE FOR CHRIST

(See also: Communion with Christ;
Meditation; Prayer)

The church has no greater
need today than to fall in
love with Jesus all over
again.   *Vance Havner*

Christ's lovers prove their
love by their obedience.
                John R. W. Stott

LOVE FOR GOD

(See also: Communion with God;
Meditation; Prayer)

Just as obedience to the
Lord is an indication of our
love for him, so is it also a
proof of our fear of God.
                Jerry Bridges

To cherish true love for God
is to be constrained by love
to yield one's ego with all
that it is and has, and to let
God be God again.
                Abraham Kuyper

The severest self-denials and
the most lavish gifts are of no
value in God's esteem unless
they are prompted by love.
                A. W. Pink

Our love for God is tested by
the question of whether we
seek him or his gifts.
                Ralph W. Sockman

Love to God is the indelible
token of the chosen seed; by
this secret seal the election of
grace is certified to the
believer.   *C. H. Spurgeon*

The primary test of life is not
service but love, both for
man and for God.
                William Still

Love to God is the essence of
all virtue.
                Augustus H. Strong

As the sunbeams united in a
burning glass burn the
hotter, so all our affections
should be united, that our
love to God may be more
ardent.   *Thomas Watson*

LOVE FOR OTHERS —
Definition

(See also: Kindness; Mercy to
Others)

The loneliest place in the
world is the human heart
when love is absent.   *Anon.*

To have the heart glow with
mutual love is vastly better
than to glare with the most
pompous titles, offices or
powers.   *Matthew Henry*

Every man feels instinctively
that all the beautiful senti-
ments in the world weigh
less than a single lovely
action.   *J. R. Lowell*

Love is that jewel of human nature which commands a valuation wherever it is found.   *John Owen*

LOVE FOR OTHERS —
Importance

If God should have no more mercy on us than we have charity one to another, what would become of us?
Thomas Fuller

Not tongues nor faith nor prophecy nor knowledge nor martyrdom nor philanthropy, but *love* is the Christian's mark of distinction.
Vance Havner

Love is the very essence and life of the Christian religion.
Matthew Henry

A man may be a good doctor without loving his patients; a good lawyer without loving his clients; a good geologist without loving science; but he cannot be a good Christian without love.
D. L. Moody

Nothing will be intentionally lacking where there is love.   *J. C. Ryle*

All men are our neighbours, and we are to love them as ourselves. We are to do this

on the basis of creation, even if they are not redeemed, for all men have value because they are made in the image of God. Therefore they are to be loved even at great cost.   *Francis Schaeffer*

Love — and the unity it attests to — is the mark Christ gave Christians to wear before the world. Only with this mark may the world know that Christians are indeed Christians and that Jesus was sent by the Father.   *Francis Schaeffer*

The primary test of life is not service but love, both for man and for God.
William Still

He who is not filled with love is necessarily small, withered, shrivelled in his outlook on life and things.
Benjamin B. Warfield

LOVE FOR OTHERS —
Measure

Love never reasons, but profusely gives; gives, like a thoughtless prodigal, its all, and trembles then lest it has done too little.
Hannah More

Love feels no loads.
William S. Plumer

Love is its own evidence.
William S. Plumer

I am determined that I am going to love everybody, even if it kills me! I have set my heart on it. I am going to do it. *A. W. Tozer*

As soon as the love of God was shed abroad in my soul, I loved all, of whatsoever denomination, who loved the Lord Jesus in sincerity of heart. *George Whitefield*

LOVE FOR OTHERS — Practical

Love not merely does not seek that which does not belong to it; it is prepared to give up for the sake of others even what it is entitled to.
C. K. Barrett

Of love there be two principal offices; one to give, another to forgive.
John Boys

Love will stammer rather than be dumb.
Robert Leighton

Love for the brethren is far more than an agreeable society whose views are the same. *A. W. Pink*

Love is not only full of benevolence but benificence. Love which enlarges the heart never straitens the hand. *Thomas Watson*

LUST
(See also: Desires; Sex)

Lust and lucre follow one another as closely akin, both seducing the heart from the Creator to the creature.
A. R. Fausset

Natural desires are at rest when that which is desired is obtained, but corrupt desires are insatiable. Nature is content with little, grace with less, but lust with nothing. *Matthew Henry*

The right way to put out the fire of lust is to withdraw the fuel of excess.
William Jenkyn

Intemperance is odious to God.
Thomas Manton

LYING
(See also: Dishonesty)

A lie is a poor substitute for the truth, but the only one discovered so far. *Anon.*

Those who are given to white lies soon become colour blind. *Anon.*

Certainly falsehood and calumnies are more deadly than swords and all other kinds of weapons.
John Calvin

There are three kinds of lies; a lie told, a lie taught, a lie acted out. *Joseph Caryl*

When a half truth is presented as a whole truth it becomes an untruth.
Walter J. Chantry

There is no form of sin in which we act more satanically than when we indulge in telling a lie. *Frank Gabelein*

The cruellest lies are often told in silence. *John Hus*

Calumny would soon starve and die of itself if nobody took it in and gave it lodging. *Robert Leighton*

No man has a good enough memory to be a successful liar. *Abraham Lincoln*

A lie is a snowball. The longer it is rolled on the ground, the larger it becomes. *Martin Luther*

Lies and false reports are among Satan's choicest weapons. *J. C. Ryle*

False words are not only evil in themselves, but they infect the soul with evil.
Socrates

Lying is a certain mark of cowardice. *Thomas Southern*

One of the most striking differences between a cat and a lie is that a cat has only nine lives.
Mark Twain

Falsehoods not only disagree with truths, but they usually quarrel among themselves.
Daniel Webster

MALICE

Malice is anger long cherished, until it becomes a settled habit of mind.
George Barlow

The malicious have a dark happiness. *Victor Hugo*

Envy and malice are quick-sighted. *Richard Sibbes*

Malice can always find a mark to shoot at, and a pretence to fire.
Charles Simmons

Malice is mental murder.
Thomas Watson

MAN — a Failure

The whole life of man until he is converted to Christ is a ruinous labyrinth of wanderings. *John Calvin*

Man is a disaster. *Cicero*

Never is a man in his right mind till he is converted, or in his right place till he sits by faith at the feet of Jesus, or rightly clothed till he has put on the Lord Jesus Christ. *J. C. Ryle*

Made in God's image, man was made to be great, he was made to be beautiful and he was made to be creative in life and art. But his rebellion has led him into making himself into nothing but a machine. *Francis Schaeffer*

Man, made in the image of God, has a purpose — to be in relationship to God, who is there. Man forgets his purpose and thus he forgets who he is and what life means. *Francis Schaeffer*

Man was created to know God but he chose the gutter. That is why he is like a bird shut away in a cage or like a fish taken from the water. *A. W. Tozer*

MAN — God's Creation and Concern

If man was not created by God in God's image, he has no more inherent dignity than a donkey.

Of all God's creatures, man alone is able to think immortality. *S. Parkes Cadman*

Man is born to have connection with God. *Clement of Alexandria*

Meditate on our making, that we may fall in love with our Maker. *David Dickson*

God defend me from ever looking at a man as an animal. *Ralph Waldo Emerson*

Our father was Adam, our grandfather dust, our greatgrandfather nothing. *William Jenkyn*

We are not begotten by God, only made by him: in our natural state we are not sons of God, only (so to speak) statues. *C. S. Lewis*

God does not love us because we are valuable, but we are valuable because God loves us. *Martin Luther*

Man was not, as created, morally neutral — indeed the whole notion of a

196

morally neutral person is a monstrosity — but his nature was positively directed to the right and opposed to the wrong.
J. Gresham Machen

Man was made of earth which was made of nothing.
Edward Marbury

Man, made in the image of God, has a purpose — to be in relationship to God, who is there. Man forgets his purpose and thus he forgets who he is and what life means.
Francis Schaeffer

My worth is what I am worth to God, and that is a marvellous great deal, for Christ died for me.
William Temple

God has made us a little lower than the angels, but he has made us a little higher than the animals.
A. W. Tozer

God made us for himself: that is the first and last thing that can be said about human existence and whatever more we add is but commentary. *A. W. Tozer*

God made us to be worshippers. That was the purpose of God in bringing us into the world. *A. W. Tozer*

I know that I take a chance of being misunderstood and perhaps of being misjudged when I state that man was more like God than any other creature ever created. Because of the nature of man's creation there is nothing in the universe so much like God as the human soul. *A. W. Tozer*

Man's only claim to importance is that he was created in the divine image; in himself he is nothing.
A. W. Tozer

MAN — a Religious Being

Man is constitutionally religious. *R. B. Kuiper*

Man is a worshipper and only in the spirit of worship does he find release for all the powers of his amazing intellect. *A. W. Tozer*

None but God can satisfy the longings of the immortal soul; as the heart was made for him, he only can fill it.
Richard C. Trench

Man is so made that he cannot ignore God. If he cannot love him he will hate him. His face is such that it haunts. *Mary Whitehouse*

197

Man in his rebellion against his Creator remains incurably religious, and he seeks to satisfy this instinct by making his own deities. He much prefers these lifeless puppets to the one true living God, because they allow him to pull the strings.
Geoffrey B. Wilson

MAN — a Sinner
(See also: Depravity; Sin; Sinful Nature)

Not only the worst of my sins, but the best of my duties speak of me as a child of Adam.
William Beveridge

We are of the world, and until Christ rescues us from it, the world reigns in us and we live unto it.
John Calvin

God created man in mint condition, but sin has seriously defaced him. Satan vandalized man.
Brian Edwards

I have never yet met any parents who admit that their child was such a perfect angel that they actually taught it one or two naughty things to make it normal!
Brian Edwards

Man lost his freedom in the garden of Eden. He is free to sin, but he is not free not to sin.
Brian Edwards

Sin is a matter of what we are, not what we learn.
Brian Edwards

Man is by nature more inclined to one sin than to another.
John Hus

Sin has left a deep and disfiguring mark on man: his life is now a moral discord.
Ernest F. Kevan

We are all murderers and prostitutes — no matter to what culture, society, class, nation one belongs; no matter how normal, moral or mature one takes oneself to be.
R. D. Laing

Fallen man is not simply an imperfect creature who needs improvement: he is a rebel who must lay down his arms.
C. S. Lewis

Fallen man is curved in on himself.
Martin Luther

Sin is not the brute in us; it is, rather, the man in us.
J. Gresham Machen

The disposition of every human heart by nature can be visually pictured as a clenched fist raised against the living God.
Al Martin

A man who is not a Christian is Satan's prisoner: Satan has him where he wants him.   *J. I. Packer*

The evil that is in us is all our own.   *J. C. Ryle*

We need no bad company to teach us, and no devil to tempt us, in order to run into sin. We have within us the beginning of every sin under heaven.   *J. C. Ryle*

Every man, so far as he is apart from God, is morally insane.   *Augustus H. Strong*

The lostness of man is not a dogma, it is a fact.
     A. W. Tozer

We are a bad lot, we sons of Adam.   *A. W. Tozer*

MARRIAGE
(See also: Family Life)

Marriages may be made in heaven, but man is responsible for the maintenance work.   *Anon.*

When a woman rules the marriage roost, she is sitting on the wrong perch!
     Anon.

The Christian married couple can be a powerful weapon in the hand of Jesus.
     John Benton

Each instance of a wife failing to defer to known wishes of her husband (unless those wishes oppose the moral law of God) subverts the divinely appointed order.
     Walter Chantry

Marriage, and the process of coming to it, is not heaven! It is the bonding together of two needy sinners in order to make a partnership which is substantially greater than either of them alone.
     Sinclair Ferguson

The powerful sexual drives which are built in to man's relationship with woman are not seen in Scripture as the foundation of marriage, but the consummation and physical expression of it.
     Sinclair Ferguson

Choose a wife rather by your ear than your eye.
     Thomas Fuller

It is not evil to marry but good to be wary.
     Thomas Gataker

Sexual desire is natural and marriage is provided for its fulfilment.   *Norman Hillyer*

There is no estate to which Satan is more opposed as to marriage.　*Martin Luther*

A successful marriage requires falling in love many times — always with the same person.
　Mignon McLaughlin

Marriage is not a concession to our sinfulness; marriage is a provision for our holiness.
　J. A. Motyer

A happy marriage is the union of two good forgivers.
　Robert Quillen

In no relation is so much earthly happiness to be found, if it be entered upon discreetly, advisedly and in the fear of God. In none is so much misery seen to follow, if it be taken in hand unadvisedly, lightly, wantonly and without thought.
　J. C. Ryle

The marriage relation lies at the very root of the social system of nations.
　J. C. Ryle

The nearer a nation's laws about marriage approach to the law of Christ, the higher has the moral tone of that nation always proved to be.
　J. C. Ryle

The heart of marriage is its communication system. It can be said that the success and happiness of any married pair is measurable in terms of the deepening dialogue which characterizes their union.
　Dwight Small

First man must choose his love, and then he must love his choice.　*Henry Smith*

The man and wife are partners, like two oars in a boat.
　Henry Smith

A gracious wife satisfies a good husband and silences a bad one.　*George Swinnock*

MARTYRDOM

(See also: Persecution)

If there be glory laid up for them that die in the Lord, much more shall they be glorified that die for the Lord.　*Richard Baxter*

Martyrs are the eldest sons of blessedness among all the sons of adoption.
　Thomas Goodwin

Martyrdom has always been a proof of the intensity, never of the correctness of a belief.　*Arthur Schnitzler*

It is far less important to die the martyr's death than to live the martyr's life.
Robert E. Speer

MATERIALISM
(See also: Possessions; Prosperity; Riches; Wealth)

Materialists know the price of everything but the value of nothing.

While we rightly recoil from materialistic Communism, pervading our society is an even more insidious materialism which makes Christians short of breath through prosperity and ill-equipped to run the race that is set before them. *J. D. Douglas*

Lives based on having are less free than lives based either on doing or on being.
William James

The most vicious aspect of the tyranny of materialism is its ability to produce merely earth-bound aspirations.
Harold B. Kuhn

The simplicity of materialism is a baneful simplicity. It is the simplicity which is arrived at by an ignoring of some of the facts.
J. Gresham Machen

The possessive clinging to things . . . must be torn from our souls in violence as Christ expelled the money changers from the temple.
A. W. Tozer

MEANNESS

The miser deprives himself of this world and God will deprive him of the next.
Thomas Adams

The only time a miser puts his hand in his pocket is during cold weather.
Anon.

A tight fist means a shrivelled soul. *Samuel Chadwick*

MEANS OF GRACE

Without the diligent use of means a lazy Christian has no right to expect to receive assurance. *Thomas Brooks*

It is far easier to speak to others than it is constantly to use and improve all holy means and duties to preserve the soul from sin and maintain it in a sweet and free communion with God.
A. W. Pink

Neither be idle in the means, nor make an idol of the means.   *William Secker*

Many live all their days under the means of grace that never get one dram of grace in the use of the means.   *George Swinnock*

Means must be neither trusted nor neglected.
John Trapp

MEDITATION

(See also: Communion with God; Love for God; Prayer)

Meditation fits a man for supplication.   *Anon.*

Meditation is the acting of all the powers of the soul.
Richard Baxter

Meditation is the life of most other duties.
Richard Baxter

Meditate on our making, that we may fall in love with our Maker.   *David Dickson*

Meditation keeps out Satan. It increases knowledge, it inflames love, it works patience, it promotes prayer, it evidences sincerity.
Philip Henry

Truths are concocted and ripened by meditation.
Thomas Manton

If I have observed anything by experience it is this: a man may take the measure of his growth and decay in grace according to his thoughts and meditations upon the person of Christ, and the glory of Christ's kingdom, and of his love.
John Owen

In meditation, the whole man is engaged in deep and prayerful thought on the true meaning and bearing of a particular biblical passage.
J. I. Packer

Meditation is not giving free rein to your imagination, nor is it reading your Bible for beautiful thoughts. Meditation is a discipline.
J. I. Packer

The minister who is to preach biblically can only do so as a result of much meditation.   *J. I. Packer*

Contemplation is a perspective glass to see our Saviour in; but examination is a looking-glass to see ourselves in.   *William Secker*

Whatever engages my attention when I should be meditating on God and things eternal does injury to my soul. *A. W. Tozer*

Reading and conversation may furnish us with many ideas of men and things, yet it is our own meditation that must form our judgement.
Isaac Watts

MEEKNESS
(See also: Humility; Self-Cruci-fixion)

Poverty of spirit is the riches of the soul. *Anon.*

Meekness is the bridle of anger. *Anon.*

The best way to outwit the devil is to be silent under the hand of God.
Thomas Brooks

The silent soul can bear a burden without a burden.
Thomas Brooks

He who is without expec-tation cannot fret if nothing comes to him. The lowly man and the meek man dominate the world because they do not care for it.
Henry Drummond

Absolute resignation to divine will baffles a thou-sand temptations, and confi-dence in our Saviour will

carry us through a thousand trials. *John Fletcher*

To be truly meek means we no longer protect ourselves because we see there is nothing worth defending.
D. Martyn Lloyd-Jones

The purest gold is the most pliable. *William Secker*

The meek man is not a human mouse afflicted with a sense of his own inferiority. Rather, he may be in his moral life as bold as a lion and as strong as Samson; but he has stopped being fooled about himself.
A. W. Tozer

Meekness is the mark of the man who has been mastered by God. His mildness towards others is the fruit of that divine discipline which brought him true self-knowledge.
Geoffrey B. Wilson

MERCY FROM GOD
(See also: Forgiveness by God)

We are saved not by merit but by mercy.

God's crumbs are better than the world's loaves.
Anon.

203

Mercy is without price and beyond all price.   *Anon.*

As there is no mercy too great for God to give, so there is no mercy too little for us to crave.
Thomas Brooks

God's mercies are above all his works, and above all ours too.   *Thomas Brooks*

The candle of mercy is set up not to play by but to work by.   *Thomas Brooks*

Without faith we are not fit to desire mercy.
Stephen Charnock

God has two sheepdogs: Goodness and Mercy. He sends them to us from his throne of grace; sometimes to bark at us, to badger us; sometimes to woo us by persuading us that his will is good and perfect for our lives.   *Sinclair Ferguson*

If God should have no more mercy on us than we have charity one to another, what would become of us?
Thomas Fuller

All the compassions of all the tender fathers in the world compared with the tender mercies of our God would be but as a candle to the sun or a drop to the ocean.
Matthew Henry

God's reasons of mercy are all drawn from himself, not from anything in us.
Matthew Henry

Christ is the mine of mercy and the gold-ore of grace and salvation.
Thomas Hooker

Mercy does not always express itself by withholding punishment.
Ernest M. Ligon

Man has no more right to mercy than a murderer has to go free.   *Fred A. Malone*

Mercy is an ocean that is ever full and ever flowing.
Thomas Manton

Mercy is a treasure that cannot easily be spent.
Thomas Manton

One spiritual mercy is worth more than all temporal blessings.   *William S. Plumer*

Clemency is one of the brightest diamonds in the crown of majesty.
William Secker

One ray of mercy is better than a sun of pleasure.
William Secker

The depths of our misery can never fall below the depths of mercy.
Richard Sibbes

All our past mercies are tokens of future mercies.
C. H. Spurgeon

Mercy may seem slow, but it is sure. The Lord in unfailing wisdom has appointed a time for the outgoings of his gracious power, and God's time is the best time.
C. H. Spurgeon

Take notice not only of the mercies of God, but of God in the mercies.
Ralph Venning

There is no reason to be given for mercy but mercy.
Ralph Venning

God's mercy can drown great sins, as the sea covers great rocks. *Thomas Watson*

Mercy's clock does not strike at the sinner's beck.
Thomas Watson

The diocese where mercy visits is very large.
Thomas Watson

MERCY TO OTHERS
(See also: Forgiveness of Others; Kindness; Love for Others)

If God should have no more mercy on us than we have charity one to another, what would become of us?
Thomas Fuller

Mercy in us is a sign of our interest in God's mercy.
Thomas Manton

The right spring of mercy is a sense of God's mercy; it is a thank-offering, not a sin-offering. *Thomas Manton*

If we refuse mercy here, we shall have justice in eternity.
Jeremy Taylor

MIND
(See also: Knowledge; Reason; Thoughts)

If the mouth be bad, the mind is not good.
Thomas Brooks

Oh, how greatly has the man advanced who has learned not to be his own, not to be governed by his own reason, but to surrender his mind to God!
John Calvin

Our minds are a beam from God. *Stephen Charnock*

The man is as the mind is.
Matthew Henry

In presenting the Christian gospel we must never, in the first place, make a direct approach either to the emotions or to the will. The emotions and the will should

always be influenced through the mind.
> *D. Martyn Lloyd-Jones*

All our minds are narrower than we think, and blind spots and obsessions abound in them like bees in clover.
> *J. I. Packer*

There is a handle to every mind, and our chief aim must be to get hold of it.
> *J. C. Ryle*

When filled with holy truth the mind rests.
> *C. H. Spurgeon*

A Christian mind is a mind which thinks Christianly about everything.
> *John R. W. Stott*

The mind of man is much wider than his mouth.
> *George Swinnock*

The human intellect, even in its fallen state, is an awesome work of God, but it lies in darkness until it has been illuminated by the Holy Spirit. *A. W. Tozer*

To possess a Spirit-indwelt mind is the Christian's privilege under grace.
> *A. W. Tozer*

MIRACLES

God never wrought miracles to convince atheism because his ordinary works convince it. *Francis Bacon*

The many signs that appear after Pentecost should make us the more careful not to set limits, in our enlightened era, to the miraculous activity of God.
> *G. C. Berkouwer*

The miracles of Jesus are signs of what lies ahead . . . for the people of God.
> *James T. Dennison*

Do not expect the supernatural when God would have you proceed in the normal, natural course of things. *Vance Havner*

Those who need miracles are men of little faith.
> *John Hus*

To strip Christianity of the supernatural is to destroy Christianity. *R. B. Kuiper*

The divine art of miracle is not an art of suspending the pattern to which events conform, but of feeding new events into that pattern.
> *C. S. Lewis*

The miracles of Jesus were the ordinary works of his

Father, wrought small and swift that we might take them in.   *George Macdonald*

A miracle is an event in the external world that is wrought by the immediate power of God.
J. Gresham Machen

God is always the first cause, but there are truly second causes; and they are the means which God uses, in the ordinary course of the world, for the accomplishment of his ends. It is the exclusion of such second causes which makes an event a miracle.
J. Gresham Machen

Without the miracles, you would have in Jesus a teacher and an example; but with the miracles you have a Saviour from your sins.
J. Gresham Machen

It is impossible on reasonable grounds to disbelieve miracles.   *Blaise Pascal*

Miracles enable us to judge of doctrine, and doctrine enables us to judge of miracles.   *Blaise Pascal*

It is more to God's glory that the world should be conquered by the force of truth than by the blaze of miracles.   *C. H. Spurgeon*

Grant me God and miracles take care of themselves!
A. W. Tozer

If God said that Jonah was swallowed by a whale, then the whale swallowed Jonah, and we do not need a scientist to measure the gullet of the whale.   *A. W. Tozer*

MODESTY

Modesty is the life-guard of chastity.   *Thomas Fuller*

Modesty is the badge of wisdom.   *Matthew Henry*

The outward modesty which makes itself known in dress, is to be accompanied by inward purity and chastity, since the former would otherwise be of no account.
J. E. Hunter

All the rules of good behaviour are contained in that one word — modesty.
John C. Ryland

MONEY
(See also: Materialism; Possessions; Prosperity; Riches; Wealth)

Money often unmakes the man who makes it.   *Anon.*

Money really adds no more to the wise than clothes to the beautiful. *Anon.*

When money speaks, the truth is silent. *Anon.*

Nearly half the parables Jesus told have the use of money as their main subject. It is sometimes said that we should give until it hurts. But Jesus teaches that it should hurt when we cease to give! *Ian Barclay*

For the proper use of no talent is self-denial more needed than for that of money. *George Barlow*

Money is never more wisely used than in forwarding the cause of God.

George Barlow

To possess money is very well; it may be a most valuable servant; to be possessed by it is to be possessed by a devil, and one of the meanest and worst kind of devils. *Tryon Edwards*

Lust and lucre follow one another as closely akin, both seducing the heart from the Creator to the creature. *A. R. Fausset*

Make money your god, it will plague you like the devil. *Henry Fielding*

Money is a miraculous thing. It is a man's personal energy reduced to portable form and endowed with powers the man himself does not possess.

Harry Emerson Fosdick

Money is no defence against the arrests of death, nor any alleviation to the miseries of the damned.

Matthew Henry

Money may be the husk of many things, but not the kernel. It brings you food, but not appetite; medicine, but not health; acquaintance, but not friends; servants, but not loyalty; days of joy, but not peace or happiness. *Henrik Ibsen*

One of the ways of manifesting and maintaining the crucifixion of the flesh is never to use money to gratify it. *Andrew Murray*

Some people are so poor they only have money! *Ivor Powell*

By doing good with his money a man, as it were, stamps the image of God upon it, and makes it pass current for the merchandise of heaven. *John Rutledge*

Although Christ's work does not depend on our money,

yet Christ is pleased to test the reality of our grace by allowing us to help him.
J. C. Ryle

It is possible to love money without having it, and it is possible to have it without loving it. *J. C. Ryle*

Money, in truth, is one of the most unsatisfying of possessions. It takes away some cares, no doubt; but it brings with it quite as many cares as it takes away. There is the trouble in the getting of it. There is anxiety in the keeping of it. There are temptations in the use of it. There is guilt in the abuse of it. There is sorrow in the losing of it. There is perplexity in the disposing of it.
J. C. Ryle

How we use our money demonstrates the reality of our love for God. In some ways it proves our love more conclusively than depth of knowledge, length of prayers or prominence of service.
Charles Caldwell Ryrie

I think when Christians get to heaven and they speak of how much they gave to missions, to build schools and so on, that the Lord is going to tell them it would have been better if they had had less money to give and had made their money with justice. *Francis Schaeffer*

There are two ways in which a Christian may view his money — 'How much of my money shall I use for God?' or 'How much of God's money shall I use for myself?'
W. Graham Scroggie

A Christian making money fast is just like a man in a cloud of dust; it will fill his eyes if he is not careful.
C. H. Spurgeon

We need not covet money, for we shall always have our God, and God is better than gold, his favour is better than fortune. *C. H. Spurgeon*

Money is an amoral instrument and like science serves good and evil alike. There is no such thing as dirty money; the stain is only on the hand that holds it as giver or taker.
A. M. Sullivan

Money is not able to buy one single necessity of the soul.
Henry David Thoreau

The two poles shall sooner meet than the love of God and the love of money.
John Trapp

MORALITY

(See also: Ethics; Goodness; Virtue)

The cost of putting a thing right can never be as great as the cost of leaving it wrong.

Moral honesty is not sufficient to keep a man out of eternal misery; all it can do is to help a man to one of the best rooms and easiest beds that hell affords.
Thomas Brooks

Morality does not make us religious, but religion makes us moral. *Charles Hodge*

Men can be moral and godless. *R. T. Kendall*

Christian morality differs radically from legalism. Legalism is obedience to the letter of the law to the neglect of the spirit; Christian morality is obedience to the spirit of the law as well as the letter. *R. B. Kuiper*

Christianity has the only true morality; no other religion conduces to true holiness. *R. B. Kuiper*

However radically definitions of goodness may, and actually do, differ, there is not a religion on this globe which does not bid its adherents to be good after a

fashion and to do good of a kind. *R. B. Kuiper*

If the God of the Bible is the one true and living God, the keeping of his precepts is the only true morality.
R. B. Kuiper

Morality is rooted in religion . . . True morality is rooted in true religion.
R. B. Kuiper

Everything that is really worth while in the morality of today has come to the world through Christ. Dismiss his standards of right and wrong and try to draw up your own ethical code, and see where you will be!
G. Campbell Morgan

A straight line is shortest in morals as well as in geometry. *I. Rahel*

Christian morality is not the product of an arbitrary God, but corresponds to the way we are made. The Ten Commandments . . . were given by a loving Creator who made us and best knows how we function. *Ian F. Shaw*

All sects differ, because they come from men; morality is everywhere the same because it comes from God.
Voltaire

Two stimuli are necessary to make man endeavour to conform with accepted moral standards: belief in an ultimate judgement and belief in the immortality of the soul.   *Wernher von Braun*

Only he who knows God is truly moral.
Friedrich W. J. von Schelling

MOTIVE

Men are more accountable for their motives than for anything else; and primarily, morality consists in the motives, that is in the affections.
Archibald Alexander

A concern for the glory of God is the ultimate motive for Christian living.   *Anon.*

It is not enough that our actions be good and praiseworthy, if our intentions are not pure and upright. It is to profane the good to do it with a bad end in view.
Jean Daillé

It is universally recognized that *what* we do matters less than *why* we do it.
John R. W. Stott

As water cannot rise higher than its source, so the moral quality in an act can never be higher than the motive that inspires it.
A. W. Tozer

The test by which all conduct must finally be judged is motive.   *A. W. Tozer*

MURMURING

Complain *to* God you may, but to complain *of* God, you must not.   *John Flavel*

The murmurer is his own martyr.   *George Swinnock*

Complain without cause and you will have cause to complain.   *Thomas Taylor*

Murmuring often ends in cursing.   *Thomas Watson*

MUSIC

The object of all music should be the glory of God and pleasant recreation.
Johann Sebastian Bach

Music is a means of giving form to our inner feelings without attaching them to events or objects in the world.   *George Santayana*

If you love and listen to the wrong kinds of music your inner life will wither and die.
A. W. Tozer

It is not overstating the case to insist that the kinds of music you enjoy will demonstrate pretty much what you are like inside.
A. W. Tozer

NATURE
(See also: Creation; Evolution)

Nature is the art of God.
Dante Alighieri

Nature is too thin a screen; the glory of the omnipresent God bursts through everywhere.
Ralph Waldo Emerson

Nature does not despise art. It is the office of art to lead back to nature.
Henry C. Fish

All nature, including the nature of man, is a wondrous instrument of many strings, delicately tuned to work God's will and upon which he plays with a master hand.
J. Gresham Machen

As the star brought the wise men to Christ, so should all the stars in the world bring up your thoughts to God.
Thomas Manton

Every formula which expresses a law of nature is a hymn of praise to God.
Maria Mitchell

Those honour nature well who teach that she can speak on everything, even on theology. *Blaise Pascal*

It is not just that God spoke: but God is speaking! He is by his nature continuously articulate. He fills the world with his speaking voice.
A. W. Tozer

Nature with open volume stands
To spread her Maker's praise abroad,
And every labour of his hands
Shows something worthy of a God.

Isaac Watts

NEGLIGENCE
(See also: Sin of Omission)

Negligence is the rust of the soul that corrodes through all her best resolves.
Owen Feltham

Nothing offends God so much as neglect of privileges. *J. C. Ryle*

NOSTALGIA

Living in the past is no way to face the future.

Nostalgia is a deadly thing if it robs us of the significance of the present.   *Paul Helm*

Learning from history and basking in nostalgia are two different things.
Roger C. Palms

OBEDIENCE —
Blessing

To pay the price of obedience is to escape the cost of disobedience.

Only in obedience can we discover the great joy of the will of God.
Sinclair Ferguson

Godly walking is the best aid to the digestion of godly truth.   *Hugh Redwood*

The way of uprightness is the way of heavenly wealth.
C. H. Spurgeon

OBEDIENCE —
Characteristics

True obedience has no lead at its heels.   *Thomas Adams*

In all true obedience there is remembrance.
William Jenkyn

Obedience is counterfeit when it is not uniform.
Thomas Manton

Doing the will of God leaves me no time for disputing about his plans.
George McDonald

What is obedience? Giving up my will to the will of another.   *Andrew Murray*

True obedience neither procrastinates nor questions.
Francis Quarles

Christian obedience is unlike every other kind of obedience. It is not the obedience of slaves or soldiers, but essentially the obedience of lovers who know, love and trust the person who issues the commands.
John R. W. Stott

The Lord is King! I own his
  power,
His right to rule each day
  and hour;
I own his claim on heart and
  will,
And his demands I would
  fulfil.
Darley Terry

The Bible recognizes no faith that does not lead to

213

obedience, nor does it recognize any obedience that does not spring from faith. The two are opposite sides of the same coin. *A. W. Tozer*

OBEDIENCE —
Importance

Christian obedience is to be the response to our acceptance, not the reason for it.

Whoever strives to withdraw from obedience withdraws from grace.
Thomas à Kempis

If God has called you, don't spend time looking over your shoulder to see who is following. *Anon.*

When Christ takes the burden of guilt off a sinner's shoulders he places the yoke of obedience upon his neck.
Anon.

Jesus has spoken; his is the Word, ours the obedience.
Dietrich Bonhoeffer

Just as obedience to the Lord is an indication of our love for him, so is it also a proof of our fear of God.
Jerry Bridges

No man obeys God truly who does not endeavour to obey God fully.
Thomas Brooks

Nothing is more fatal to us than to refuse to give ourselves in obedience to God.
John Calvin

God marks with sorrow the point in the history of any one of his servants where there is failure to yield him implicit, unquestioning, heroic obedience.
Leslie Carter

The rugged obedience of the cross may still be seen in our creeds, but it is hard to find in our lives.
Robert E. Coleman

Obedience to God is the most infallible evidence of sincere and supreme love to him. *Nathanael Emmons*

Be obedient even when you do not know where obedience may lead you.
Sinclair Ferguson

Perfect obedience is God's right as God.
Graham Heaps

The opposite of ignorance in the spiritual realm is not knowledge but obedience.
Howard Hendricks

Those who would have the blessings of God's testimonies must come under the bonds of his statutes.
Matthew Henry

All moral obligation resolves itself into the obligation of conformity to the will of God. *Charles Hodge*

Obedience to legitimate authority is one of the fruits and evidences of Christian sincerity. *Charles Hodge*

Justification supplies the only efficient motive to obedience. *Ernest F. Kevan*

The strongest inducement for a Christian to obey the divine law is the fact that he has been graciously pardoned for having broken it.
Ernest F. Kevan

God is a totalitarian Ruler who demands full allegiance from his subjects.
R. B. Kuiper

Obedience is the crown and honour of all virtue.
Martin Luther

Partial obedience is an argument of insincerity.
Thomas Manton

The life of sanctification is the life of obedience.
J. A. Motyer

Legal obedience was approved by *justice*; evangelical obedience is acceptable unto *mercy*. *A. W. Pink*

Not only does God require obedience, but an obedience which issues from, is animated by, and is an expression of, love.
A. W. Pink

Sincere obedience, though it be not sinless, is acceptable unto God; if it were not, then it would be impossible for any of his children to perform a single act in this life which was pleasing in his sight. *A. W. Pink*

It is our bounden duty to live *in* obedience, but it would prove our utter ruin to live *on* obedience.
William Secker

We have been born under a monarchy; to obey God is freedom. *Seneca*

A life under the rule of Christ can alone prove that we are the objects of our Lord's delight.
C. H. Spurgeon

Obedience is the hallmark of faith. *C. H. Spurgeon*

Christ's lovers prove their love by their obedience.
John R. W. Stott

God being who he is must have obedience from his creatures. Man being who he is must render that obedience, and he owes God complete obedience whether or not he feels for him the faintest trace of love in his heart. *A. W. Tozer*

Theological truth is useless until it is obeyed. The purpose behind all doctrine is to secure moral action! *A. W. Tozer*

OLD AGE

In old age life's shadows are meeting eternity's day. *Anon.*

It is not how many years we live, but what we do with them. *Evangeline Booth*

When grace is joined with wrinkles, it is adorable. There is an unspeakable dawn in happy old age. *Victor Hugo*

Age is not all decay; it is the ripening, the swelling, of the fresh life within, that withers and bursts the husk. *George Macdonald*

Old age is a blessed time. It gives us leisure to put off our earthly garments one by one and dress ourselves for heaven. *Ray Palmer*

Seek that your last days be your best days, and so you may die in a good old age, which may be best done when you die good in old age. *Ralph Venning*

OPINION

Modesty in delivering our opinions leaves us the liberty of changing them without humiliation. *Anon.*

Only where there is no direct teaching in the Word of God on any matter may we hold opinions, subject to change. *Donald Grey Barnhouse*

Every man has a right to his opinion, but no man has a right to be wrong in his facts. *Bernard M. Baruch*

The number of people who believe a thing to be true does not even create a presumption about it one way or the other. *William G. Sumner*

Every man has a right to his opinion, but his opinion may not be right. *Arthur H. Townsend*

ORTHODOXY

Orthodoxy of words is blasphemous unless it is backed up by superiority of character. *Blaise Pascal*

There is nothing more ugly than orthodoxy without understanding or compassion. *Francis Schaeffer*

There is no pride so insidious and yet so powerful as the pride of orthodoxy.
A. W. Tozer

Orthodoxy is my doxy; heterodoxy is another man's doxy. *William Warburton*

PAIN

(See also: Sickness; Suffering; Trials)

There is a pain that is productive of life itself.
Eric Alexander

Pain makes men think and forces us to ask questions.
Brian Edwards

The experience of God's people shows that bodily pain has a special office to perform in the work of sanctification. *Charles Hodge*

Even pain pricks to livelier living. *Amy Lowell*

PASSION

(See also: Anger; Zeal)

Some men's passion is for gold. Some men's passion is for art. Some men's passion is for fame. My passion is for souls. *William Booth*

Passion does not compensate for ignorance.
Samuel Chadwick

Serving one's own passions is the greatest slavery.
Thomas Fuller

Passions are spiritual rebels and raise rebellion against the understanding.
Ben Jonson

When passion is up, true zeal is usually asleep.
Thomas Manton

The ruling passion, be it what it will,
The ruling passion conquers reason still.
Alexander Pope

PATIENCE

Patience is a quality that is most needed when it is exhausted. *Anon.*

Patience is a virtue that carries a lot of wait!
Anon.

Patience is not passive: on the contrary it is active; it is concentrated strength.

Anon.

Patience is the livery of Christ's servants. *Anon.*

Patience is the ballast of the soul that will keep it from rolling and tumbling in the greatest storms.

Ezekiel Hopkins

Cheerful patience is a holy art and skill, which a man learns from God.

Thomas Manton

All true servants of Christ must be content to wait for their wages. *J. C. Ryle*

PEACE

All men desire peace, but very few desire those things that make for peace.

Thomas à Kempis

Peace is rarely denied to the peaceful. *Anon.*

Rest is not a hallowed feeling that comes over us in church; it is the repose of a heart set deep in God.

Anon.

The best tranquillizer is a clear conscience. *Anon.*

I hear the words of love,
I gaze upon the blood,
I see the mighty sacrifice,
And I have peace with God.

Horatius Bonar

I have taken my good deeds and bad deeds and thrown them together in a heap, and fled from them both to Christ, and in him I have peace. *David Dickson*

It is the religion of Jesus alone that can bring peace to a man. *François Fenelon*

Peace does not dwell in outward things, but within the soul. *François Fenelon*

We sleep in peace in the arms of God when we yield ourselves up to his providence. *Franççois Fenelon*

Better a lean peace than a fat victory. *Thomas Fuller*

Grace is the free favour of God; peace is the condition which results from its reception. *H. L. Goudge*

The peace of God will keep us from sinning under our troubles and from sinking under them.

Matthew Henry

When we lack the peace *of* God, we should turn to our peace *with* God.

Robert M. Horn

The mere absence of war is not peace. *John F. Kennedy*

Peace if possible, but truth at any rate. *Martin Luther*

Peace comes not from the absence of trouble, but from the presence of God.
Alexander Maclaren

Peace without righteousness is but a sordid compliance; righteousness without peace is but a rough austerity.
Thomas Manton

There is no grace unless God bestows it, and there is no real peace unless it flows forth from God's reconciliation with sinful man.
J. J. Muller

All peace with God is resolved into a purging atonement made for sin.
John Owen

Nothing can give perfect peace of conscience with God but what can make atonement for sin. And whoever attempts it in any other way but by virtue of that atonement will never attain it, in this world or hereafter.
John Owen

I thank thee, Lord, that here
    our souls,
Though amply blest,

Can never find, although
    they seek,
A perfect rest,
Nor ever shall, until they
    lean
On Jesus' breast.
Adelaide Anne Proctor

There will be no universal peace till the Prince of peace appears. *J. C. Ryle*

If we lose inward peace, we lose more than a fortune can buy. *C. H. Spurgeon*

It is in the way of truth that real peace is found.
C. H. Spurgeon

When filled with holy truth the mind rests.
C. H. Spurgeon

There is no kind of peace that can be purchased on the bargain counter.
Carey Williams

Peace of heart is the natural outcome of purity of heart.
Spiros Zodhiates

PENITENCE
(See also: Confession; Contrition; Conviction of Sin; Repentance)

Holiness is a Christian's ornament, and peaceableness is the ornament of holiness. *Thomas Manton*

Anything is good for us if it makes us loathe ourselves and penitently sue for mercy.   *William S. Plumer*

PERFECTION

Perfection demands perfection; that is why salvation must be by grace, and why works are not sufficient.
Donald Grey Barnhouse

Fully aware that he will not reach the goal of moral perfection in this life, the Christian must yet press on with might and main towards that very mark.
R. B. Kuiper

It is of the essence of Christianity to strive for the unattainable.   *R. B. Kuiper*

PERSECUTION
(See also: Martyrdom)

It is the suffering church that is the growing church.
A. Jack Dain

Scars are the price which every believer pays for his loyalty to Christ.
William Hendriksen

Persecution and opposition ought to encourage rather than discourage us, for we are faithfully warned by our Lord that the natural man and the religionist will not receive the gospel of the grace of God.
Henry T. Mahan

When men try to extinguish the light of the gospel it burns more brightly.
Henry T. Mahan

Storms cannot shipwreck the gospel; they waft it forward.
F. B. Meyer

Persecution . . . is like the goldsmith's hallmark on real silver and gold: it is one of the marks of a converted man.   *J. C. Ryle*

The assaults of persecution from without have never done half so much harm to the church as the rise of false doctrines within.
J. C. Ryle

Take care if the world does hate you that it hates you without cause.
C. H. Spurgeon

The wind of persecution often fans the torch of truth.
David Thomas

Suffering for Christ's sake is to be viewed as a privilege. As God has bestowed the gift of salvation so he has also bestowed the gift of suffering. *Howard F. Vos*

PERSEVERANCE

He who gives over never truly began.
William Jenkyn

The will to persevere is often the difference between failure and success.
Donald Sarnoff

PHILOSOPHY

Any philosophy, though championed by the most brilliant intellects, that tends to lure the soul from Christ, that puts anything in the place of him, or depreciates in any way our estimate of his glorious character, is false and full of peril.
George Barlow

The exhortations of the philosophers are cold and lifeless, if compared with the convictions, affections and boundless energy of the real believers. *John Calvin*

The sublimest virtue according to philosophy is to live the life of nature, but Scripture points us to the perfect Christ as our example.
John Calvin

There is nothing so strange and so unbelievable that it has not been said by one philosopher or another.
René Descartes

Human philosophy, the wisdom of the world, has never converted a soul.
Henry C. Fish

Philosophy has been a quest, and never a conquest.
G. Campbell Morgan

No philosophy that will not teach us how to master death is worth twopence to us. *J. I. Packer*

PIETY

There is no solid wisdom but in true piety. *John Evelyn*

Piety requires us to renounce no ways of life where we can act reasonably and offer what we do to the glory of God. *William Law*

True piety hath true plenty.
George Swinnock

PLEASURES
(See also: Hedonism)

He whose main pursuit is pleasure will never attain to righteousness.
Walter J. Chantry

221

Sinful and forbidden pleasures are like poisoned bread; they may satisfy appetite for the moment, but there is death in them at the end.
Tryon Edwards

The pleasures of sense are puddle-water; spiritual delights are rock water.
Matthew Henry

Fly the pleasure that bites tomorrow. *George Herbert*

Life in worldly pleasure is only life in appearance.
H. J. Holtzmann

All sins are rooted in love of pleasure. Therefore be watchful. *Thomas Manton*

All the pleasure that wicked men have is upon earth; here, and nowhere else.
Thomas Manton

God allows us to use pleasures, but not to live in them; to take delights, but not that they should take us.
Thomas Manton

POPULARITY

Popularity has killed more prophets than persecution.
Vance Havner

Avoid popularity; it has many snares, and no real benefits. *William Penn*

Nothing is so fickle and uncertain as popularity. It is here today and gone tomorrow. It is a sandy foundation, and sure to fail those who build upon it.
J. C. Ryle

POSSESSIONS
(See also: Materialism; Money; Prosperity; Riches; Wealth)

Worldly possessions, through human depravity, are often not helps but hindrances in the way of religion. *Anon.*

To be content with one's possessions is one of the most strongly worded exhortations in Scripture.
Jerry Bridges

To possess what Christ would not have us to possess is waste; to possess anything instead of Christ and his will is waste. *Sinclair Ferguson*

The real value of a thing is the price it will bring in eternity. *John Wesley*

POVERTY

The two great tests of character are wealth and poverty.   *Anon.*

There are worse things than poverty.   *Vance Havner*

There is no sin in poverty.
J. C. Ryle

The Saviour of sinners knows what it is to be poor.
J. C. Ryle

We never need be ashamed of our poverty unless our own sins have brought it upon us.   *J. C. Ryle*

Wealth is no mark of God's favour. Poverty is no mark of God's displeasure.
J. C. Ryle

Poverty and affliction take away the fuel that feeds pride.   *Richard Sibbes*

Whatever a man amasses by the way is in the nature of luggage, no part of his truest personality, but something he leaves behind at the toll-bar of death.
E. K. Simpson

Poverty is a hard heritage; but those who trust in the Lord are made rich by faith.
C. H. Spurgeon

No one in this world has ever been saved and gone to heaven because he was poor. You can be as poor as a church mouse and still be as bad as a church rat.
A. W. Tozer

The pilgrim is not to despise the comforts which he may meet with by the way, but he is not to tarry among them, or leave them with regret.   *Geoffrey B. Wilson*

POWER

Power in the Christian life depends upon our communication with the source of power.   *L. Nelson Bell*

We are not to think that, where we see no possibility, God sees none.   *Marcus Dods*

We must learn to cease from measuring the power of God by our own, and reasoning from the one to the other.
Marcus Dods

The power to live a new life depends upon daily communion with the living Lord.   *John Eadie*

It is amazing how strong we become when we begin to understand what weaklings we are!   *François Fenelon*

The same power that brought Christ back from the dead is operative within those who are Christ's. The resurrection is an ongoing thing.   *Leon Morris*

Now that I am in Christ, God's moral demands have not altered, but it is no longer I who meets them.
       Watchman Nee

There is no telling how much power God can put into a man.
       C. H. Spurgeon

The greatest power today is not atomic but spiritual power; not Communism but communion; not the machinations of men but the might of God.   *J. Charles Stern*

PRAISE
(See also: Worship)

Be not hot in prayer and cold in praise.   *Anon.*

Bless God heartily though he afflict you heavily.   *Anon.*

Bless the Lord today; he blesses you every day.
       Anon.

Hem your blessings with praise, lest they unravel.
       Anon.

God listens for nothing more tenderly as when his children help each other by their testimonies to his goodness and the way in which he has brought them deliverance.   *Horace Bushnell*

Praise is the best of all sacrifices and the true evidence of godliness.   *John Calvin*

It is a bad sign when a newborn babe has not lungs enough to make itself heard over the whole house. It is equally a bad symptom when the new convert is born dumb and cannot find his voice to praise God audibly.   *T. L. Cuyler*

In praising a creature, we may easily exceed the truth; but in praising God we have only to go on confessing what he really is to us. Hence it is impossible to exceed the truth: here is genuine praise.
       A. R. Fausset

In thanking God, we fasten upon his favours to us; in praising and adoring God, we fasten upon his perfections in himself.
       Matthew Henry

Praise God, from whom all
    blessings flow,
Praise him, all creatures
    here below,

Praise him above, ye heavenly host,
Praise Father, Son and Holy Ghost.

Thomas Ken

Praising and adoring God is the noblest part of the saint's work on earth, as it will be his chief employ in heaven.

A. W. Pink

Let us keep a catalogue of God's blessings.

Richard Sibbes

The water of saints' praises is drawn out of a deep spring, the heart. *George Swinnock*

No duty almost is more pressed in both Testaments than this, of rejoicing in the Lord. It is no less a sin not to rejoice than not to repent.

John Trapp

Praise is a soul in flower.

Thomas Watson

I'll praise my Maker while I've breath,
And when my voice is lost in death,
Praise shall employ my nobler powers;
My days of praise shall ne'er be past,
While life, and thought, and being last
Or immortality endures.

Isaac Watts

Praise, more divine than prayer; prayer points our ready way to heaven; praise is already there.

Edward Young

PRAYER — Answers

No answer to prayer is an indication of our merit; every answer to prayer is an indication of God's mercy.

Be not hot in prayer and cold in praise. *Anon.*

It is entirely of his free grace that God is propitious, and that our prayers are not wholly ineffectual.

John Calvin

The answer of our prayers is secured by the fact that in rejecting them God would in a certain sense deny his own nature. *John Calvin*

Answered prayers cover the field of providential history as flowers cover western prairies. *T. L. Cuyler*

The firmament of the Bible is ablaze with answers to prayer. *T. L. Cuyler*

Never was a faithful prayer lost. Some prayers have a longer voyage than others, but then they return with

225

their richer lading at last, so that the praying soul is a gainer by waiting for an answer.　*William Gurnall*

Our prayers run along one road, and God's answers by another, and by and by they meet. God answers all true prayer, either in kind or in kindness.　*Adoniram Judson*

Prayer is a serious thing. We may be taken at our words.
　　　　　D. L. Moody

Beyond our utmost wants
His love and power can bless;
To praying souls he always grants
More than they can express.
　　　　　John Newton

Those who trade with heaven by prayer grow rich by quick returns.
　　　　　William S. Plumer

God's chief gift to those who seek him is himself.
　　　　　E. B. Pusey

I seldom made an errand to God for another but I got something for myself.
　　　　　Samuel Rutherford

Prayer, among sane people, has never superseded practical efforts to secure the desired end.
　　　　　George Santayana

God can pick sense out of a confused prayer.
　　　　　Richard Sibbes

Because God is the living God, he can hear; because he is a loving God, he will hear; because he is our covenant God, he has bound himself to hear.
　　　　　C. H. Spurgeon

Grass cannot call for dew as I do. Surely the Lord who visits the unpraying plant will answer to his pleading child.　*C. H. Spurgeon*

The granting of prayer, when offered in the name of Jesus, reveals the Father's love to him, and the honour which he has put upon him.
　　　　　C. H. Spurgeon

We must hear Jesus speak if we expect him to hear us speak.　*C. H. Spurgeon*

If God gives you a rose without giving you himself he is giving you a thorn.
　　　　　A. W. Tozer

God never denied that soul anything that went as far as heaven to ask it.
　　　　　John Trapp

PRAYER —
Earnestness

Do not pray *by* heart but *with* the heart. *Anon.*

Work as if everything depended upon work and pray as if everything depended upon prayer.
William Booth

Prayer requires more of the heart than of the tongue.
Adam Clarke

The act of praying is the very highest energy of which the human mind is capable; praying, that is, with the total concentration of the faculties.
Samuel Taylor Coleridge

Prayers not felt by us are seldom heard by God.
Philip Henry

There must be fired affections before our prayers will go up. *William Jenkyn*

Let me burn out for God. After all, whatever God may appoint, prayer is the great thing. Oh, that I may be a man of prayer!
Henry Martyn

Pray till you pray.
D. M. McIntyre

We must wrestle earnestly in prayer, like men contending with a deadly enemy for life.
J. C. Ryle

Do not work so hard for Christ that you have no strength to pray, for prayer requires strength.
J. Hudson Taylor

Prayer is the most difficult and costly activity of the Christian. *Alan Walker*

Prayer is the gymnasium of the soul.
Samuel M. Zwemer

PRAYER — Essence

Intercession is standing in other people's shoes and representing them before God. *Anon.*

Private prayer conscientiously performed is the privy key of heaven.
Thomas Brooks

Prayer is the language of a man burdened with a sense of need. *E. M. Bounds*

Prayer puts God's work in his hands — and keeps it there. *E. M. Bounds*

Prayer is a shield to the soul, a sacrifice to God, and a scourge to Satan.

John Bunyan

Prayer is a sincere, sensible, affectionate pouring out of the soul to God, through Christ, in the strength and assistance of the Spirit, for such things as God has promised. *John Bunyan*

When we present ourselves before God ... the finest rhetoric ... is pure simplicity. *John Calvin*

As air is the breath of life, so prayer is the breath of faith.

Paul Yonggi Cho

When we seek the Lord, we soon discover that he has never been far away.

Chan Hie Kim

He prays well who is so absorbed with God that he does not know he is praying.

François de Sales

Prayer is the simplest form of speech
That infant lips can try;
Prayer the sublimest strains that reach
The Majesty on high.

James Montgomery

Prayer is one hand with which we grasp the invisible; fasting the other, with which we let loose and cast away the visible. *Andrew Murray*

Real prayer seeks an *audience* and an *answer*.

William S. Plumer

Prayer should be definite. What a lot of praying there is that prays for everything in general and nothing in particular! *C. H. Spurgeon*

Praying is learnt by praying.

L. A. T. van Dooren

Prayer is the soul's breathing itself into the bosom of its heavenly Father.

Thomas Watson

PRAYER — and Faith

God's ear lies close to the believer's lip. *Anon.*

The prayer of faith is the only power in the universe to which the great Jehovah yields. *Robert Hall*

We lie to God in prayer if we do not rely on him afterwards. *Robert Leighton*

Faith is the fountain of prayer, and prayer should be nothing else but faith exercised. *Thomas Manton*

What an excellent ground of hope and confidence we have when we reflect upon these three things in prayer — the Father's love, the Son's merit and the Spirit's power! *Thomas Manton*

The great thing in prayer is to feel that we are putting our supplications into the bosom of omnipotent love.
Andrew Murray

An intrepid faith in prayer will always give it unction.
Austin Phelps

Good prayers never come weeping home. I am sure I shall receive either what I ask or what I should ask.
Austin Phelps

God may turn his ears from prattling prayers, or preaching prayers, but never from penitent, believing prayers.
William S. Plumer

A saint is to put forth his faith in prayer, and afterwards follow his prayer with faith. *Vavasor Powell*

PRAYER — and Fasting

Prayer is one hand with which we grasp the invisible; fasting the other, with which we let loose and cast away the visible. *Andrew Murray*

By fasting, the body learns to obey the soul; by praying the soul learns to command the body. *William Secker*

PRAYER — Hindrances

Nothing is discussed more and practised less than prayer. *Anon.*

The devil enjoys hearing a prayer that is addressed to an audience. *Anon.*

It is not well for a man to pray cream and live skim milk. *Henry Ward Beecher*

Other duties become pressing and absorbing and crowd out prayer. 'Choked to death' would be the coroner's verdict in many cases of dead praying if an inquest could be secured on this dire, spiritual calamity.
E. M. Bounds

Straight praying is never born of crooked conduct.
E. M. Bounds

Cold prayers shall never have any warm answers.
Thomas Brooks

Look, as a painted man is no man, and as painted fire is no fire, so a cold prayer is no prayer. *Thomas Brooks*

Many pray with their lips for that for which their hearts have no desire.
Jonathan Edwards

Prayer as a means to effect a private end is theft and meanness.
Ralph Waldo Emerson

Dealing in generalities is the death of prayer.
J. H. Evans

God is not mocked. He does not answer prayers if he has already given us the answer and we are not willing to use it. *William Macdonald*

If we be empty and poor, it is not because God's hand is straitened, but ours is not opened. *Thomas Manton*

When we make self the end of prayer, it is not worship but self-seeking.
Thomas Manton

As long as we just pour out our hearts in a multitude of petitions without taking time to see whether every petition is sent with the purpose and expectation of getting an answer, not many will reach the mark.
Andrew Murray

Saying prayers without praying is blasphemy.
Brownlow North

Most Christians expect little from God, ask little and therefore receive little and are content with little.
A. W. Pink

We may as well not pray at all as offer our prayers in a lifeless manner.
William S. Plumer

No prayers can be heard which do not come from a forgiving heart. *J. C. Ryle*

Most commit the same mistake with God that they do with their friends: they do all the talking.
Fulton J. Sheen

Selfishness is never so exquisitely selfish as when it is on its knees ... Self turns what would otherwise be a pure and powerful prayer into a weak and ineffective one. *A. W. Tozer*

A wicked man in prayer may lift up his hands, but he cannot lift up his face.
Thomas Watson

The prayer that is faithless is fruitless. *Thomas Watson*

Sincerity is the prime requisite in every approach to the God who requires 'truth in the inward parts' and who hates all hypocrisy, falsehood and deceit.
Geoffrey B. Wilson

PRAYER — and Holy Living

Prayer is humbling work. It abases intellect and pride, crucifies vainglory and signs our spiritual bankruptcy, and all these are hard for flesh and blood to bear.
E. M. Bounds

None can pray well but he that lives well.
Thomas Fuller

Honest dealing becomes us when we kneel in God's pure presence. *David McIntyre*

Do not work so hard for Christ that you have no strength to pray, for prayer requires strength.
J. Hudson Taylor

Prayer at its best is the expression of the total life, for all things else being equal, our prayers are only as powerful as our lives.
A. W. Tozer

PRAYER — Importance

The secret of reaching men is to know the secret of reaching God.

When we miss out on prayer we cause disappointment to Christ, defeat to ourselves and delight to the devil.

God tells us to burden him with whatever burdens us.
Anon.

When a good man falls, he falls on his knees. *Anon.*

When the knees are not often bent the feet soon slide.
Anon.

Let the day have a blessed baptism by giving your first waking thoughts into the bosom of God. The first hour of the morning is the rudder of the day.
Henry Ward Beecher

No heart thrives without much secret converse with God, and nothing will make amends for the want of it.
John Berridge

The prime need of the church is not men of money nor men of brains, but men of prayer. *E. M. Bounds*

What is the life of a Christian but a life of prayer?
David Brown

The Christian will find his parentheses for prayer even in the busiest hours of life.
Richard Cecil

Prayer is the acid test of devotion. *Samuel Chadwick*

231

Even if no command to pray had existed, our very weakness would have suggested it.
François Fenelon

Time spent in prayer is never wasted.
François Fenelon

Prayer should be the key of the day and the lock of the night. *Thomas Fuller*

You can do more than pray *after* you have prayed, but you cannot do more than pray *until* you have prayed.
S. D. Gordon

If you can't pray as you want to, pray as you can. God knows what you mean.
Vance Havner

Prayer-time must be kept up as duly as meat-time.
Matthew Henry

Though we cannot by our prayers give God any information, yet we must by our prayers give him honour.
Matthew Henry

We read of preaching the Word out of season, but we do not read of praying out of season, for that is never out of season.
Matthew Henry

He who has learned to pray has learned the greatest secret of a holy and a happy life. *William Law*

I have many times been driven to my knees by the utter conviction that I had nowhere else to go.
Abraham Lincoln

I have to hurry all day to get time to pray.
Martin Luther

Prayer is a strong wall and fortress of the church; it is a goodly Christian's weapon.
Martin Luther

Men of God are always men of prayer.
Henry T. Mahan

Let us see God before man every day.
Robert Murray M'Cheyne

The spirit of prayer is the fruit and token of the Spirit of adoption. *John Newton*

I had rather learn what some men really judge about their own justification from their prayers than their writings. *John Owen*

We are never more like Christ than in prayers of intercession. *Austin Phelps*

A man's state before God may always be measured by his prayers. *J. C. Ryle*

232

Never, never may we forget that if we would do good to the world, our first duty is to pray! *J. C. Ryle*

No time is so well spent in every day as that which we spend upon our knees. *J. C. Ryle*

Whatever else you make a business of, make a business of prayer. *J. C. Ryle*

One cannot get deep into religion until one gets deep into prayer. *W. E. Sangster*

God has no dumb children. *C. H. Spurgeon*

Sometimes we think we are too busy to pray. That is a great mistake, for praying is a saving of time. *C. H. Spurgeon*

Whether we like it or not, asking is the rule of the Kingdom. *C. H. Spurgeon*

Of all things, guard against neglecting God in the secret place of prayer. *William Wilberforce*

PRAYER — Power

Prayers are the leeches of care. *Anon.*

The men who have done the most for God in this world have been early on their knees. *E. M. Bounds*

Prayer is the key to heaven's treasures. *John Gerhard*

Prayer is the sovereign remedy. *Robert Hall*

I had rather stand against the cannons of the wicked than against the prayers of the righteous. *Thomas Lye*

Prayer is the great engine to overthrow and rout my spiritual enemies, the great means to procure the graces of which I stand in hourly need. *John Newton*

Thou art coming to a King;
Large petitions with thee bring;
For his grace and power are such,
None can ever ask too much. *John Newton*

The prayers of the Christian are secret, but their effect cannot be hidden. *Howard Chandler Robbins*

I know no blessing so small as to be reasonably expected without prayer, nor any so great but may be obtained by it. *Robert South*

233

PRAYER — and the Promises of God

(See also: Promises of God)

Prayer is a sincere, sensible, affectionate pouring out of the soul to God, through Christ, in the strength and assistance of the Spirit, for such things as God has promised. *John Bunyan*

All the prayers in the Scripture you will find to be reasoning with God, not a multitude of words heaped together. *Stephen Charnock*

The mightier any is in the Word, the more mighty he will be in prayer.
William Gurnall

God's promises are to be our pleas in prayer.
Matthew Henry

God's promises are the cork to keep faith from sinking in prayer. *Thomas Watson*

PRAYER — Unanswered

In reality, the denial of prayer is a denial of God himself. *E. M. Bounds*

How good is God to deny us mercies in mercy!
William Jenkyn

PRAYER — and the Will of God

God likes to see his people shut up to this, that there is no hope but in prayer. Herein lies the church's power against the world.
Andrew Bonar

When we disclose our wants
in prayer,
May we our wills resign;
That not a thought may
enter there
Which is not wholly thine.
Joseph Dacre Carlyle

PREACHING AND PREACHERS — Aim

A sheep must be fed on the ground. *Anon.*

It is no easy matter to speak so plain that the ignorant may understand us, so seriously that the deadest hearts may feel us and so convincingly that contradictory cavaliers may be silenced. *Richard Baxter*

He is the best preacher, not that tickles the ear, but that breaks the heart.
Thomas Brooks

234

The job of a pastor is to gather the people in his arms and draw them near to God.
Michael Buss

If ministers wish to do any good, let them labour to form Christ, not to form themselves, in their hearers.
John Calvin

Let the preacher hold before him, through the whole preparation of the sermon, the one practical effect intended to be produced upon the hearer's will.
R. L. Dabney

Ministers are not cooks but physicians, and therefore should not study to delight the palate but to recover the patient; they must not provide sauce but physic.
Jean Daillé

Christ is the native subject, upon which all preaching should run. *James Durham*

My pulpit work must go from law to grace. It must never rush at grace as if, to unconvicted men, grace can ever be a 'harmonious sound'. *Guy R. Finnie*

The excellency of a sermon lies in the plainest discoveries and liveliest applications of Jesus Christ. *John Flavel*

Ministers are but interpreters; they cannot make the thing otherwise than it is.
Matthew Henry

The minister's task is not to coddle the saints but to collar the sinners.
Hugh Price Hughes

What is the chief end of preaching? I like to think it is this: it is to give men and women a sense of God and his presence.
D. Martyn Lloyd-Jones

A preacher must be both soldier and shepherd.
Martin Luther

When I preach, I regard neither doctors nor magistrates, of whom I have above forty in my congregation. My eyes are on the servant maids and the children.
Martin Luther

Ministers are not managing directors, administrators or counsellors. They are heralds of God. *Donald MacLeod*

We must tell men to embrace Christ as prophet, priest and king and as preachers we need to work hard to attain a theological vocabulary that is both accurate and contemporary.
Donald MacLeod

I see a man cannot be a faithful minister until he preaches Christ for Christ's sake.

Robert Murray M'Cheyne

Those who make comfort the great subject of their preaching seem to mistake the end of their ministry. Holiness is the great end.

John Henry Newman

Aim at the conscience. Soldiers aim at the faces.

John Newton

The purpose of preaching is to humble the sinner, exalt the Saviour and promote holiness. *Charles Simeon*

It should be our ambition, in the power of the Holy Ghost, to work the entire church into a fine missionary condition. *C. H. Spurgeon*

If we can but teach *Christ* to our people, we teach them all. *John R. W. Stott*

The aim of exposition is to make man understand what God wants him to understand, feel as God wants him to feel and do as God wants him to do. *Andrew Swanson*

Teach the tractable, command the obstinate, lay God's charge upon all.

John Trapp

The ultimate aim of all ministry is to give further cause for glorying in Christ Jesus. *Geoffrey B. Wilson*

PREACHING AND PREACHERS — Dangers

Herod was eaten by worms because he refused to give God the glory. I am afraid there are a lot of worms being fattened in our churches today.

A sermon's length is not its strength. *Anon.*

He who thinks by the inch and talks by the yard deserves to be kicked by the foot. *Anon.*

A man who does not practise what he preaches destroys what he builds.

Bonaventura

The preacher may lose God in his sermon.

E. M. Bounds

In the work of the ministry, the word *work* forbids loitering and the word *ministry* lording. *John Boys*

One prayerless interpretation of an important text may result in most disastrous consequences ever after to

the flippant expounder himself and to all the souls whom he is addressing.
John Burne

A sermon that has more head infused into it than heart will not come home with efficacy to the hearers.
Richard Cecil

In pulpit eloquence, the grand difficulty is to give the subject all the dignity it deserves without attaching any importance to ourselves.
C. C. Colton

Is God so intensely real to us that those who meet us meet him? Or are we little manikins capering professionally through our duties with no true realization of the awesome glory of our Master?
Edward Donnelly

An unconverted ministry and unconverted membership are the devil's chief weapons to oppose the work of God.   *Jonathan Edwards*

Omitting any truth intentionally in a sermon leads to the denial of it.
John Elias

The mature man is not threatened by other people's ministries.   *Donald English*

A holy office does not make one holy.   *Henry C. Fish*

If the love of fame be our governing principle, our whole ministry will be tainted by it.
Andrew Fuller

A lot of what goes for Bible teaching and evangelism is but religious entertainment.
Vance Havner

There is a lot of difference between pouring out one's heart and getting something off one's chest.
Vance Havner

To become ordained is not necessarily to escape from one's passion for power. It may only serve to canonize it.   *Ian Henderson*

I don't like those mighty fine preachers who round off their sentences so beautifully that they are sure to roll off the sinner's conscience.
Rowland Hill

Rash preaching disgusts; timid preaching leaves poor souls fast asleep; bold preaching is the only preaching that is owned by God.   *Rowland Hill*

When our zeal is beginning to flag and our ministry becomes formal and professional, we are to go back to the cross.
David N. Jones

237

Let the preacher beware of any affectation of feeling which he does not possess.
D. P. Kidder

The minister who preaches for his own glory rather than God's glory is guilty of idolatry; but so is the minister who preaches for God's glory *and* his own.
R. B. Kuiper

If any preacher of the gospel, myself included, gives an impression of cleverness, it is bad preaching.
D. Martyn Lloyd-Jones

In presenting the Christian gospel we must never, in the first place, make a *direct* approach either to the emotions or to the will. The emotions and the will should always be influenced through the mind.
D. Martyn Lloyd-Jones

A sermon-subject is like a greased pig. It can slip through the hands with incredibly elusive wriggles.
Halford Luccock

Recreation to a minister must be as whetting is with the mower, that is, only to be used so far as is necessary for his work.
Robert Murray M'Cheyne

A man may preach every day of the week and not have his heart engaged once.
John Owen

If the truth were known, many sermons are prepared and preached with more regard for the sermon than the souls of the hearers.
George F. Pentecost

It is but poor eloquence which only shows that the orator can talk.
Joshua Reynolds

An unpreaching minister is of little use to the church of Christ. He is a lampless light-house, a silent trumpeter, a sleeping watchman, a painted fire.
J. C. Ryle

Half the diseases of Christianity have arisen from mistaken notions about the minister's office.
J. C. Ryle

None do such injury to the cause of Christianity as unconverted, worldly ministers. They are a support to the infidel, a joy to the devil, and an offence to God.
J. C. Ryle

A man may be a false prophet and yet speak the truth. *Richard Sibbes*

238

As every sound is not music, so every sermon is not preaching.   *Henry Smith*

I know a minister who is great upon the ten toes of the beast, the four faces of the cherubim, the mystical meaning of the badgers' skins and the typical bearings of the staves of the ark, and the windows of Solomon's temple: but the sins of businessmen, the temptations of the times, and the needs of the age, he scarcely ever touches upon.
                                   C. H. Spurgeon

The plodding multitudes will never be benefited by preaching which requires them to bring a dictionary to church.   *C. H. Spurgeon*

To men of prodigious jaw it may seem a hardship to be confined to time, but a broad charity will judge it better that one man should suffer than that a whole congregation should be tormented.   *C. H. Spurgeon*

It is not too much to say that the preacher who loves to be before the public is hardly prepared spiritually to be before them.   *A. W. Tozer*

We who witness and proclaim the gospel must not think of ourselves as public relations agents sent to establish good will between Christ and the world.
                                   A. W. Tozer

Mere promise-mongers are no gospel preachers.
                                   John Wesley

No ministry can afford to become a museum that embalms the past, but neither can it afford to become a chameleon that spends all its time adjusting to the present.   *Warren Wiersbe*

Jealousy is the dominating temptation of the ministry.
                                   Dinsdale T. Young

PREACHING AND PREACHERS — Divine Calling

There are moments when the minister can derive stimulus and courage for his work only by falling back upon the irrefutable fact of his divine call.
                                   George Barlow

God never sent a messenger with an empty envelope.
                                   Joel Horne

A godly preacher is not the organ of a human fraternity but the oracle of a divine gospel.   *H. D. McDonald*

239

Two keys are committed to us by Christ: the one the key of doctrine, by means of which we unlock the treasures of the Bible; the other the key of discipline, by which we open or shut the way to the sealing ordinances of the faith.
Robert Murray M'Cheyne

The only way in which a man can possibly enter the ministry is when the Holy Spirit of God bestows upon him a gift from the Head of the church. By that gift he is made a minister of Jesus Christ. *G. Campbell Morgan*

Every man who is divinely called to the ministry is divinely equipped.
A. W. Pink

Do not be a minister if you can help it. *C. H. Spurgeon*

The true minister is not one by his own choice but by the sovereign commission of God. *A. W. Tozer*

PREACHING AND PREACHERS — Doctrine

Preaching should consist in a simple exhibition of the truth. *Albert Barnes*

There is no deceit in the gospel itself; and there should be none in exhibiting it. It should consist of a simple statement of things as they are. *Albert Barnes*

The power of all genuine ministry is the power of its content, compared with which the most splendid endowments of human ministers are only trivial and irrelevant. *G. W. Bromley*

Preaching is not a matter of parts, words or wit; it is Scripture demonstration that works upon the conscience, and that God owns and crowns. *Thomas Brooks*

The doctrine of a minister must credit his life and his life adorn his doctrine.
Jean Daillé

Preach the gospel of the grace of God intelligently, affectionately and without shame — all the contents of the great box, from predestination to glorification.
Christmas Evans

Preachers who saturate their sermons with the Word of God never wear out.
Henry C. Fish

All true Christian preaching must place its emphasis upon something already done by God and offered to the hearers, something which remains true and all-important even if they reject it. *Bryan Green*

Preaching is theology coming through a man who is on fire. *D. Martyn Lloyd-Jones*

It is disgraceful for the lawyer to desert his brief; it is even more disgraceful for the preacher to desert his text. *Martin Luther*

I like those expositions that take the wings of a dove and fly to the uttermost parts of the text. *Edward Marbury*

I am just an interpreter of Scripture in my sermons; and when the Bible runs dry then I shall.
Robert Murray M'Cheyne

The man who preaches the Word of God has an inexhaustible supply to draw from. *A. W. Pink*

Doctrinal preaching is the only way to get a congregation to know what it believes. *Klaas Runia*

We have the truth and we need not be afraid to say so.
J. C. Ryle

That which cost thought is likely to excite thought.
C. H. Spurgeon

Preaching is indispensable to Christianity . . . For Christianity is, in its essence, a religion of the Word of God.
John R. W. Stott

The Christian preacher is to be neither a speculator who invents new doctrines which please him, nor an editor who excises old doctrines which displease him, but a steward, God's steward, dispensing faithfully to God's household the truths committed to him in the Scriptures, nothing more, nothing less and nothing else.
John R. W. Stott

PREACHING AND PREACHERS — Earnestness

A God who cares cannot be represented by those who don't.

Deal with sin as sin, and speak of heaven and hell as they are, and not as if you were in jest. *Richard Baxter*

I seldom come out of the pulpit but my conscience smiteth me that I have been no more serious and fervent.
Richard Baxter

I preached what I did feel, what I smartingly did feel.
John Bunyan

There is no rest for a messenger till the message is delivered. *Joseph Conrad*

I would have every minister of the gospel address his audience with the zeal of a friend, the generous energy of a father and the exuberant affection of a mother.
François Fenelon

Sermons from burning hearts set others on fire.
Henry C. Fish

Speak for eternity.
Robert Murray M'Cheyne

How much more would a few good and fervent men effect in the ministry than a multitude of lukewarm ones!
Oecolampadius

Genius is not essential to good preaching, but a live man is. *A. Phelps*

Pray the Lord to save your hearers, then drive at them as though you could save them yourselves.
C. H. Spurgeon

The preacher who talks lightly of sin and punishment does a work strikingly analogous to Satan, when he told Eve, 'Ye shall not surely die.' *Augustus H. Strong*

PREACHING AND PREACHERS — Glory of Preaching

In the ministry God has committed to a man an office as high as heaven, as deep as hell, as broad as space. *B. H. Carroll*

Preaching is God in action: it is his chosen method and therefore that which he will honour more than any other. *Brian Edwards*

Preaching is the miracle of God communicating himself to a fallen world through the words of a fallen man.
Brian Edwards

With its preaching Christianity stands or falls.
P. T. Forsyth

God had but one Son in the world and he made him a minister. *Thomas Goodwin*

When the chariot of humanity gets stuck ... nothing will lift it out except great preaching that goes straight to the mind and heart. *David Lloyd-George*

I would say without hesitation that the most urgent need in the Christian church is true preaching; and as it is the greatest and the most urgent need in the church, it

is obviously the greatest need of the world also.
D. Martyn Lloyd-Jones

No restoration of biblical standards in worship or evangelism, spirituality or church growth is possible without a restoration of biblical preaching. *Dick Lucas*

The pulpit is the throne for the Word of God.
Martin Luther

The church cannot live above the level of its expository preaching.
Bruce Milne

Preaching is an ordinance of Christ. *Iain H. Murray*

A true sermon is an act of God, and not a mere performance by man.
J. I. Packer

We have no lack of preachers of prophecy, but we are pitiably short of prophetic preachers.
Leonard Ravenhill

The issues of life and death are in the pulpit.
John Ruskin

A minister is a merchant of invaluable jewels.
Abraham Wright

PREACHING AND PREACHERS — Humility

It takes more grace for a preacher to listen to preaching than to preach.

The Christian ministry is not a lordship, but a stewardship. *George Barlow*

No man can preach Jesus when self fills his vision.
B. H. Carroll

If ministers know aright what they are, and what they should be, they will be ever throwing themselves on God's mercy.
Patrick Fairbairn

I can say quite honestly that I would not cross the road to listen to myself preaching.
D. Martyn Lloyd-Jones

A Christian pastor can rule, or he can have the reputation of ruling; but he cannot do both. Real ruling involves a sinking of self, a working through others, a doing of nothing that someone else can be got to do.
Augustus H. Strong

Reverence and boasting cannot be found on the same platform. *A. W. Tozer*

243

As ministers commend the mercy of God to others, they must never forget that they need to be partakers of it themselves.

Geoffrey B. Wilson

PREACHING AND PREACHERS — The Preacher's Life

An exposition of the truth is no substitute for an exhibition of it.

The minister's life is the life of his ministry.   *Anon.*

We must not only speak faithfully to our people in our sermons, but live faithfully for them, too.

A. A. Bonar

Life-giving preaching costs the preacher much — death to self, crucifixion to the world, the travail of his own soul. Crucified preaching only can give life. Crucified preaching can only come from a crucified man.

E. M. Bounds

Preaching is not the performance of an hour. It is the outflow of a life.

E. M. Bounds

The preacher's sharpest and strongest preaching should be to himself.

E. M. Bounds

The sermon cannot rise in its life-giving forces above the man. Dead men give out dead sermons, and dead sermons kill.   *E. M. Bounds*

Ministers give occasion of stumbling when by their own faults they hinder the progress of the gospel in those who hear them.

John Calvin

The man who wishes to make himself useful in Christ's service must devote all his energies to maintaining the honour of his ministry.   *John Calvin*

A minister of Christ is often in highest honour with men for the performance of one half of his work, while God is regarding him with displeasure for the neglect of the other half.

Richard Cecil

Example is more forceful than precept. People look at me six days a week to see what I mean on the seventh day.   *Richard Cecil*

The world looks at ministers out of the pulpit to know what they mean when in it.

Richard Cecil

Let the preacher influence himself; let him reach his own heart if he would reach the hearts of others; if he would have others feel, he must feel himself.

Christmas Evans

I have never preached a sermon to others that I have not first preached to my own soul. *Henry C. Fish*

Many a church thinks it needs a new pastor when it needs the same pastor renewed. *Vance Havner*

Ministers are likely to preach most to the purpose when they can press their hearers to follow their example. *Matthew Henry*

Before God asks evangelists about their faithfulness in preaching the gospel he will ask them about their faithfulness as fathers.

Leo Janz

Our own spiritual fitness is of first importance.

Dick Lucas

As a preacher I find it much easier to put the church and the world to rights in a sermon than to hold at bay the dark powers of evil that continually threaten my own soul. *David Orrock*

No man preaches that sermon so well to others who does not preach it first to his own heart. *John Owen*

The most effective preaching comes from those who embody the things they are saying. *John Poulton*

Laziness and frivolity are bad enough in any profession, but worst of all in that of a watchman for souls. *J. C. Ryle*

Whatever 'call' a man may pretend to have, if he has not been called to holiness, he certainly has not been called to the ministry.

C. H. Spurgeon

PREACHING AND PREACHERS — Prayer

A prayerless ministry is the undertaker for all God's truth and for God's church. He may have the most costly casket and the most beautiful flowers, but it is a funeral, notwithstanding the charmful array.

E. M. Bounds

As the engine never moves until the fire is kindled, so preaching, with all its machinery, perfection and polish, is at a dead standstill, as far as spiritual results are concerned, till prayer has kindled and created the steam. *E. M. Bounds*

Prayer puts the preacher's heart into the preacher's sermon; prayer puts the preacher's sermon into the preacher's heart.

E. M. Bounds

Preachers who are great thinkers, great students, must be the greatest of prayers, or else they will be the greatest of backsliders, heartless professionals.

E. M. Bounds

I never in my life stood up to preach except once — which exception I profoundly regret — without first isolating myself from all human company, even the dearest, and prostrating myself in spirit before the dread and awful God, imploring him, in deepest humility, to bless me that one time.

B. H. Carroll

Prayer . . . is one half of a man's ministry; and it gives to the other half all its power and success.

Henry C. Fish

Prayer is the principal work of a minister, and it is by this he must carry on the rest.

Thomas Hooker

If we spent twice as much time listening to God as we spend speaking to God, the effectiveness of our sermons would increase a thousandfold.

Ivor Powell

I do not know how a preacher can be much blessed of God who does not feel an agony when he fears that some of his hearers will pass into the next world impenitent and unbelieving.

C. H. Spurgeon

No man should stand before an audience who has not first stood before God.

A. W. Tozer

PREACHING AND PREACHERS — Qualifications

The first qualification for being a spiritual shepherd is to be a good sheep.

The preachers who have moved the world never sold their liberty for a comfortable cage in some ecclesiastical menagerie. Better be a free preacher who can walk into any pulpit responsible only to God, immune to praise or blame, than a ventriloquist's dummy!

Vance Havner

He is the best teacher that preaches most plainly.

Martin Luther

The minister who is to preach biblically can only do so as a result of much meditation.   *J. I. Packer*

He who would be a faithful minister of the gospel must deny the pride of his heart, be emptied of ambition, and set himself wholly to seek the glory of God in his calling.
William Perkins

Trees which stand on top of a cliff need to send their roots deep.   *Ivor Powell*

Tearless hearts can never be the heralds of the passion.
James S. Stewart

The servant of the evangel must be possessed by the message; possessed, heart and mind and soul by the momentous enterprise that has laid its compulsion upon him.   *James S. Stewart*

PREACHING AND PREACHERS — Results

In a faithful ministry, success is the rule; want of it the exception.   *A. A. Bonar*

Every preacher is, or ought to be, a prophet of God who preaches as God bids him without regard to results.
A. C. Dixon

The hearer's life is the preacher's best commendation.   *Thomas Manton*

If true preaching does not subdue us it is sure to exasperate us.
Alexander Whyte

PREACHING AND PREACHERS — Unction

Scintillating eloquence may captivate people, but it is the power of God that changes lives.   *Ivor Powell*

Unction is God's knighthood for the soldier-preacher who has wrestled in prayer and gained the victory.
Leonard Ravenhill

We are tired of men in soft raiment and softer speech who use rivers of words with but a spoonful of unction.
Leonard Ravenhill

Whom God appoints he anoints.   *J. H. Thornwell*

PREDESTINATION
(See also: Election — and Conversion)

The Christian's place in heaven was assured before there was a

247

single angel there to help in arranging his accommodation.

Far from relegating the doctrine of predestination to some secondary place, the Bible puts it right at the heart of all its teaching.
J. Gresham Machen

The doctrine of predestination is just the doctrine of the divine decrees applied to the special sphere of salvation. *J. Gresham Machen*

The doctrine of predestination, so distasteful to human pride, is really the only solid ground of hope for this world and for the next.
J. Gresham Machen

When the final result is fore-ordained by God all the steps to it are also fore-ordained.
J. Gresham Machen

PREJUDICE

Beware of letting prejudices become principles.

Prejudice is a lazy man's substitute for thinking.
Anon.

Prejudice, which sees what it pleases, cannot see what is plain. *Aubrey de Vere*

Prejudice is the child of ignorance. *William Hazlitt*

There is no prejudice so strong as that which arises from a fancied exemption from all prejudice.
Wiliam Hazlitt

Prejudice, not being founded on reason, cannot be removed by argument.
Samuel Johnson

All our minds are narrower than we think, and blind spots and obsessions abound in them like bees in clover.
J. I. Packer

All looks yellow to the jaundiced eye. *Alexander Pope*

PRIDE — Characteristics

If you want to please the devil, begin to admire yourself. *Anon.*

When a proud man hears another praised, he thinks himself injured. *Anon.*

The proud are ever most provoked by pride.
William Cowper

If the love of fame be our governing principle our whole ministry will be tainted by it. *Andrew Fuller*

You never knew a man full of self-confidence and self-abasement together.
William Gurnall

Pride is the inmost coat, which we put off last and which we put on first.
Joseph Hall

Pride is a vice, which cleaves so fast unto the hearts of men, that if we were to strip ourselves of all faults, one by one, we should undoubtedly find it the very last and hardest to put off.
Thomas Hooker

A proud man is always looking down on things and people; and, of course, as long as you are looking down you can't see something that is above you.
C. S. Lewis

The more pride we have, the more other people's pride irritates us.
C. S. Lewis

The flesh ever seeks to be glorified before it is crucified.
Martin Luther

No sin is so deeply rooted in our nature as pride. It cleaves to us like our skin.
J. C. Ryle

Arrogancy is a weed that ever grows in dunghills.
George Swinnock

The worm of pride breeds soonest in rotten wood.
George Swinnock

Guard especially against those little tricks by which a vain man seeks to bring around the conversation to himself to gain the praise or notice which his thirsty ears drink in so greedily.
Samuel Wilberforce

PRIDE — Description

Spiritual pride is a white devil.
Thomas Brooks

Pride is over-estimation of oneself by reason of self-love.
Baruch Spinoza

Pride is the shirt of the soul, put on first and put off last.
George Swinnock

PRIDE — Effects

Proud man would perish unless a lowly God found him.
Augustine

The proud man lives halfway down the slope to hell.
George Barlow

A proud man is seldom a grateful man, for he never

249

thinks he gets as much as he deserves.
Henry Ward Beecher

The most effective poison to lead men to ruin is to boast in themselves, in their own wisdom and will power.
John Calvin

Pride of gifts robs us of God's blessing in the use of them.
William Gurnall

The wind of pride is the life and soul of error; it is the element in which it moves and breathes.
William Jenkyn

Pride will make hell insufferable.
William S. Plumer

Pride destroys all symmetry and grace, and affectation is a more terrible enemy to fine faces than the small-pox.
Richard Steele

PRIDE — Essence
(See also: Conceit; Vanity)

Pride is a denial of dependence upon God.

Pride is the mask of one's own faults.
Anon.

Everyone flatters himself and carries a kingdom in his breast.
John Calvin

Humility is the ornament of angels and pride the deformity of devils.
William Jenkyn

You can have no greater sign of a confirmed pride than when you think you are humble enough.
William Law

A man needs above all to be saved from what is the root of all sin — his self-will and his pride.
Andrew Murray

Pride is a sinner's torment, but humility is a saint's ornament.
William Secker

There is no pride so insidious and yet so powerful as the pride of orthodoxy.
A. W. Tozer

PRIDE — Folly

He who is proud of his knowledge . . . has gout in the wrong end.
Thomas Adams

If we are proud of our talents we betray our lack of gratitude to God.
John Calvin

Proud men surpass every kind of drunkenness.
John Calvin

This one word 'evil' is a thunderbolt which lays low all human pride.
John Calvin

Of all the marvellous works of God perhaps there is nothing that angels behold with such astonishment as a proud man. *C. C. Colton*

The sun should not set upon our anger, neither should it rise upon our confidence.
C. C. Colton

Goodness that preaches undoes itself.
Ralph Waldo Emerson

The one-eyed is easily king among the blind.
A. R. Fausset

High places . . . are slippery places. *Matthew Henry*

The Lord would give us great things if only he could trust us not to steal the glory for ourselves.
David Morgan

That which is begun in self-confidence will end in shame. *Richard Sibbes*

Neither God nor man will care to lift up a man who lifts up himself; but both God and good men unite to honour modest worth.
C. H. Spurgeon

PRIDE — Opposed by God

Nothing that comes from God will minister to my pride or self-congratulation.
A. W. Tozer

Pride is a sin the Lord hates, because it is a sin that sets itself most against him. Other sins are against God's laws, this is against his being and sovereignty.
Spiros Zodhiates

PRIDE — Remedy

Swallowing of pride seldom leads to indigestion. *Anon.*

The cure of boasting is to boast in the Lord all the day long. *C. H. Spurgeon*

PRINCIPLES

Expedients are for the hour; principles for the ages.
Henry Ward Beecher

Good principles fixed in the head will produce good resolutions in the heart and good practices in the life.
Matthew Henry

251

One may be better than his reputation, but never better than his principles.
Nicolas Valentin de Latena

PROCRASTINATION

Hell is truth seen too late.
H. G. Adams

One of these days is none of these days. *Anon.*

'Too late' is written on the gates of hell. *Anon.*

For an individual to procrastinate and reject Christ makes his sins more heinous and angers God who was so gracious in giving him an overture of mercy.
Earl Blackburn

Not to decide is to decide.
Harvey Cox

Delay is a kind of denial.
Timothy Cruso

The Bible, which ranges over a period of four thousand years, records but one instance of a death-bed conversion — one that none may despair, and but one that none may presume.
William Guthrie

The procrastinating man is for ever struggling with ruin.
Hesiod

Some people treat Christian truth like chewing gum. They will chew it over in discussion for hours, but never swallow it.
Kenneth W. Prior

A second lease of life is granted to no man. Then let us resist procrastination as we would resist the devil.
J. C. Ryle

Procrastination is the thief of time. *Edward Young*

PROMISES OF GOD

(See also: Prayer — and the Promises of God)

The carrying out of God's promises is as certain as if already in the past tense.

A little saint may enjoy a great promise. *Anon.*

God never promises us an easy time, only a safe arrival.
Anon.

The promises of God will eat their way over all the Alps of opposition. *Thomas Brooks*

The whole covenant is a bundle of promises.
Thomas Brooks

We are refugees from the sinking ship of this present

world-order, so soon to disappear; our hope is fixed in the eternal order, where the promises of God are made good to his people in perpetuity. *F. F. Bruce*

Whatever God can do, he unquestionably will do, if he has promised it.
John Calvin

The being of God may as well fail as the promise of God. *Timothy Cruso*

The greatness of the Promiser enhances the greatness of the promises.
A. R. Fausset

God does not parcel himself out by retail, but gives his saints leave to challenge whatever he has as theirs.
William Gurnall

God's promise is never out of his thoughts.
William Gurnall

Oh, it is sad for a poor Christian to stand at the door of the promise in the dark night of affliction afraid to draw the latch!
William Gurnall

The wise Christian will store himself with promises in health for sickness, and in peace for future perils.
William Gurnall

God never promises more than he is able to perform.
Matthew Henry

God's promises are to be our pleas in prayer.
Matthew Henry

God's promise is better than any bond or note on any bank, financial institution, or most stable government, for all these may have to repudiate their bond; God never does so.
R. C. H. Lenski

We cannot close with Christ without a promise; and we must not close with a promise without Christ.
Thomas Manton

Learn to put your hand on all spiritual blessings in Christ and say 'Mine'.
F. B. Meyer

God's promises are like the stars; the darker the night the brighter they shine.
David Nicholas

It is a blessed fact that God's promises are as large as his exhortations, and for each of the latter there is one of the former exactly meeting it.
A. W. Pink

Have faith in God, my heart,
Trust and be unafraid;

God will fulfil in every part
Each promise he has made.
Bryn Austin Rees

Faith always sees the bow of covenant promise whenever sense sees the cloud of affliction. *C. H. Spurgeon*

If we would venture more upon the naked promise of God, we should enter a world of wonders to which as yet we are strangers.
C. H. Spurgeon

My own weakness makes me shrink, but God's promise makes me brave.
C. H. Spurgeon

Upon the two hinges of faith and repentance do all the promises of the Bible hang.
George Swinnock

A great part of a Christian's estate lies in bonds and bills of God's hand. *John Trapp*

Faith and the promise meeting make a happy mixture, a precious confection.
John Trapp

The promises are good freehold. *John Trapp*

The promises are not made to strong faith but to true.
Thomas Watson

Engraved as in eternal brass,
The mighty promise shines;
Nor can the powers of darkness rase
Those everlasting lines.
Isaac Watts

I believe the promises of God enough to venture an eternity on them.
Isaac Watts

Christ is the fulfiller and fulfilment of all the promises of God because he is the sum and substance of them.
Geoffrey B. Wilson

PROPHECY

No Bible subject holds more practical implications than the matter of prophecy.
Vance Havner

It is greatly to be desired that Christians who are so much given to speculate upon the prophecies would turn their thoughts to the perishing myriads by whom we are surrounded and sow in the fields of evangelization rather than in the cloudland of guesswork interpretation.
C. H. Spurgeon

Much of the Bible is devoted to prediction. Nothing God has yet done for us can

254

compare with all that is written in the sure word of prophecy.   *A. W. Tozer*

PROSPERITY

(See also: Materialism; Money; Possessions; Riches; Wealth)

Prosperity is not a sign that all is well.

A full cup must be carried steadily.   *Anon.*

Watch lest prosperity destroy generosity.
        Henry Ward Beecher

For every one hundred men who can stand adversity there is only one who can withstand prosperity.
        Thomas Carlyle

The comforts of this life are as candles that will end in a snuff.   *Stephen Charnock*

If prosperity is regarded as the reward of virtue, it will be regarded as the symptom of virtue.   *G. K. Chesterton*

Prosperity is only an instrument to be used; not a deity to be worshipped.
        Calvin Coolidge

To see a man humble under prosperity is one of the greatest rarities in the world.
        John Flavel

Prosperity is a great mercy, but adversity is a greater one, if it brings us to Christ.
        J. C. Ryle

Prosperity teaches men themselves.   *Richard Sibbes*

It is hard to carry a full cup without a spill.
        C. H. Spurgeon

Uninterrupted prosperity is a thing to cause fear and trembling.   *C. H. Spurgeon*

Few of us can stand prosperity. Another man's, I mean.   *Mark Twain*

Prosperity is a state full of danger. Both the wise and pious have been ensnared by it.   *Daniel Wilson*

PROVIDENCE

(See also: Will of God)

God has his hours and his delays.   *J. A. Bengel*

Every blade of grass in the field is measured; the green cups and the coloured crowns of every flower are curiously counted; the stars of the firmament wheel in cunningly calculated orbits; even the storms have their laws.   *William Blaikie*

I have lived, seen God's hand through a lifetime, and all was for best.
Robert Browning

Providence is crowned by the end of it.
Stephen Charnock

God moves in a mysterious way
His wonders to perform;
He plants his footsteps in the sea,
And rides upon the storm.
William Cowper

The longer I live, the more faith I have in providence, and the less faith in my interpretation of providence.
Jeremiah Day

While providence supports,
Let saints securely dwell;
That hand which bears all nature up
Shall guide his children well.
Philip Doddridge

He that will watch providences will never want providences to watch.
John Flavel

Sometimes providences, like Hebrew letters, must be read backwards.
John Flavel

God's providences often seem to contradict his purposes, even when they are serving them.
Matthew Henry

What is corrupt, though of God's permitting, is not of his planting.
Matthew Henry

Everything that happens to me can help me along in my Christian life.
E. Stanley Jones

Nothing is or can be accidental with God.
Henry W. Longfellow

Our Lord God doeth work like a printer, who setteth the letters backwards; we see and feel well his setting, but we shall see the print yonder — in the life to come.
Martin Luther

Our spirits are most satisfied when we discern God's aim in everything.
Thomas Manton

God not only orders our steps; he orders our stops.
George Müller

God is at no loss for means, instruments or agents. Heaven and earth, sea and land, mind and matter are full of them.
William S. Plumer

God rules and overrules.
William S. Plumer

God's government will never fail in any part of the world,

in any event of life, or in any tumult of the nations..
William S. Plumer

We need never fear that God will be dethroned, or over-reached or defeated.
William S. Plumer

Nothing was too little for God to create. Nothing is too little for God to preserve.
J. C. Ryle

God's providence is all exercised through Christ.
Augustus H. Strong

I do not know why God does some things, but I am convinced that nothing is accidental in his universe.
A. W. Tozer

God is always previous.
Friedrich von Hugel

God would never permit evil if he could not bring good out of evil. *Thomas Watson*

It is a sin as much to quarrel with God's providence as to deny his providence.
Thomas Watson

Providence is a Christian's diary but not his Bible ... We must not think the better of what is sinful because it is successful. *Thomas Watson*

If a Christian has to change his plans, it is always because God has something better in store. *Phil Webb*

PURITY

Our chastity should be as dear to us as our lives, and we should be as much afraid of that which defiles the body as of that which destroys it. *Matthew Henry*

Those who keep themselves pure in times of common impurity God will keep safe in times of common calamity.
Matthew Henry

The outward modesty which makes itself known in dress is to be accompanied by inward purity and chastity, since the former would otherwise be of no account.
J. E. Hunter

The pure in heart shall see God; all others are but blind bats. *C. H. Spurgeon*

PURPOSE

Apart from the bright hope of the gospel everything would be meaningless.
Poul Madsen

257

The will itself is not itself weak or strong; it is our motivation that is weak or strong. *John Powell*

Man, made in the image of God, has a purpose — to be in relationship to God, who is there. Man forgets his purpose and thus he forgets who he is and what life means.
Francis Schaeffer

God made us for himself; that is the first and last thing that can be said about human existence and whatever more we add is but commentary. *A. W. Tozer*

God made us to be worshippers. That was the purpose of God in bringing us into the world. *A. W. Tozer*

REASON
(See also: Knowledge; Mind)

A religion small enough for our understanding would not be big enough for our needs. *Anon.*

We may as well judge of colours by moonlight as of spiritual things by natural reason. *Elisha Coles*

The supreme achievement of reason is to bring us to see that there is a limit to reason. *Blaise Pascal*

Consideration is the high road to conversion.
J. C. Ryle

To bring our minds under Christ's yoke is not to deny our rationality but to submit to his revelation.
John R. W. Stott

The devil labours to put out the right eye of faith and to leave us only the left eye of reason. *John Trapp*

RECREATION
(See also: Amusements)

When recreation gets ahead of re-creation, then God's house has become a den of thieves. *Vance Havner*

Recreation to a minister must be as whetting is with the mower, that is, only to be used so far as is necessary to his work.
Robert Murray M'Cheyne

Recreation is not the highest kind of enjoyment, but in its time and place is quite as proper as prayer.
S. I. Prime

REDEMPTION

(See also: Atonement; Salvation)

No one is redeemed except through unmerited mercy, and no one is condemned except through merited judgement. *Augustine*

Life is not worth living apart from redemption.
Oswald Chambers

Jesus came not only to teach but to save, not only to reveal God to mankind, but also to redeem mankind for God. *John R. W. Stott*

The purpose and work of redemption in Christ Jesus is to raise man as much above the level of Adam as Christ himself is above the level of Adam. *A. W. Tozer*

There can be no thought of 'cheap' forgiveness when we remember that our redemption cost God the life of his beloved Son.
Geoffrey B. Wilson

REFORMATION

Reformation which springs from any source other than regeneration washes only the outside of the cup.
L. Nelson Bell

The foundation of every reformation of the Holy Spirit is the Word of God made plain to the people.
Frank Cooke

The only true reformation is that which emanates from the Word of God.
J. H. Merle d'Aubigné

REGENERATION

(See also: Conversion; Faith — Saving)

Man's basic need is not a grasp of logic but the gift of life.

Regeneration is God's mysterious prerogative.

The new birth is infinite in its beginning because its beginning lies in infinity.

The new birth is not only a mystery that no man can understand, it is a miracle that no man can undertake.

Seeing we are born God's enemies we must be newborn his sons. *Richard Baxter*

Regeneration is a universal change of the whole man . . . it is as large in renewing as sin was in defacing.
Stephen Charnock

Regeneration is the communication of the divine nature to man by the operation of the Holy Spirit through the Word.

A. J. Gordon

God's work of regeneration is never directly perceived by the soul: it takes place in man within the region of what has now come to be called the subconscious.

Ernest F. Kevan

Whatever man may do after regeneration, the first quickening of the dead must originate with God.

A. A. Hodge

The genesis of Christianity as an experience is that of being born again of the Spirit. *G. Campbell Morgan*

Regeneration is inseparable from its effects and one of its effects is faith.

John Murray

The embrace of Christ in faith is the first evidence of regeneration and only thus may we know that we have been regenerated.

John Murray

We are not born again by repentance or faith or conversion: we repent and believe because we have been born again.

John Murray

Regeneration has made our hearts a battlefield.

J. I. Packer

There is no regeneration without spiritual activities.

J. I. Packer

Regeneration is the transforming not only of an unlovely object, but of one that *resists* with all its might the gracious designs of the heavenly Potter.

A. W. Pink

The regenerate have a spiritual nature within that fits them for holy action, otherwise there would be no difference between them and the unregenerate.

A. W. Pink

Grace does not run in families. It needs something more than good examples and good advice to make us children of God. *J. C. Ryle*

Though Christ a thousand times in Bethlehem be born,
If he's not born in thee, thy soul is still forlorn.

Johannes Scheffler

The very first and indispensable sign of regeneration is self-loathing and abhorrence. *Charles Simeon*

Every generation needs regeneration. *C. H. Spurgeon*

260

Regeneration is a change which is known and felt: known by works of holiness and felt by a gracious experience.   *C. H. Spurgeon*

God regenerates the soul by uniting it to Jesus Christ.
Augustus H. Strong

Regeneration is a restoration of the original tendencies towards God which were lost by the Fall.
Augustus H. Strong

Man's need can only be met by a new creation.
Geoffrey B. Wilson

RELIGION

If we make religion our business, God will make it our blessedness.
H. G. J. Adam

Religion is man's search for God, but Christianity is God's search for man.
Anon.

Religion is neither a winter resort nor a last resort.
Anon.

Religion without Christ is a lamp without oil.   *Anon.*

Still water and still religion freeze the quickest.   *Anon.*

Your daily duties are a part of your religious life just as much as your devotions are.
Henry Ward Beecher

Religion is as requisite as reason to complete a man.
Stephen Charnock

Men will wrangle for religion, write for it, fight for it, die for it, anything but *live* for it.   *C. C. Colton*

Religion's home is in the conscience.   *T. L. Cuyler*

As science is the verification of the ideal in nature, so religion is the verification of the spiritual in human life.
A. J. Dubois

True religion is a powerful thing . . . a ferment, a vigorous engagedness of the heart.
Jonathan Edwards

The religion that is afraid of science dishonours God and commits suicide.
Ralph Waldo Emerson

If religion be worth anything it is worth everything.
Matthew Henry

The root of religion is the fear of God reigning in the heart, a reverence of his majesty, a deference to his authority and a dread of his wrath.   *Matthew Henry*

261

I would give nothing for that man's religion whose very dog and cat were not the better for it. *Rowland Hill*

Morality does not make us religious, but religion makes us moral. *Charles Hodge*

Man is constitutionally religious. *R. B. Kuiper*

Religion is not a matter of fits, starts and stops, but an everyday affair.
David Livingstone

Religion is not adorned with ceremonies, but purity and charity. *Thomas Manton*

Most of modern evangelical religion is rotten to the core, because its aim is happiness, not holiness. *Al Martin*

The basic religious question is that of our relation to God. *John Murray*

Men never do evil so completely and cheerfully as when they do it from religious conviction.
Blaise Pascal

A consciousness of the absence of God is one of the standard incidents of religious life. *Austin Phelps*

A religion which costs nothing is worth nothing.
J. C. Ryle

Those who fancy that true religion has any tendency to make men unhappy are greatly mistaken. It is the absence of it that does this, and not the presence.
J. C. Ryle

Belief in the immortality of the soul and belief in the accountability of the soul are fundamental beliefs in all religion. *O. J. Smith*

Frankly, I would much rather have no religion at all than to have just enough to deceive me. *A. W. Tozer*

Religion can be a front or a fount. *A. W. Tozer*

Religion, so far as it is genuine, is in essence the response of created personalities to the creating personality, God. *A. W. Tozer*

Religion will either make us very tender of heart, considerate and kind, or it will make us very hard.
A. W. Tozer

The essence of true religion is spontaneity, the sovereign movings of the Holy Spirit upon and in the free spirit of redeemed man.

A. W. Tozer

REPENTANCE — Blessings

Real repentance produces confession and forsaking of sin, reconciliation and restitution, separation from the world, submission to the lordship of Christ and filling of the Holy Spirit.
Vance Havner

The grief of repentance is never loss in any way; not to experience this grief, that is loss indeed.
R. C. H. Lenski

Holy tears are the sponge of sin.
Thomas Manton

Upon the two hinges of faith and repentance do all the promises of the Bible hang.
George Swinnock

Those who make their eyes a fountain to wash Christ's feet in shall have his side to wash their souls in.
John Trapp

It is better to meet God with tears in your eyes than with weapons in your hands.
Thomas Watson

REPENTANCE — Essence

(See also: Confession; Contrition; Penitence; Conviction of Sin)

True repentance is being broken for sin and from sin.

True repentance is personal, permanent, painful and profitable.

True repentance arises from the sight by faith of the crucified Saviour.
A. R. Fausset

True repentance does not substitute sacrifice for obedience.
Vance Havner

Repentance is the turning of the whole heart from sin and Satan to serve God in newness of life.
Erroll Hulse

Repentance is no fun at all. It is something harder than merely eating humble pie. It means unlearning the self-conceit and self-will that we have been training ourselves into for thousands of years.
C. S. Lewis

It is impossible to disentangle faith and repentance. Saving faith is permeated with repentance and repentance is permeated with faith.
John Murray

The broken spirit and the contrite heart are the

263

abiding marks of the believing soul.   *John Murray*

The faith that is unto salvation is a penitent faith and the repentance that is unto life is a believing repentance.
John Murray

Repentance unto life will be repentance in the life.
William Nevins

True repentance begins with knowledge of sin. It goes on to work sorrow for sin. It leads to confession of sin before God. It shows itself before man by a thorough breaking off from sin. It results in producing a habit of deep hatred for all sin.
J. C. Ryle

True repentance takes God's part against ourselves.
Augustus H. Strong

True repentance has a double aspect; it looks upon things past with a weeping eye, and upon the future with a watchful eye.
Robert South

True repentance hates the sin, and not merely the penalty; and it hates the sin most of all because it has discovered and felt God's love.
W. M. Taylor

I have discovered that truly repentant men never quite get over it, for repentance is not a state of mind and spirit that takes its leave as soon as God has given forgiveness and as soon as cleansing is realized.   *A. W. Tozer*

Repentance is primarily a change of moral purpose, a sudden and often violent reversal of the soul's direction.   *A. W. Tozer*

Amendment of life is the best repentance.   *John Trapp*

Repentance, that fair and happy daughter of an ugly and odious mother.
John Trapp

Repentance with man is the changing of his will; repentance with God is the willing of a change.   *John Trapp*

Repentance and faith are both humbling graces; by repentance a man abhors himself, by faith he goes out of himself.   *Thomas Watson*

REPENTANCE — False

Repentance without moral change is a contradiction in terms.

There is more to repentance than apologizing to God.

Esau wept that he lost the blessing, not that he sold it.
William Gurnall

Repentance is not a change of opinion but of attitude, and there is very little repentance nowadays because of our attitude towards sin. *Vance Havner*

Evangelical repentance is not at the beck and call of the creature. It is the gift of God. *A. W. Pink*

Multitudes desire to be saved from hell (the natural instinct of self-preservation) who are quite unwilling to be saved from sin.
A. W. Pink

Multitudes seem to think that it is about as easy for a sinner to purify his heart as it is to wash his hands.
A. W. Pink

Of himself, the fallen sinner can no more repent evangelically, believe in Christ savingly, come to him effectually, than he can create a world. *A. W. Pink*

Let us beware of a repentance without evidence.
J. C. Ryle

This is like weeping with an onion; the eye sheds tears because it smarts.
William Secker

The teaching and the hope of being forgiven while persisting in sin is a great moral impossibility. *A. W. Tozer*

The teaching of forgiveness without any turning from sin is a great error and it has filled the churches with deceived members and helped to fill hell with deceived souls. *A. W. Tozer*

To teach pardon and cleansing where there is no intention to change the life would upset heaven and turn it into a moral insane asylum, and in a hundred years you would not know heaven from hell!
A. W. Tozer

REPENTANCE — and Holiness

Remorse is being sorry. Repentance is being sorry enough to stop. *Anon.*

A sincere repentance from the heart does not guarantee that we shall not wander from the straight path and sometimes become bewildered. *John Calvin*

Repentance, to be of any avail, must work a change of heart and conduct.
T. L. Cuyler

Sleep with clean hands, either kept clean all day by integrity or washed clean at night by repentance.

John Donne

I will take my repentance to the gates of heaven.

Philip Henry

When our Lord and Master Jesus Christ said 'Repent' he called for the entire life of believers to be one of repentance.

Martin Luther

REPENTANCE — Importance

Whatever the cost of putting a thing right, it can never be more than the cost of leaving it wrong.

When a person becomes a Christian, the repentant sinner becomes a repenting saint.

When man fell into sin he changed his mind – and until he changes it again he can never be right with God.

Let the quantity of thy sins be the measure of thy repentance.

Isaac Bargrave

I have carried a penitent form around in my heart for half a century or more, and if there is ever any need, instantly I fly there. Jesus waits, loves, pities and never turns away the seeking soul.

Samuel Logan Brengle

Of all acts of man repentance is the most divine. The greatest of all faults is to be conscious of none.

Thomas Carlyle

Never will Christ enter into that soul where the herald of repentance hath not been before him.

Joseph Hall

The church can do many things after she repents, but she can do nothing else until she repents.

Vance Havner

You should never think of sin without repenting.

Philip Henry

Christianity starts with repentance.

D. Martyn Lloyd-Jones

The first reason for leaving sin is that God commands me to do so.

D. Martyn Lloyd-Jones

Repentance may be old-fashioned, but it is not outdated as long as there is sin.

J. C. Macaulay

Repentance is one of the foundation stones of Christianity.

J. C. Ryle

We are all responsible to God for repentance.

J. C. Ryle

Sackcloth and ashes are the court robes of those blessed mourners who shall be comforted. *C. H. Spurgeon*

You can pray till doomsday for revival, but you will never get it without repentance and confession of sin in the Christian life.
Erlo Stegan

Do a thorough job of repenting. *A. W. Tozer*

REPENTANCE — Urgency

The Lord has made a promise *to* late repentance, but where has he made a promise *of* late repentance?
Thomas Brooks

Death-bed repentance is burning the candle of life in the service of the devil, then blowing the snuff in the face of heaven. *Lorenzo Dow*

You cannot repent too soon, because you do not know how soon it may be too late.
Thomas Fuller

Fair-weather repentance might save us many a cloudy day. *Vance Havner*

Whoever delays his repentance does in effect pawn his soul with the devil.
Thomas Manton

If we put off repentance another day, we have a day more to repent of, and a day less to repent. *W. Mason*

What insanity is it that persuades multitudes to defer the effort to repent till their death-beds? Do they imagine that when they are so weak that they can no longer turn their bodies they will have strength to turn their souls from sin? Far sooner could they turn themselves back to perfect physical health.
A. W. Pink

Whatever stress some may lay upon it, a death-bed repentance is but a weak and slender plank to trust our all upon.
Lawrence Sterne

Late repentance is seldom true, but true repentance is never too late.
Ralph Venning

REPUTATION

Reputation is sometimes as wide as. the horizon when character is the point of a needle.
Henry Ward Beecher

One may be better than his reputation, but never better than his principles.
Nicolas Valentin de Latena

RESPONSIBILITY

(See also: Duty; Service)

One bird cannot fly to heaven with another bird's wings. *Thomas Adams*

Some people grow under responsibility, others swell.
Anon.

Man facing God is an encounter in responsibility.
Martin Buber

The hours which come fresh to you out of the mercy of your heavenly Father will carry for ever the imprint which your life leaves on them, until all accounts are closed at his Last Assize.
Sinclair Ferguson

It is not what you have that matters. It is what you do with what you have.
Wilfred Grenfell

We are not born for ourselves. *Matthew Henry*

Responsibility walks hand in hand with capacity and power. *John G. Holland*

One cannot be religious by proxy. *William Ralph Inge*

If God were less than sovereign, man would be less than responsible. Since God is absolutely sovereign, man is wholly responsible to him.
R. B. Kuiper

The history of America will be written in three phases: the passing of the Indian, the passing of the buffalo and the passing of the buck.
Will Rogers

Let it be a settled principle in our religion, that man's salvation, if saved, is wholly of God; and that man's ruin, if lost, is wholly of himself.
J. C. Ryle

If God created man then there is someone outside of man to whom he becomes responsible.
Charles Caldwell Ryrie

RESURRECTION OF CHRIST

Death died when Christ rose. *Anon.*

The angel rolled away the stone from Jesus' tomb, not to let the living Lord out, but to let unconvinced outsiders in.
Donald Grey Barnhouse

The stone at the tomb of Jesus was a pebble to the Rock of Ages inside.
Fred Beck

The resurrection is the first and last and dominating element in the Christian consciousness of the New Testament. *James Denney*

If Christ be not risen, the dreadful consequence is not that death ends life, but that we are still in our sins.
G. A. Studdert Kennedy

The man in Christ rose again, not only the God.
C. S. Lewis

Easter is to our faith what water is to the ocean, what stone is to the mountain, what blood is to the body.
Raymond Linquist

I know that my Redeemer lives!
What joy the blest assurance gives!
He lives, he lives, who once was dead;
He lives, my everlasting Head!
Samuel Medley

The same power that brought Christ back from the dead is operative within those who are Christ's. The resurrection is an ongoing thing. *Leon Morris*

Everything antecedent in the incarnate life of our Lord moves towards the resurrection and everything subsequent rests upon it and is conditioned by it.
John Murray

In an age of abounding unbelief and scepticism, we shall find that the resurrection of Christ will bear any weight that we can lay upon it. *J. C. Ryle*

This is no appendix to the faith. This is the faith. He is risen! The Lord is risen indeed! *James S. Stewart*

Christianity is in its very essence a resurrection religion. The concept of resurrection lies at its heart. If you remove it, Christianity is destroyed.
John R. W. Stott

Before Christ's resurrection, it was twilight; it is sunrise now. *Augustus H. Strong*

Christ's resurrection is not only the best proof of immortality, but we have no certain evidence of immortality without it.
Augustus H. Strong

The account of the life of Jesus Christ is the only biography known to man that does not end with death

and burial — the only record of human life that joyfully hastens on to the next chapter after the last!
A. W. Tozer

The moral obligation of the resurrection of Christ is the missionary obligation, the responsibility and the privilege of carrying the message and telling the story, of praying and interceding, and of being involved personally and financially in the cause of this great commission. *A. W. Tozer*

The resurrection morning was only the beginning of a great, grand and vast outreach that has never ended and will not end until our Lord Jesus Christ comes back again. *A. W. Tozer*

The resurrection of Christ and the fact of the empty tomb are not part of the world's complex and continuing mythologies. This is not a Santa Claus tale — it is history and it is reality.
A. W. Tozer

Never was there as great an imposture put upon the world as Christianity, if Christ be yet in the grave.
John Trapp

The resurrection of Jesus is something to shout about. It is an explosive event whose fall-out affects the whole human race.
Douglas Webster

Taking all the evidence together, it is not too much to say that there is no single historic incident better or more variously supported than the resurrection of Christ. *Brooke Foss Westcott*

The Gospels cannot explain the resurrection; it is the resurrection which alone explains the Gospels.
John S. Whale

The resurrection is the proof of our reconciliation.
Geoffrey B. Wilson

RESURRECTION OF CHRISTIANS

Our bodies shall be *like* Christ's glorious body, not *equal* to it. *Richard Sibbes*

At the close of every obituary of his believing children God adds the word 'henceforth!' *A. W. Tozer*

The resurrection and the judgement will demonstrate before all worlds who won and who lost. We can wait!
A. W. Tozer

REVELATION

(See also: Bible — Divine Authorship; Knowledge of God)

God has not been discovered by reasoning but . . . has disclosed himself, unexpectedly and dramatically, in the history of a chosen people.
J. C. P. Cockerton

God wants us to reason together with him on the basis of revelation, not on the basis of our poor logic.
Vance Havner

By the light of nature we see God as a God above us; by the light of the law we see him as a God against us; but by the light of the gospel we see him as Emmanuel, God with us.   *Matthew Henry*

To dust-begotten creatures like ourselves, God is unknowable. The only things we can ever know of him are the things he himself reveals to us.   *John Hercus*

Revelation is the act of communicating divine knowledge by the Spirit to the mind. Inspiration is the act of the same Spirit, controlling those who make the truth known.   *Charles Hodge*

Nothing is to be introduced as doctrine which is not according to revelation.
Henry T. Mahan

Unless thou show us thine own true way, none can find it; Father, thou must lead!
Michaelangelo

Revelation is a disclosure of the divine righteousness.
P. S. Moxom

Scripture . . . is the only revelation of the mind and will of God available to us. This is what the finality of Scripture means to us; it is the only extant revelatory Word of God.
John Murray

God takes us into his confidence and shares his secrets with us; God finds us ignorant, and gives us knowledge. That is what revelation means.   *J. I. Packer*

In revelation, God is the agent as well as the object. It is not just that men speak about God, or for God; God speaks for himself, and talks to us in person.
J. I. Packer

Since the apostolic age God has said nothing new to men, for he has in fact no more to say to us than he said then. But it is also true that God has not ceased to say to man all that he said then.   *J. I. Packer*

No man can know the Father any farther than it pleaseth the Son to reveal him.   *John Penry*

God's design in all that he has revealed to us is to the purifying of our affections and the transforming of our characters.   *A. W. Pink*

The Lord has more truth yet to break forth out of his holy Word.   *John Robinson*

The nearer we come to God, the more graciously will he reveal himself to us.
     C. H. Spurgeon

No man has any right to pick and choose among revealed truths.
     A. W. Tozer

Unless God give sight as well as light, and enlighten both organ and object, we can see nothing.   *John Trapp*

That which we know about God is not what we have been clever enough to find out, but what divine charity has secretly revealed.
     Evelyn Underhill

God is beyond human examination and can be known only by those to whom he chooses to reveal himself.
     Geoffrey B. Wilson

In the goodness of God, what could never be discovered by human reason has been revealed to Christians by the Holy Spirit.
     Geoffrey B. Wilson

The only revelation from God which Christians still await is the revelation of Jesus Christ at his second coming.   *Geoffrey B. Wilson*

REVIVAL

When God is about to do a great work, he pours out a spirit of supplication.
     Jonathan Edwards

Revival is nothing else than a new beginning of obedience to God ... a deep repentance, a breaking down of heart, a getting down into the dust before God with deep humility, and a forsaking of sin.
     Charles G. Finney

There can be no revival when Mr Amen and Mr Wet-Eyes are not found in the audience.
     Charles G. Finney

It may seem mysterious that God should permit a work of his own holy and blessed Spirit to be accompanied, marred and perverted by errors and abuses. But so it has been from the beginning. *Ashbel Green*

Revival is God rending the heavens and coming down upon his people. *Vance Havner*

In every period when God has awakened his people, the gospel of justification has come to the fore. *Robert M. Horn*

An indispensable sign of true revival is that the Word of God grows mightily and prevails — it spreads widely and grows in power. *Erroll Hulse*

The chief mark of authentic revival is enduring repentance. *Erroll Hulse*

Revive thy work, O Lord,
Thy mighty arm make bare;
Speak with the voice that wakes the dead
And make thy people hear. *Albert Midlane*

You can have evangelism without revival, but you cannot have revival without evangelism. *Brian Mills*

The devil keeps step with God, and when revival comes it is always a mixed work, hard to identify just because so much error,

fanaticism and disorder are mixed up in it. *J. I. Packer*

Revival is the inrush of God's Spirit into a body which threatens to become a corpse. *D. M. Paton*

Revival is never the end of the church's problems, nor is it intended to be ... but better the problems of life than of death! *Derek Prime*

The most important motive for prayer for revival is the glory of God. *Derek Prime*

There is no revival possible in any fellowship without a price being paid. *Alan Redpath*

You can pray until doomsday for revival, but you will never get it without repentance and confession of sin in the Christian life. *Erlo Stegan*

By definition, revival is not meant to last, though it can pass sooner than intended on account of Christians quenching and grieving the Holy Spirit. *H. N. J. Waite*

There is nothing in the whole scene of religion that is of the order of revival. *H. N. J. Waite*

Revival is divine intervention in the normal course of spiritual things. It is God revealing himself to man in awful holiness and irresistible power.   *Arthur Wallis*

It may be said that revivals thrive on the Word and the Word is exalted in revivals.
Arthur Skevington Wood

Revival is a sad necessity.
Arthur Skevington Wood

Revival is not something we have and must seek to keep, but something we lack and must plead to receive.
Arthur Skevington Wood

Revival makes the ideal real within the church of God.
Arthur Skevington Wood

The greatest hindrance to revival is pride amongst the Lord's people.
Arthur Skevington Wood

RICHES
(See also: Materialism; Money; Possessions; Prosperity; Wealth)

Riches and content are like two buckets; while one comes up full the other goes down empty.
Thomas Adams

Gold can no more fill the spirit of man than grace his purse.   *Anon.*

No man can tell whether he is rich or poor by turning to his ledger. It is the heart that makes a man rich. He is rich or poor according to what he is, not according to what he has.   *Henry Ward Beecher*

As it is not the great cage that makes the bird sing, so it is not the great estate that makes the happy life, nor the great portion that makes the happy soul.   *Thomas Brooks*

Earthly riches are called thorns, and well they may; for as thorns, they pierce both head and heart; the head with cares in getting them, and the heart with grief in parting with them.
Thomas Brooks

It is the best riches not to desire riches.
Thomas Brooks

You may as well fill a bag with wisdom, a chest with riches, or a circle with a triangle, as the heart of man with anything here below. A man may have enough of the world to sink him, but he can never have enough to satisfy him.
Thomas Brooks

Where there is no want there is usually much wantonness.
John Flavel

The pride of dying rich raises the loudest laugh in hell.   *John Foster*

Riches have made more covetous men than covetousness has made rich men.
Thomas Fuller

Riches rather enlarge than satisfy appetites.
Thomas Fuller

The truly godly person is not interested in becoming rich. He possesses inner resources which furnish riches far beyond that which earth can offer.   *William Hendriksen*

Riches, like dust, slip through our fingers even when we hold them fast.
Matthew Henry

There is a burden of care in getting riches, fear in keeping them, temptation in using them, guilt in abusing them, sorrow in losing them, and a burden of account at last to be given concerning them.   *Matthew Henry*

It is better being rich in grace than rich in purse.
James Janeway

God commonly gives riches to foolish people to whom he gives nothing else.
Martin Luther

A man may be rich and godly, but it is because now and then God will work some miracles of grace.
Thomas Manton

God gave us riches as a means to escape wrath, by a liberal and charitable distribution of them to his glory.
Thomas Manton

Riches with a blessing are so far from being a hindrance to grace that they are an ornament to it.
Thomas Manton

Nobody leaves the world richer than when he came in.   *Stuart Olyott*

Many a millionaire, after choking his soul with gold-dust, has died from melancholia!   *E. K. Simpson*

Riches are no curse when they are blessed of the Lord.
C. H. Spurgeon

I'm glad I did not inherit a fortune. It would have ruined me.   *R. A. Torrey*

Riches, as glass, are bright but brittle.   *John Trapp*

A shoe may have a silver lace on it, yet pinch the foot.
Thomas Watson

Riches are not evil but they are dangerous. *John White*

RITUALISM
(See also: Formalism; Hypocrisy)

Ritualism supplants Jesus Christ. *George Barlow*

Christ and ritualism are opposed to each other, as light is to darkness. The cross and crucifix cannot agree. Either ritualism will banish Christ or Christ will banish ritualism.
Horatius Bonar

RUMOUR
(See also: Gossip; Slander; Speech)

Rumour is one thing that gets thicker as you spread it.
Anon.

Rumour is a loud liar, like a snowball that gathers as it goes. *John Trapp*

The first tale is good till the second be heard.
John Trapp

SACRIFICE

A religion which costs nothing is worth nothing.
J. C. Ryle

God knows all about my health and need of a rest and need of many other things regarded as absolutely necessary . . . I gladly laugh at being without them, and rejoice in a living death with a marvellous joy in order to fill the place that others have left unoccupied whatever their reasons for so doing.
C. T. Studd

SALVATION
(See also: Atonement; Redemption)

We are saved not by merit but by mercy.

The surest token of God's good will towards us is his good work in us. *Anon.*

Perfection demands perfection; that is why salvation must be by grace, and why works are not sufficient.
Donald Grey Barnhouse

Anyone can devise a plan by which good people may go to heaven. Only God can devise a plan whereby sinners, who are his enemies, can go to heaven.
Lewis Sperry Chafer

The soul was made for God. He who is saved from sin possesses the utmost felicity that the soul can enjoy, in this or the coming world.
Adam Clarke

The death-struck sinner, like the wan, anaemic, dying invalid, is saved by having poured into his veins the healthier blood of Christ.
Henry Drummond

If there be ground for you to trust in your own righteousness, then all that Christ did to purchase salvation, and all that God did to prepare the way for it is in vain.
Jonathan Edwards

Souls are not saved in bundles.
Ralph Waldo Emerson

God did not save us to make us happy but to make us holy.   *Vance Havner*

Our salvation includes more than pardon from sin, deliverance from hell and a ticket to heaven. It includes all that we shall need on our journey.   *Vance Havner*

Salvation does not come from assent of the head but by the consent of the heart.
Vance Havner

Salvation is a happy security and a secure happiness.
William Jenkyn

A chain is as strong as its weakest link. If but one link of the ten thousand is of the sinner's making, he is hopelessly lost.   *R. B. Kuiper*

Nowhere does the Bible tell us that salvation is by a faith that does not work.
R. B. Kuiper

Salvation is only by a working faith. In short, good works are the fruit of saving faith. They are also the proof of saving faith.   *R. B. Kuiper*

The scriptural doctrine of God and scriptural doctrine of salvation are inseparable and interdependent.
R. B. Kuiper

Whatever contribution men make to their salvation they make by the grace of God. And that makes salvation the work of grace a hundred per cent.   *R. B. Kuiper*

A man cannot be thoroughly humbled until he comes to know that his salvation is utterly beyond his own powers, counsel, endeavours, will and works and is absolutely dependent upon the will, counsel and pleasure of another.   *Martin Luther*

277

No man stands so tall as when he kneels and asks God to set the record straight.
Roy O. McClain

Christ is the final word about salvation. Here, he is not only without a peer, he is without a competitor.
G. Campbell Morgan

The casting out of demons is ascribed to God's 'finger'; his delivering of Israel from Egypt to his 'hand'; but when the Lord saves a sinner it is his 'holy arm' which gets him the victory.
A. W. Pink

The will of the Father is the originating cause of our salvation, the worth of the Son's redemption its meritorious cause and the work of the Spirit its effectual cause.
A. W. Pink

We are not saved by our giving; we are saved by God's giving. *A. W. Pink*

Salvation excels all the miracles ever wrought.
William S. Plumer

All that is necessary for salvation is accomplished in Christ's work, even the guarantee of its application.
Ernest Reisinger

That Christ and a forgiven sinner should be made one, and share heaven between them, is the wonder of salvation; what more could love do? *Samuel Rutherford*

Who could be saved if God were not God, and if he were not such a God as he is?.
Samuel Rutherford

Let it be a settled principle in our religion that men's salvation, if saved, is wholly of God; and that man's ruin, if lost, is wholly of himself.
J. C. Ryle

Salvation is no precarious half-measure but a foundation laid in heaven.
E. K. Simpson

If there is to be in our celestial garment but one stitch of our own making we are all of us lost.
C. H. Spurgeon

Many people think that when we preach salvation, we mean salvation from going to hell. We do mean that, but we mean a great deal more: we preach salvation from *sin*. We say that Christ is able to save a man, and we mean by that that he is able to save him from sin and to make him holy, to make him a new man.
C. H. Spurgeon

God does not owe you salvation. You deserve damnation, but he provides salvation.   *Billy Sunday*

We need to be delivered from the freedom which is absolute bondage into the bondage which is perfect freedom.   *William Temple*

It is God alone who saves, and that in every element of the saving process.
     Benjamin B. Warfield

SATAN
(See also: Hell)

Nothing promotes the activity of the devil more than the Christian's proximity to God.

To deny the fact of Satan is to deny the truth of Scripture.

The devil is old, but not infirm.   *Anon.*

The devil's boots don't creak.   *Anon.*

There is no need for ignorance concerning the devices of the devil, for they are set forth plainly in the Word of God, and they are also visible all around us.
     Donald Grey Barnhouse

If God were not my friend, Satan would not be so much my enemy.   *Thomas Brooks*

Satan has only a persuading sleight, not an enforcing might.   *Thomas Brooks*

The devil is most devilish when respectable.
     Elizabeth Barrett Browning

Adam's fall was the devil's masterpiece.   *Elisha Coles*

God's makes the devil a polisher while he intends to be a destroyer.
     Stephen Charnock

Satan paints God with his own colours.
     Stephen Charnock

The devil was educated in the best divinity school in the universe, viz the heaven of heavens.
     Jonathan Edwards

I think the devil has made it his business to monopolize on three elements: noise, hurry, crowds ... Satan is quite aware of the power of silence.   *Jim Elliot*

The devil has got to be resisted, not merely deprecated.   *Michael Green*

Did the Christian consider what Satan's power is, and

who dams it up, this would always be a song of praise in his mouth. *William Gurnall*

God sets the devil to catch himself. *William Gurnall*

Satan, as in his first temptation, is still on the losing side. *William Gurnall*

The devil is a great student in divinity. *William Gurnall*

The devil shall never lift his head higher than the saint's heel. *William Gurnall*

The devil's *nature* shows his power; it is angelical. *William Gurnall*

Satan does far more harm as an angel of light than as a roaring lion. *Vance Havner*

Satan produces mental and spiritual anaesthetics more potent than any shot from a needle. *Vance Havner*

Satan, the great adversary, directs all his energy to prevent men becoming the subject of that illumination of which the gospel, as the revelation of the glory of Christ, is the source. *Charles Hodge*

The devil will rather play at small game than no game at all. *Christopher Love*

The devil allows no Christian to reach heaven with clean feet all the way. *Martin Luther*

There is no estate to which Satan is so opposed as to marriage. *Martin Luther*

The devil's greatest asset is the doubt people have about his existence. *John Nicola*

Satan has no constructive purpose of his own: his tactics are simply to thwart God and destroy men. *J. I. Packer*

Satan was the original sinner. *J. I. Packer*

The natural response to denials of Satan's existence is to ask, who then runs his business? *J. I. Packer*

Satan is very clever; he knows exactly what bait to use for every place in which he fishes. *A. W. Pink*

Satan has three titles in the Scriptures, setting forth his malignity against the church of God: a dragon, to note his malice; a serpent, to note his subtlety; and a lion, to note his strength. *Edward Reynolds*

The devil's war is better than the devil's peace. Sus-

pect dumb holiness. When the dog is kept out of doors he howls to be let in again.
Samuel Rutherford

Nowhere pehaps is the devil so active as in a congregation of gospel-hearers.
J. C. Ryle

The devil has more knowledge than any of us, and yet is no better for it.
J. C. Ryle

There is no enemy worse than an enemy who is never seen and never dies, who is near to us wherever we live and goes with us wherever we go.
J. C. Ryle

Sometimes the devil is a gentleman.
Percy Bysshe Shelley

If men's trades can be called crafts, the devil's trade may be called craft.
Henry Smith

The devil deserves his name.
Henry Smith

The devil, that great peripatetic.
John Trapp

Satan has spite against the new creature.
Thomas Watson

The devil does not care how many sermon pills you take,

so long as they do not work upon your conscience.
Thomas Watson

The devil hunts more as a fox than as a lion; his snares are worse than his darts.
Thomas Watson

The devil is a busy bishop in his diocese. *Thomas Watson*

It is only by posing as the champion of truth that the prince of darkness is able to persuade men to swallow his lies. *Geoffrey B. Wilson*

Satan's malice is always frustrated by God and made to minister a blessing to his people. The 'all things' of Romans 8:28 admit of no exceptions.
Geoffrey B. Wilson

The work of Satan is overruled so that it assists in bringing to pass the divine purpose, though Satan on his part uses his utmost powers to thwart that purpose. *Geoffrey B. Wilson*

SCIENCE

Science is but a mere heap of facts, not a golden chain of truths, if we refuse to link it to the throne of God.
F. B. Cobbe

We have done wrong to set up any sharp antithesis between science and religion . . . There is no other way out of our impasse than to assert that science is one aspect of God's presence.
C. A. Coulson

The religion that is afraid of science dishonours God and commits suicide.
Ralph Waldo Emerson

Science and religion no more contradict each other than light and electricity.
William Hiram Foulkes

God pity the man of science who believes in nothing but what he can prove by scientific methods; for if ever a human being needed divine pity he does.
J. G. Holland

There is nothing in modern science that invalidates the teaching of the Bible regarding God's care for his creatures; nay, there is much that wonderfully confirms it, if only we had eyes to see. Something other than true science has put the mist and darkness over men's eyes.
J. Gresham Machen

Every formula which expresses a law of nature is a hymn of praise to God.
Maria Mitchell

There is no ascertained fact of science with which the Bible is out of harmony. There are some hypotheses of scientific investigators which are out of harmony with the biblical revelation. But there is a great difference between hypotheses and established fact.
G. Campbell Morgan

Science cannot determine origin and so cannot determine destiny. As it presents only a sectional view of creation, it gives only a sectional view of everything in creation.   *T. T. Munger*

Whenever I find men running to science to find support for the Bible, I know they are rationalists and not true believers.
A. W. Tozer

SECOND COMING OF CHRIST

The Christ who rose from the earth and now reigns over the earth will one day return to the earth.

When Christ returns, the second advent will no longer be a subject for discussion.

When it comes to belief in the Lord's return there are two

kinds of Christians — gazers and goers. *Anon.*

The only remedy for all this mass of misery is the return of our Lord Jesus Christ. Why do we not plead for it every time we hear the clock strike? *Anthony Ashley Cooper*

The subject of the second coming of Christ has never been popular to any but the true believer. *Billy Graham*

Oh, the joy to see thee reigning,
Thee, my own beloved Lord!
Every tongue thy name confessing,
Worship, honour, glory, blessing,
Brought to thee with glad accord —
Thee, my Master and my Friend,
Vindicated and enthroned,
Unto earth's remotest end
Glorified, adored and owned!
Frances Ridley Havergal

Christ will come when he pleases, to show his sovereignty, and will not let us know when, to teach us our duty. *Matthew Henry*

When Jesus comes there will be instant job satisfaction for us. *David N. Jones*

There is such a danger of our being so occupied with the things that are to come more than with him who is to come. *Andrew Murray*

In all our thoughts about Christ, let us never forget his second advent. *J. C. Ryle*

There shall be no time for parting words or a change of mind when the Lord appears. *J. C. Ryle*

Uncertainty about the date of the Lord's return is calculated to keep believers in an attitude of constant expectation and to preserve them from despondency. *J. C. Ryle*

When Christ comes again, the remains of ignorance shall be rolled away. *J. C. Ryle*

Oh, that the Lord would come! He *is* coming! He is on the road and travelling quickly. The sound of his approach should be as music to our hearts! *C. H. Spurgeon*

He who came in humility and shame will return in spectacular magnificence. *John R. W. Stott*

The imminent return of our Lord is the great Bible

argument for a pure, unself-ish, devoted, unworldly, active life of service.

R. A. Torrey

This is pinned as a badge to the sleeve of every true believer — that he looks for and longs for Christ's coming to judgement.

John Trapp

The brightness of Christ's advent will reveal the true character of those things which were previously hidden by darkness.

Geoffrey B. Wilson

SECURITY

If the Father has the king-dom ready for us, he will take care of us on the way.

Andrew Bonar

If God has said, 'I will never leave,' we may well say, 'What shall man do?'

John Brown

Anyone who has the firm conviction that he will never be forsaken by the Lord will not be unduly anxious, because he will depend on his providence. *John Calvin*

Everyone who is a man of God has omnipotence as his guardian, and God will

sooner empty heaven of angels than leave a saint without defence.

C. H. Spurgeon

This only can my fears control,
And bid my sorrows fly;
What harm can ever reach my soul
Beneath my Father's eye?

Anne Steele

Should all the hosts of death,
And powers of hell unknown,
Put their most dreadful forms
Of rage and malice on,
I shall be safe, for Christ displays
Superior power and guard-ian grace.

Isaac Watts

SELF

(See also: Conceit; Pride)

Self-will is so ardent and active that it will break a world in pieces to make a stool to sit on.   *Anon.*

The person who is all wrapped up in himself is overdressed.   *Anon.*

The self-made man usually admires his maker.   *Anon.*

You never cultivate self into anything but self.   *Anon.*

O Lord, deliver me from the lust of always vindicating myself.   *Augustine*

The biggest problem with me is 'I'.   *Doug Barnett*

It is the desiring of one's own way which leads to every other sin in the world.
Donald Grey Barnhouse

The truest self-respect is not to think of self.
Henry Ward Beecher

The Christian needs a reminder every hour; some defeat, surprise, adversity, peril; to be agitated, mortified, beaten out of his course, so that all remains of self will be sifted out.
Horace Bushnell

To live happily the evils of ambition and self-love must be plucked from our hearts by the roots.   *John Calvin*

If you open your mouth to vindicate yourself you will lose what you might gain.
Oswald Chambers

If one devil of self-interest is swept from the soul, seven self-schemes worse than the first will return with it unless the soul is fully employed with living unto him who died and rose again.
Walter J. Chantry

'Self-centred Christian' is a term of impossible contradiction.   *Walter J. Chantry*

Self is the poise of the unsanctified heart.
John Flavel

That household god, a man's own self.
John Flavel

Self is the most abominable principle that ever was.
Thomas Goodwin

Self is the soul, the spirit of unregeneracy.
Thomas Goodwin

Self-love is king in unregenerate hearts.
Thomas Goodwin

I am more afraid of my own heart than of the pope and all his cardinals. I have within me the great pope — Self.   *Martin Luther*

Nowhere does the self-centred heart of man more quickly take control than when it comes to the machinery of criticism and the promptings of self-interest.   *J. A. Motyer*

My true knowledge of self comes not from my searching myself but from God searching me.
Watchman Nee

Sin is a man's self. Just as 'I' is the centre letter of sin, so sin is the centre, the moving-power, the very life of self.
A. W. Pink

Oh, wretched idol, myself!
Samuel Rutherford

Sinful self is to be destroyed and natural self is to be denied. *William Secker*

How can self drive out self? As well expect Satan to drive out Satan! *John R. W. Stott*

Self-will is a close relative of pride. *A. W. Tozer*

Self is the only prison that can bind the soul.
Henry Van Dyke

SELF-CONTROL
(See also: Discipline)

The beginning of self-mastery is to be mastered by Christ, to yield to his lordship. *D. G. Kehl*

True spiritual self-discipline holds believers in bounds but never in bonds; its effect is to enlarge, expand and liberate. *D. G. Kehl*

No man is free who cannot command himself.
Pythagoras

SELF-CRUCIFIXION
(See also: Humility; Meekness)

Self is to be dealt with by crucifixion, not forgiveness.
Donald Grey Barnhouse

If we truly place ourselves beneath the cross, then we will throw off lives of masquerade, of make-believe, of bluffing, of emptiness and of secret sin.
Gerhard Bergmann

Put relentless hands down into your hearts, and tear out by the roots everything that will not advance the interests of the Redeemer's kingdom. *B. H. Carroll*

God does not want us to think less of ourselves. He wants us not to think of ourselves at all. *Andrew Dhuse*

You may ask me what is the cure of this love of self. There is no question of a cure; the thing must be killed. *François Fenelon*

We read in Scripture of taking up the cross, but never of laying it down.
J. Ford

Self is the tumour of the soul, and it grows by what it feeds on. You cannot cure it by a few good resolutions. It requires the most drastic treat-

ment, and Christ prescribes crucifixion as the only way of destroying this root of every kind of bitterness.
R. Moffatt Gantry

Let ... corrupt affections ... be mortified and not gratified. *Matthew Henry*

If you're dead to self you can't hurt any more.
Kay Long

One of the ways of manifesting and maintaining the crucifixion of the flesh is never to use money to gratify it. *Andrew Murray*

The vigour and power and comfort of our spiritual life depends on the mortification of the deeds of the flesh.
John Owen

Mortification is war.
J. I. Packer

We cannot save ourselves and save others; there must be a destruction of self for the salvation of men.
C. H. Spurgeon

You will never glory in God till first of all God has killed your glorying in yourself.
C. H. Spurgeon

Self-sacrifice brought Christ into the world, and self-sacrifice will lead his follow-

ers, not away from but into the midst of men.
Benjamin B. Warfield

SELF-DELUSION

Nothing is so easy to deceive as one's self. *Demosthenes*

There is much self-delusion in our estimation of ourselves when we are untried, and in the midst of Christian friends, whose warm feelings give a glow to ours which they do not possess in themselves.
Robert Murray M'Cheyne

SELF-DENIAL

You deny Christ when you fail to deny yourself for Christ. *Anon.*

For the proper use of no talent is self-denial more needed than for that of money. *George Barlow*

All who have not been influenced by the principle of self-denial have followed virtue merely from the love of praise. *John Calvin*

Show me a single man who does not believe in the Lord's law of self-denial, and who yet willingly practises virtue among men.

John Calvin

The denial of ourselves will leave no room for pride, haughtiness, or vainglory, nor for avarice, licentiousness, love of luxury, wantonness, or any sin born from self-love.   *John Calvin*

There is no end and no limit to the obstacles of the man who wants to pursue what is right and at the same time shrinks back from self-denial.   *John Calvin*

All of the great spiritual delights we long for come into the world of a Christian's experience attended with the birth-pangs of self-denial.   *Walter J. Chantry*

Whoever will labour to get rid of self, to deny himself according to the instruction of Christ, strikes at once at the root of every evil and finds the germ of every good.

François Fenelon

Self-renunciation is the cardinal ethic of the Christian church.   *Charles Inwood*

The severest self-denials and the most lavish gifts are of no value in God's esteem unless they are prompted by love.

A. W. Pink

We are to rise above our fellows by a superior self-forgetfulness.

C. H. Spurgeon

SELF-EXAMINATION

The best eyes look inwards and upwards.   *Anon.*

He who knows himself best esteems himself least.

Henry G. Bohn

Nearly all the wisdom we possess, that is to say, true and sound wisdom, consists of two parts: the knowledge of God and of ourselves.

John Calvin

Those who know themselves best will fear themselves most.   *Donald Cargill*

Search others for their virtues and thyself for thy vices.   *Thomas Fuller*

No man can produce great things who is not thoroughly sincere in dealing with himself.   *James Russell Lowell*

Gracious hearts reflect most upon themselves; they do not seek what to reprove in others, but what to lament in themselves.

Thomas Manton

Until men know themselves better, they will care very little to know Christ at all.
John Owen

The worst ignorance in the world is not to know ourselves.
J. C. Ryle

Contemplation is a perspective glass to see our Saviour in; but *examination* is a looking-glass to view ourselves in.
William Secker

The reason why there is so little self-condemnation is because there is so little self-examination.
William Secker

Examination is the eye of the soul.
Henry Smith

The Holy Spirit would lead us to think much upon our own sins. It is a dangerous thing for us to dwell upon the imperfections of others.
Ichabod Spencer

A frequent reckoning with ourselves will pluck up sin before it is rooted in the soul.
George Swinnock

Self-knowledge is so critically important to us in our pursuit of God and his righteousness that we lie under heavy obligation to do immediately whatever is necessary to remove the disguise and permit our real selves to be known.
A. W. Tozer

Self-examination is a spiritual inquisition set up in the soul.
Thomas Watson

SELFISHNESS

Selfishness follows the line of least resistance.
Galen

No indulgence of passion destroys the spiritual nature so much as respectable selfishness.
George Macdonald

Where self is the end of our actions, there Satan is the rewarder of them.
William Secker

He who lives to benefit himself confers on the world a benefit when he dies.
Tertullian

Selfishness is never so exquisitely selfish as when it is on its knees ... Self turns what would otherwise be a pure and powerful prayer into a weak and ineffective one.
A. W. Tozer

SELF-PITY

Self-pity can be as addictive as alcohol – and just as deadly.

Self-pity is a prison without walls — a sign pointing to nowhere.   *Anon.*

SEPARATION

The Christian must live in the world, but he must not let the world live in him.
                                    Anon.

We are strangers here. Don't make yourself at home.
                    Vance Havner

We must dare to be peculiar.
                    J. C. Ryle

SERVICE — Dignity

Christian service has been digni-fied by Deity.

Love is the *motive* for work-ing; joy is the *strength* for working.   *Andrew Bonar*

Service to God through ser-vice to mankind is the only motivation acceptable to God for diligence and hard work in our vocational call-ing.   *Jerry Bridges*

There are no trivial assign-ments in the work of the Lord.   *Vance Havner*

Service can never become slavery to one who loves.
                    J. L. Massee

You do not do God a favour by serving him. He honours you by allowing you to serve him.   *Victor Nyquist*

The world's idea of greatness is to rule, but Christian greatness consists in serving.
                    J. C. Ryle

To serve God is to reign.
                Richard Sibbes

If you cannot be great, be willing to serve God in that which is small. *S. F. Smith*

It is better to be God's dog than the devil's darling.
                C. H. Spurgeon

God's work does not need pious lies to support it.
                    A. W. Tozer

SERVICE — God's Part

Spirituality is a work of God for his child; service is a work of the child for his God, which can be accom-plished only in the power of the indwelling Spirit.
                Lewis Sperry Chafer

Spirituality is not gained by service; it is *unto* service.
                Lewis Sperry Chafer

Those whom God will employ are first struck with a sense of their unworthiness to be employed.
Matthew Henry

Whatever you do, begin with God. *Matthew Henry*

Nothing serves God or worships and adores him but that which wills and works with him. *William Law*

The most significant gifts in the church's life in every era are ordinarily natural abilities sanctified. *J. I. Packer*

Human sweat can add nothing to the work of the Spirit, especially when it is nerve sweat. *A. W. Tozer*

God is more interested in the workman than in the work.
Warren Wiersbe

SERVICE — Prayer

Life is fragile — handle it with prayer. *Anon.*

You can do more than pray *after* you have prayed, but you cannot do more than pray *until* you have prayed.
S. D. Gordon

SERVICE — Responsibility

Men who love much will work much. *Anon.*

No man's life is for his private use. *Anon.*

Pray for a good harvest, but keep on hoeing. *Anon.*

The world is full of willing workers; some willing to work, and others willing to let them work. *Anon.*

God made me for himself, to
serve him here,
With love's pure service and
in filial fear;
To show his praise, for him
to labour now;
Then see his glory where the
angels bow.
Henry William Baker

Christianity is not a sedentary profession or employment. *Richard Baxter*

Church greatness consists in being greatly serviceable.
Richard Baxter

The candle of mercy is set up not to play by but to work by. *Thomas Brooks*

The Lord first of all wants sincerity in his service, simplicity of heart without guile and falsehood. *John Calvin*

291

Whatever ability a faithful Christian may possess, he ought to possess it for his fellow believers, and he ought to make his own interest subservient to the well-being of the church in all sincerity.   *John Calvin*

We are born into permanent service.   *David H. Chilton*

What is my being but for thee,
Its sure support, its noblest end;
Thy ever-smiling face to see,
And serve the cause of such a Friend?
    Philip Doddridge

We do not trust God, but tempt him, when our expectations slacken our exertions.
    Matthew Henry

Christ keeps no servants only to wear a livery.
    William Jenkyn

God never gave man a thing to do concerning which it were irreverent to ponder how the Son of God would have done it.
    George Macdonald

The measure of a man is not the number of his servants, but in the number of people whom he serves.
    Paul D. Moody

Any man or woman in the church who does not know what it is to share the travail that makes his kingdom come is dishonest and disloyal to Jesus Christ.
    G. Campbell Morgan

Unless a man's faith saves him out of selfishness into service it will certainly never save him out of hell into heaven.   *Mark Guy Pearce*

Activity is the mark of the holy spirits and should be the mark of holy men.
    C. H. Spurgeon

The imminent return of our Lord is the great Bible argument for a pure, unselfish, devoted, unworldly, active life of service.   *R. A. Torrey*

SERVICE — Rewards

Work for the Lord. The pay isn't much, but the retirement benefit is out of this world.   *Anon.*

The best part of all Christian work is that part which only God sees.   *Andrew Bonar*

The service of the Lord does not only include implicit obedience, but also a willingness to put aside our sinful desires, and to surrender completely to the leadership of the Holy Spirit.   *John Calvin*

The gospel teaches us that while believers are not rewarded on account of their works, they are rewarded according to their works.
R. L. Dabney

Men who expect to be paid in this world for serving God have mistaken God for mammon.
Thomas V. Moore

The fruit of Christian service is never the result of allowing the natural energies and inclinations to run riot.
Leon Morris

God is a sure paymaster, though he does not always pay at the end of every week.
C. H. Spurgeon

The labourer, not the loiterer, is worthy of his hire.
Henry Wilkinson

Faithful service is sure to be rewarded, yet this is the reward of grace and not a merited award.
Geoffrey B. Wilson

SERVICE — Wholeheartedness

(See also: Zeal)

You cannot be too active as regards your own efforts; you cannot be too dependent as regards divine grace. Do everything as if God did nothing; depend upon God as if he did everything.
John Angell James

The man who tries to do something and fails is infinitely better than the man who tries to do nothing and succeeds.
D. Martyn Lloyd-Jones

The oil of the lamp in the temple burnt away in giving light; so should we.
Robert Murray M'Cheyne

Though you cannot do what you ought, yet you ought to do what you can.
Christopher Nesse

Do little things as if they were great, because of the majesty of the Lord Jesus Christ who dwells in thee; and do great things as if they were little and easy, because of his omnipotence.
Blaise Pascal

Only a burdened heart can lead to fruitful service.
Alan Redpath

God deserves to be served with all the energy of which we are capable.
C. H. Spurgeon

If the service of God is worth anything, it is worth everything.
C. H. Spurgeon

When you have kindled your love to Christ at his love to you, then let it burn and spend ... in his service and to his praise.
Robert Traill

God does sometimes accept of willingness without the work, but never the work without the willingness.
Thomas Watson

The most willing service to men is rendered by those who are bent on pleasing Christ!
Geoffrey B. Wilson

SEX
(See also: Lust)

The first sexual thought in the universe was God's, not man's.
Doug Barnett

In nothing did early Christianity so thoroughly revolutionize the ethical standards of the pagan world as in regard to sexual relationships.
George S. Duncan

The powerful sexual drives which are built into man's relationship with woman are not seen in Scripture as the foundation of marriage, but the consummation and physical expression of it.
Sinclair Ferguson

Sexual desire is natural and marriage is provided for its fulfilment.
Norman Hillyer

Homosexual practices are against nature and against revealed truth ... Homosexual indulgence is something which God condemns as the ultimate sign of decadence and degradation in any culture.
O. R. Johnston

No sinful act desecrates the body like fornication and sexual abuse. In this sense fornication has a deadly eminence.
R. C. H. Lenski

What a man or woman does with his or her sexual energy will decide not only the quality of their own lives, but the kind of world in which they live.
Mary Whitehouse

When sex is deformed, cheapened and exploited then the potentiality of life and the whole social fabric of society deteriorates.
Mary Whitehouse

SICKNESS

(See also: Pain; Suffering; Trials)

The decay of the outward man in the godless is a melancholy spectacle, for it is the decay of everything; in the Christian it does not touch that life which is hid with Christ in God, and which is in the soul itself a well of water springing up to life eternal.   *James Denny*

Sickness is God's messenger to call us to meet with God.
Thomas Manton

The chief care of a sick man should be for his soul.
Thomas Manton

Health is a good thing, but sickness is far better if it leads us to God.
J. C. Ryle

Sickness is a great leveller.
J. C. Ryle

There is no commentary that opens up the Bible so much as sickness and sorrow.
J. C. Ryle

Sanctified sickness is far better than unsanctified soundness.   *George Swinnock*

SILENCE

Blessed is the man who having nothing to say abstains from giving wordy evidence of the fact.
George Eliot

I think the devil has made it his business to monopolize on three elements: noise, hurry, crowds ... Satan is quite aware of the power of silence.   *Jim Elliot*

How rare it is to find a soul quiet enough to hear God speak!   *François Fenelon*

Silence is one great art of conversation.
William Hazlitt

I always feel it a blessed thing when the Saviour takes me aside from the crowd.
Robert Murray M'Cheyne

Often silence is the sum of our duties.
William S. Plumer

In a still night every voice is heard, and when the body is quiet the mind most commonly is quiet also ... and when our minds are quiet we are fit to deal with heavenly matters.   *Henry Smith*

God can be known in the tumult if his providence has

for the time placed us there, but he is known best in the silence.   *A. W. Tozer*

SIN — and the Christian

The lost leap into sin and love it; the saved lapse into sin and loathe it.

If I grapple with sin in my own strength, the devil knows he may go to sleep.
                    H. G. J. Adams

Believers sin less but they are not sinless.   *Anon.*

It is a great sin to love a small sin.   *Anon.*

The Christian has sin in him but not on him.   *Anon.*

If sin comes into the life of the believer, he should immediately become concerned about it. It should cause him to rush to the Lord in confession and repentance, and it should cause him to build every bulwark possible against the recurrence of the sin.
                Donald Grey Barnhouse

A godly man doth mourn for another's sin as well as for his own, because he mourns for sin as sin.
                    William Bridge

It is not falling into the water, but lying in the water that drowns.
                    Thomas Brooks

It was sin that made our bodies mortal . . . therefore do not yield obedience to such an enemy.
                    Matthew Henry

A sinner falls into sin as a fish, the saint as a child does into the water.
                    William Jenkyn

This is one of the sorest trials of a renewed life, that it is built over dark dungeons, where dead things may be buried but not forgotten, and where through open grating rank vapours still ascend.   *John Ker*

Even the sinning of the regenerate man differs essentially from that of the unregenerate man.
                    R. B. Kuiper

Whatever sin he may commit, the regenerate person always sins against his will.   *R. B. Kuiper*

No figure of speech can represent my utter want of power to resist the torrent of sin.
                Robert Murray M'Cheyne

The seeds of all sins are in my heart, and perhaps all the more dangerously that I do not see them.
Robert Murray M'Cheyne

It is one thing for sin to live in us; it is another for us to live in sin. *John Murray*

It is not the absence of sin but the grieving over it which distinguishes the child of God from empty professors. *A. W. Pink*

The Christian does not have to live in defeat, but he does have to live all his life with the sin nature ... and ... because God has not made the flesh any better in the believer, because it has not been refined, it is a powerful enemy with which we have to live.
Charles Caldwell Ryrie

The way we can thank Jesus the most in this life for his act of redemption is no longer to tolerate sin.
Basilea Schlink

Of two evils, choose neither.
C. H. Spurgeon

Sin in a Christian is like a diver's dress on land — awkward and harassing.
John Trapp

Better starve than go to the devil for provender.
Thomas Watson

The sins of the godly are worse than others, because they bring a greater reproach upon religion.
Thomas Watson

Though we [as Christians] are like Christ, having the firstfruits of the Spirit, yet are we unlike him, having the remainders of the flesh.
Thomas Watson

SIN — Deceitfulness

No sin is to be regarded as small, because the God who forbids all sin is so great.

Evil enters like a needle and spreads like an oak tree.
Anon.

Though Satan's apples may have a fair skin, yet they certainly have a bitter core.
William Secker

A sin is two sins when it is defended. *Henry Smith*

Sin may open bright as the morning, but it will end dark as night.
Thomas de Witt Talmage

'Evil' is Hebrew for a fool.
John Trapp

SIN — Effects

Our vices have voices; they testify against us.

Sin denies man the power of God in this life and the presence of God in the next.

The real horror of being outside of Christ is that there is no shelter from the wrath of God. *Eric Alexander*

A little sin will add to your trouble, subtract from your energy and multiply your difficulties. *Anon.*

Nothing will stop your song quicker than your sin.
Anon.

Sin always ruins where it reigns. *Anon.*

Sin puts hell into the soul and the soul into hell.
Anon.

Sin has turned the world from a paradise into a thicket; there is no getting through without being scratched. *Thomas Boston*

The wicked have the seeds of hell in their own hearts.
John Calvin

This one word 'evil' is a thunderbolt which lays low all human pride.
John Calvin

Sin is the greatest robber that this world will ever know. *Peter Clement*

No marvel that our sorrows are multiplied when our sins are. *Matthew Henry*

Sin lessens men.
Matthew Henry

Sins are like circles in the water when a stone is thrown into it; one produces another. *Philip Henry*

It is the tendency of righteousness to produce blessings, as it is the tendency of evil to produce misery.
Charles Hodge

Sin and shame came in both together. *Christopher Nesse*

Of all trades, sin is the most unprofitable. *J. C. Ryle*

God has set it down for an eternal rule that vexation and sin shall be inseparable.
Richard Sibbes

He cannot smell sweetly who sleeps in a bed of garlic.
C. H. Spurgeon

Sin is no little thing. It girded the Redeemer's head with thorns, and pierced his heart ... Look upon all sin as that which crucified the Saviour, and you will see it to be 'exceeding sinful'.
C. H. Spurgeon

All misery calls sin mother.
George Swinnock

Sin is the weight on the clock which makes the hammer to strike. *George Swinnock*

One sin liked and loved will make way for every other.
John Trapp

Pollution is the forerunner of perdition. *John Trapp*

Sin is like the Jerusalem artichoke; plant it where you will, it overruns the ground and chokes the heart.
John Trapp

All offences against God will either be forgiven or avenged. *A. W. Tozer*

Sin makes sad convulsions in the conscience.
Thomas Watson

SIN — Essence

Sin is moral mutiny by man.

There is no right way to do a wrong thing. *Anon.*

Sin is energy in the wrong channel. *Augustine*

Sin is a serious business to God, and it becomes serious business to us when we reflect upon the fact that every sin, regardless of how seemingly insignificant it appears to us, is an expression of contempt towards the sovereign authority of God. *Jerry Bridges*

Every sin is an election of the devil to be our Lord.
Stephen Charnock

Sinful man does not wish to know God; he wishes himself to be the self-sufficient centre of his universe.
P. E. Hughes

Put sin into its best dress, it is but gilded damnation.
William Jenkyn

At the heart of everything that the Bible says are two great truths, which belong inseparably together — the majesty of the law of God, and sin as an offence against that law.
J. Gresham Machen

Sin is not the brute in us; it is, rather, the man in us.
J. Gresham Machen

In the ways of sin you have a bad master, worse work and the worst wages.
Thomas Manton

Sin is a kind of allergy in the moral and spiritual system of fallen man. *J. I. Packer*

We shall never know what sin really is till we learn to think of it in terms of our relationship with God.
J. I. Packer

Sin is a man's self. Just as 'I' is the centre letter of 'sin', so sin is the centre, the moving-power, the very life of self.
A. W. Pink

No man ever dreaded or hated sin excessively.
William S. Plumer

The worst thing in every sin is that it is against God.
William S. Plumer

Sin as a state is unlikeness to God, as a principle is opposition to God, and as an act is transgression of God's law.
E. G. Robinson

Opposition to the divine will is the very essence of all sin.
David Thomas

Sin has the devil for its father, shame for its companion and death for its wages. *Thomas Watson*

SIN — Fact

The two greatest facts in life are sin and death.

Sin is a matter of what we are, not what we learn.
Brian Edwards

How could a holy God, if he is all-powerful, have permitted the existence of sin? What shall we do with the problem? I am afraid we shall have to do with it something that is not very pleasing to our pride; I am afraid we shall just have to say that it is insoluble.
J. Gresham Machen

Many have puzzled themselves about the origin of evil; I observe that there *is* evil, and that there is a way to escape it, and with this I begin and end.
John Newton

Good and evil are not the same to the living God: whichever side you are on, and for whatever reason you do it, evil is evil, and the nature of the cause you support makes no difference to the evils you perform.
James Philip

The right measure of sin's sinfulness is the dignity of him who came into the world to save sinners. If

Christ is so great, then sin must indeed be sinful!
J. C. Ryle

Men's sins feast the devil.
Thomas Watson

Sin is an irrational thing.
Thomas Watson

Sin is worse than hell; for the pains of hell are a burden to the creature only, but sin is a burden to God.
Thomas Watson

The evil of sin is not so much seen in that one thousand are damned for it, as that Christ died for it.
Thomas Watson

SIN OF OMISSION
(See also: Negligence)

Sinful omissions lead to sinful commissions.
Thomas Brooks

Sins of omission are aggravated by knowledge.
Thomas Manton

Not doing good fits the heart for doing evil.
George Swinnock

Some sins of omission are like great men, that never go without great followers.
George Swinnock

Every man is guilty of all the good he didn't do. *Voltaire*

SIN — Power

Those sins that seem most sweet in life will prove most bitter in death.
Thomas Brooks

Our sin is a step to another more heinous. *David Dickson*

Sin cannot be reduced to manageable proportions.
Sinclair Ferguson

God's wounds cure; sin's kisses kill. *William Gurnall*

Sin has turned the world upside down; the earth has become quite a different thing to man from what it was when God made it to be his habitation.
Matthew Henry

The way of sin is downhill; a man cannot stop himself when he will.
Matthew Henry

Duty is the greatest liberty, and sin the greatest bondage.
Thomas Manton

He that hath slight thoughts of sin never had great thoughts of God.
John Owen

There is no death of sin without the death of Christ.
John Owen

Sin is worse than all other evils. It makes earth like hell, and it makes hell what it is. *William S. Plumer*

Sin is sovereign until sovereign grace dethrones it.
C. H. Spurgeon

Sin will reign if it can: it cannot be satisfied with any place below the throne of the heart. *C. H. Spurgeon*

No sin is small. It is against an infinite God and may have consequences immeasurable. No grain of sand is small in the mechanism of a watch. *Jeremy Taylor*

Pollution is the forerunner of perdition. *John Trapp*

Little sins unrepented of will damn thee as well as greater. Not only great rivers fall into the sea, but little brooks; not only greater sins carry men to hell, but lesser; therefore do not think pardon easy because sin is small.
Thomas Watson

SINCERITY
(See also: Honesty)

Be what you seem! Live your creed! *Horatius Bonar*

The Lord first of all wants sincerity in his service, simplicity of heart without guile and falsehood. *John Calvin*

Sincerity is the salt which seasons every sacrifice.
Stephen Charnock

Sincerity is the face of the soul. *S. Dubay*

Sincerity is the highest compliment you can pay.
Ralph Waldo Emerson

Be as you would seem to be.
Thomas Fuller

Sincerity! It is the life of all our graces and puts life into all our duties.
William Gurnall

Sincerity makes the soul willing. *William Gurnall*

No one can produce great things who is not thoroughly sincere in dealing with himself. *James Russell Lowell*

Never has there been one possessed of complete sincerity who did not move others. *Mencius*

Sincerity is of the essence of the life of godliness.

Iain Murray

We are to receive our reward not according to our success, but according to our sincerity. *John Oldfield*

To be true to convictions is the life of sincerity.

John Owen

The strength of every grace lies in the sincerity of it.

A. W. Pink

Whatever we are in our religion, let us resolve never to wear a cloak. Let us by all means be honest and real.

J. C. Ryle

Sincerity is the prime requisite in every approach to the God who requires 'truth in the inward parts' and who hates all hypocrisy, falsehood and deceit.

Geoffrey B. Wilson

SINFUL NATURE

(See also: Depravity; Guilt; Man — a Sinner; Sin)

Our sinful natures are neither removed at our regeneration nor refined by our sanctification.

Not only the worst of my sins, but the best of my duties speak me a child of Adam. *William Beveridge*

Man without God is a beast, and never more beastly than when he is most intelligent about his beastliness.

Whittaker Chambers

It is easier to denature plutonium than to denature the evil spirit of man.

Albert Einstein

Embellished nature is nature still. *John Flavel*

I have never heard of a sin being committed without knowing full well that I had the seed of it within myself.

Johann Wolfgang von Goethe

The flesh is the womb where all sin is conceived and formed, the anvil upon which all is wrought, the Judas that betrays us, the secret enemy within that is ready on all occasions to open the gates to the besiegers. *Thomas Jacomb*

All the old primitive sins are not dead but are crouching in the dark corners of our modern hearts — still there, and still as ghastly as ever.

Carl Gustav Jung

Original sin is in us, like the beard. We are shaved today and look clean, and have a

303

smooth chin; tomorrow our beard has grown again, nor does it cease growing while we remain on earth.
Martin Luther

No figure of speech can represent my utter want of power to resist the torrent of sin.
Robert Murray M'Cheyne

None but God knows what an abyss of corruption is in my heart.
Robert Murray M'Cheyne

The seeds of all sin are in my heart, and perhaps all the more dangerously that I do not see them.
Robert Murray M'Cheyne

It is one thing for sin to live in us; it is another for us to live in sin. *John Murray*

Flesh is an affection which focuses on the enjoyment of the creature, without primary reverence for and worship of the Creator.
Tom J. Nettles

The flesh is radically and wholly evil. *A. W. Pink*

No prayer is complete which does not contain a petition to be kept from the devil.
J. C. Ryle

The evil that is in us is all our own. *J. C. Ryle*

There is far more wickedness in all our hearts than we know. *J. C. Ryle*

The seeds of every wickedness lie hidden in our hearts. They only need the convenient season to spring forth into a mischievous vitality. *J. C. Ryle*

The Christian does not have to live in defeat, but he does have to live all his life with the sin nature ... and ... because God has not made flesh any better in the believer, because it has not been refined, it is a powerful enemy with which we have to live. *Charles Caldwell Ryrie*

All the devils in hell and tempters on earth could do us no injury if there were no corruption in our own natures. *C. H. Spurgeon*

Human nature ... is not a green apple to be perfected by mere growth, but an apple with a worm at the core, which left to itself will surely rot and perish.
Augustus H. Strong

The human personality has ... been invaded by an alien army which is always campaigning within it.
R. V. G. Tasker

Though we (as Christians) are like Christ, having the firstfruits of the Spirit, yet we are unlike him, having the remainders of the flesh.
Thomas Watson

SLANDER
(See also: Gossip; Rumour; Speech)

Slander is almost invariably verbal cowardice.

Slander, like coal, will either dirty your hand or burn it.
Anon.

The surest method against slander is to live it down by perseverance in well-doing.
Hermann Boerhaave

No one should say behind a man's back what he dare not, or would not, say to his face. *William Booth*

If you are slandered, never mind; it will all come off when it is dry.
Charles G. Finney

Lies and false reports are among Satan's choicest weapons. *J. C. Ryle*

SLEEP

For what else is sleep but a daily death which does not completely remove man hence nor detain him too long? And what else is death, but a very long and very deep sleep from which God arouses man? *Augustine*

Sleep is, in fine, so like death I dare not trust it without my prayers. *Thomas Fuller*

SOCIAL RESPONSIBILITY

However we do it, the Christian faith requires us to have sensitivity to social need and oppression. This is not a social gospel. This is not the gospel. It is a fruit of the gospel. *Alan Kreider*

A born-again Christian without a social conscience is irrelevant, and a social activist without a regenerate heart is irresponsible.
Gordon Moyes

Christianity was never meant to interfere with a man's obedience to the civil power. *J. C. Ryle*

Whatever makes men good Christians makes them good citizens. *Daniel Webster*

SORROW

Every lock of sorrow has a key of promise to fit it.
Anon.

Joys are our wings; sorrows are our spurs. *Anon.*

How fast we learn in a day of sorrow! *Horatius Bonar*

The heaviest thing in the world is a heavy heart.
John Burroughs

Sorrow is given us on purpose to cure us of sin.
Chrysostom

Christ takes no more delight to dwell in a sad heart than we do to live in a dark house.
William Gurnall

No marvel that our sorrows are multiplied when our sins are. *Matthew Henry*

Weeping must never hinder worship. *Matthew Henry*

Sorrows and joys alike are temporary. In a moment all may be changed. Therefore to one who judges rightly, earthly grief is not over grievous and earthly joy not over joyous. *J. B. Lightfoot*

There is no commentary that opens up the Bible so much as sickness and sorrow.
J. C. Ryle

This only can my fears control,
And bid my sorrows fly;
What harm can ever reach my soul
Beneath my Father's eye?
Anne Steele

All misery calls sin mother.
George Swinnock

There are such things as consecrated griefs, sorrows that may be common to everyone but which take on a special character when accepted intelligently and offered to God in loving submission. *A. W. Tozer*

Melancholy gives the devil great advantages; it pulls off the chariot wheels.

Thomas Watson

SOUL
(See also: Heart)

As God's eternal decrees have an end without a beginning, so the souls of men have a beginning without an end. *John Boys*

Soul is that by which we live naturally; spirit is that by which we live through grace supernaturally. *John Boys*

The soul is the breath of God, the beauty of man, the

wonder of angels and the envy of devils.
Thomas Brooks

As the man is more noble than the house he dwells in, so is the soul more noble than the body.
John Bunyan

The body is the prison of the soul. *John Calvin*

The soul, being a spirit, conveys more to the body than the body can to it.
Stephen Charnock

If the soul be lost, the man is lost. *John Flavel*

The soul pays a dear rent for the tenement it now lives in.
John Flavel

The soul is the man.
Matthew Henry

The real value of an object is that which one who knows its worth will give for it. He who made the soul knew its worth, and gave his life for it. *Arthur Jackson*

Your own soul is your first and greatest care.
Robert Murray M'Cheyne

Where the eternal interests of the soul are concerned, only a fool will give himself the benefit of the doubt.
A. W. Pink

The whole world cannot make up to a man for the loss of his soul. *J. C. Ryle*

Our souls are like the mill that grinds what is put into it. *Richard Sibbes*

None but God can satisfy the longings of the immortal soul; as the heart was made for him, he only can fill it.
Richard C. Trench

SOUL-WINNING
(See also: Evangelism; Witnessing)

A good fisherman keeps himself out of sight. *Anon.*

The greatest thing in life is to bring others to Jesus Christ. *Henry Ward Beecher*

Go for souls — and go for the worst! *William Booth*

Some men's passion is for gold. Some men's passion is for art. Some men's passion is for fame. My passion is for souls. *William Booth*

I cared not where or how I lived, or what hardships I went through, so that I could but gain souls to Christ. *David Brainerd*

There was nothing of any importance to me but holiness of heart and life, and the conversion of the Indians to God.   *David Brainerd*

Nothing is more useless than a Christian who does not try to save others ... I cannot believe in the salvation of anyone who does not work for his neighbour's salvation.
Chrysostom

The best publicity the gospel will ever have is a new Christian out to win others.
Vance Havner

If we do not catch men we are in danger of losing even the desire to catch them.
John Henry Jowett

I feel there are two things it is impossible to desire with sufficient ardour — personal holiness and the honour of Christ in the salvation of souls.
Robert Murray M'Cheyne

What would I not give for the power to make sinners love *him!*   *Edward Payson*

A man's religion may well be suspected when he is content to go to heaven alone.
J. C. Ryle

One single soul saved shall outlive and outweigh all the kingdoms of the world.
J. C. Ryle

What are all your kings, all your nobles, all your diadems, when you put them together, compared with the dignity of winning souls to Christ?   *C. H. Spurgeon*

You do not love the Lord at all unless you love the souls of others.   *C. H. Spurgeon*

I would rather win souls than be the greatest king or emperor on earth; I would rather win souls than be the greatest general that ever commanded an army ... My one ambition in life is to win as many as possible. Oh, it is the only thing worth doing, to save souls; and, men and women, we can all do it.   *R. A. Torrey*

SPEECH
(See also: Eloquence; Gossip; Rumour; Slander)

A sharp tongue is no evidence of a keen mind.
Anon.

No physician can heal the wounds inflicted by the tongue.   *Anon.*

One thing you can give and still keep is your word.
Anon.

The Christian should learn two things about his tongue: how to hold it and how to use it. *Anon.*

The tongue is but three inches long, yet it can kill a man six feet high. *Anon.*

Words are leaves — deeds are fruit. *Anon.*

It is a sad fact that the tongues of professing Christians are often all too busy doing the devil's work.
Donald Grey Barnhouse

Gentle words fall lightly, but they have great weight.
Derick Bingham

The vice of the tongue spreads and prevails over every part of life. It is as active and potent for evil in old age as ever it was in the days of our youth.
John Calvin

Kind words are the music of the world.
Frederick W. Faber

A sanctified heart is better than a silver tongue.
Thomas Goodwin

If the mouth be bad, the mind is not good.
Matthew Henry

There will come a time when three words, uttered with charity and meekness, shall receive a far more blessed reward than three thousand volumes written with disdainful sharpness of wit. *Richard Hooker*

Many people would be more truthful were it not for their uncontrollable desire to talk.
Edgar Watson Howe

An evil speaker is his own scourge. *William Jenkyn*

When the hands are idle, the tongue is usually very active.
Henry T. Mahan

A tongue that is set on fire from hell shall be set on fire in hell. *Thomas Manton*

Evil words show a wicked heart, and idle words a vain mind. *Thomas Manton*

A word spoken is physically transient but morally permanent. *J. C. Ryle*

Our words are the evidence of the state of our hearts as surely as the taste of the water is an evidence of the state of the spring.
J. C. Ryle

By the striking of the clapper we guess at the metal of the bell. *William Secker*

Speech

The word of a man is as powerful as himself.
Richard Sibbes

Tongues are more terrible instruments than can be made with hammers and anvils, and the evil which they inflict cuts deeper and spreads wider.
C. H. Spurgeon

The heart is the metal of the bell, the tongue but the clapper. *George Swinnock*

SPIRITUAL DARKNESS

It is no advantage to be near the light if the eyes are closed. *Augustine*

The blindness of unbelievers in no way detracts from the clarity of the gospel; the sun is no less bright because blind men do not perceive its light. *John Calvin*

A blind man will not thank you for a looking-glass.
Thomas Fuller

Man lives in the dark and even his nuclear flashlight cannot pierce it.
Vance Havner

Spiritual darkness is spiritual bondage.
Matthew Henry

Those that love darkness rather than light shall have their doom accordingly.
Matthew Henry

The penalty of living in the darkness is not merely that one does not see, but that one goes blind.
David Smith

Blindness is the cause of unbelief, whoever the unbeliever may be.
John R. W. Stott

The human intellect, even in its fallen state, is an awesome work of God, but it lies in darkness until it has been illuminated by the Holy Spirit. *A. W. Tozer*

A blind eye is worse than a lame foot. *Thomas Watson*

SPIRITUAL GIFTS

If we are proud of our talents we betray our lack of gratitude to God. *John Calvin*

If we listen to the instruction of Scripture we must remember that our talents are not of our own making, but free gifts of God.
John Calvin

Whatever ability a faithful Christian may possess, he

310

ought to possess it for his fellow believers, and he ought to make his own interest subservient to the well-being of the church in all sincerity.   *John Calvin*

To claim credit for the Lord's gifts to us or to undervalue our particular charisma is in either case to lose sight of the essential nature of any gift.
Herbert M. Carson

Salvation is promised to those who have the graces of the Spirit, but not to those who have merely the extraordinary gifts. Many have these last, and yet go to hell.
Jonathan Edwards

There is a great deal of unmapped country within us.   *George Eliot*

Grace is too much neglected where gifts are too highly prized.   *William Gurnall*

We cannot get Christ's gifts without himself.
Alexander Maclaren

All through the New Testament, when God's work in human lives is spoken of, the ethical takes priority over the charismatic.
J. I. Packer

The most significant gifts in the church's life in every era are ordinarily natural abilities sanctified.   *J. I. Packer*

It is very hard to behold our own gifts without pride, and the gifts of others without envy.   *Vavasor Powell*

Men forget that gifts without grace save no one's soul, and are the characteristics of Satan himself.   *J. C. Ryle*

We are all talented people. Anything whereby we may glorify God is a talent.
J. C. Ryle

SPIRITUAL HUNGER

A deep and sober daily concern to please God is the rarest of rareties.
Vance Havner

Desires for more grace, and groanings which cannot be uttered, are growing pains, and we should wish to feel them more and more.
C. H. Spurgeon

SPIRITUALITY

Spirituality is a work of God for his child; service is a work of the child for his

God, which can only be accomplished in the power of the indwelling Spirit.
Lewis Sperry Chafer

Spirituality is not gained by service; it is *unto* service.
Lewis Sperry Chafer

Spirituality is the genius of the gospel.
Stephen Charnock

No man is living at his best who is not living at his best spiritually.
W. Marshall Craig

The carnal mind sees God in nothing, not even in spiritual things. The spiritual mind sees him in everything, even in natural things.
Robert Leighton

In the biblical sense, the spiritual man is the man who has been begotten again, and has not had part of his nature but all of his nature transformed by the supernatural act of the Spirit of God.
J. Gresham Machen

Spirituality begins to have real meaning in our lives as we begin to exhibit simultaneously the holiness of God and the love of God.
Francis Schaeffer

In spiritual things there is no envy.
Richard Sibbes

SPIRITUAL RICHES

The saint's enduring riches are in the future, locked up in the heavenly casket.
George Barlow

Union with Christ entitles to all that is his.
Elisha Coles

Learn to put your hand on all spiritual blessings in Christ and say, 'Mine'.
F. B. Meyer

If ever you are tempted to say, 'I wish someone were to die and leave me something in his will,' allow me to tell you, 'Someone has!'
David Shepherd

There's a huge inheritance to be claimed by repenting sinners.
David Shepherd

God is the portion of his people, and the chosen people are the portion of their God.
C. H. Spurgeon

The All-Sufficient is sufficient for my largest want. He who is sufficient for earth and heaven is certainly able to meet the case of one poor worm like me.
C. H. Spurgeon

The way of uprightness is the way of heavenly wealth.
C. H. Spurgeon

SPIRITUAL WARFARE

All whom the Lord has chosen and received into the society of his saints ought to prepare themselves for a life that is hard, difficult, laborious and full of countless griefs. *John Calvin*

Scars are the price which every believer pays for his loyalty to Christ.
William Hendriksen

Regeneration has made our hearts a battlefield.
J. I. Packer

The believer may be known by his inward warfare as well as by his inward peace.
J. C. Ryle

Where there is grace there will be a conflict.
J. C. Ryle

STEWARDSHIP
(See also: Giving; Tithing)

Our temporary stewardship will determine our permanent ownership.

Stewardship is the acceptance from God of personal responsibility for all of life and life's affairs.
Roswell C. Long

STUBBORNNESS

A stiff neck usually supports an empty head. *Anon.*

Nothing is more like real conviction than simple obstinacy. *Anon.*

Man's impotency lies in his obstinacy. *Thomas Brooks*

SUBMISSION

Shall I, I pray Thee, change
  thy will my Father
Until it be according unto
  mine?
But no Lord, no, that never
  shall be, rather
I pray thee blend my human
  will with thine.
Amy Carmichael

The Lord is King! Who then
  shall dare
Resist his will, distrust his
  care,
Or murmur at his wise
  decrees,
Or doubt his royal promises?
Josiah Conder

Submission

Let him rule man who said,
'Let us make man.'
Matthew Henry

It has always been my ambition to have no plans as regards myself.
Robert Murray M'Cheyne

What I have to do, as his child, is to be satisfied with what my Father does, that I may glorify him.
George Müller

Man is most truly himself, not when he struts about in pride of ability and possession, but when he sees himself as a creature of God and submits to the will of his Creator which is his true happiness.
Warren A. Quanbeck

To bring our minds under Christ's yoke is not to deny our rationality but to submit to his revelation.
John R. W. Stott

We are not truly converted if we are not intellectually and morally converted, and we are not intellectually and morally converted if we have not subjected our minds and wills to the yoke of Jesus Christ.
John R. W. Stott

SUCCESS

The highest branch is not the safest roost.
Anon.

Even success in the Lord's work is a broken reed if we lean on it for security.
John W. Sanderson

The mania to succeed is a good thing perverted.
A. W. Tozer

The man who is elated by success and cast down by failure is still a carnal man. At best his fruit will have a worm in it.
A. W. Tozer

The resurrection and the judgement will demonstrate before all worlds who won and who lost. We can wait!
A. W. Tozer

Success without God only makes temporary friends and admirers.
Spiros Zodhiates

SUFFERING
(See also: Pain; Sickness; Trials)

Tears are often the telescope by which men see far into heaven.
Henry Ward Beecher

Those who sing loudest in the kingdom will be those who on earth had the great-

est bodily suffering. We pity them now, but then we shall almost envy them.
Andrew Bonar

Suffering . . . is the badge of the true Christian.
Dietrich Bonhoeffer

We must suffer patiently, because impatience is rebellion against the justice of God. *John Calvin*

Tears are part of existence on this earth. They have flowed from Eden right down through history to the present day. *Wayne Detzler*

I am convinced that the Christian answer to the question of suffering is positive and hopeful.
Brian Edwards

There is no authentic Christian service that does not have suffering written into it. *Donald English*

A Christian never moves so swiftly to heaven as when he is under a sanctified cross.
Andrew Gray

Suffering often awakens a consciousness of sin in the sufferer. *D. Edmond Hiebert*

Many parts of religion relate entirely to suffering, and every part receives a lustre from it. *William Jay*

There is a sanctity in suffering when meekly borne.
D. Jerrold

Suffering is a choice instrument for shaping character, and without its touch the most delicate chasing on the vessel would be impossible.
Ian Maclaren

There is a great want about all Christians who have not suffered. Some flowers must be broken or bruised before they emit any fragrance.
Robert Murray M'Cheyne

It is and should be the care of a Christian not to suffer for sin, nor sin in suffering.
Vavasor Powell

We must shed tears if we would hereafter have them wiped away.
Richard Sibbes

The best of saints have borne the worst of sufferings.
George Swinnock

It is worth noting that suffering only becomes a problem when we accept the existence of a good God.
David Watson

Suffering can often produce great depths of character, mature understanding, warm compassion and rich spirituality. *David Watson*

SUICIDE

We may not ourselves loose our souls, but let God let them out of prison.
John Boys

He that would not die when he must, and he that would die when he must not, are both of them cowards alike.
George Swinnock

SYMPATHY

God does not comfort us to make us comfortable but to make us comforters.
J. H. Jowett

It is good manners to be an unbidden guest at a house of mourning. *George Swinnock*

TEMPTATION — Avoiding and Resisting

Never invite trouble — it always accepts. *Anon.*

To realize God's presence is the one sovereign remedy against temptation.
François Fenelon

Unless there is within us that which is above us, we shall soon yield to that which is about us. *P. T. Forsyth*

If you don't want to trade with the devil, stay out of his shops. *Vance Havner*

Those that would avoid sin must not parley with temptation. *Matthew Henry*

Those that would be kept from harm must keep out of harm's way.
Matthew Henry

In the line of duty adult Christians are bound to face many temptations, but to expose oneself needlessly to temptation is to tempt God.
R. B. Kuiper

The more of the divine nature in you, the more you are able to stand against temptations. We are easily carried aside, because we have more of man than God in us. *Thomas Manton*

Temptation is like a knife, that may either cut the meat or the throat of a man; it may be his food or poison.
John Owen

Temptations . . . put nothing into a man, but only draw out what was in him before.
John Owen

He cannot smell sweetly who sleeps in a bed of garlic.
C. H. Spurgeon

Learn to say 'No'; it will be of more use to you than to be able to read Latin.

C. H. Spurgeon

One reason that sin flourishes is that it is treated like a cream-puff instead of a rattle-snake. *Billy Sunday*

It is not laying the bait that hurts the fish if the fish do not bite. *Thomas Watson*

Temptation is a trial of our sincerity. *Thomas Watson*

TEMPTATION — Blessing

Find out what your temptations are and you will find out largely what you are yourself.

Henry Ward Beecher

Temptation has its uses. As we grapple we grow.

E. Stanley Jones

TEMPTATION — Certainty

Temptations, like foul weather, come before we send for them. *Anon.*

Christ is no sooner out of the waters of baptism than he is in the fires of temptation; whence we learn that great manifestations of the love of God are usually followed with great temptations from Satan. *Francis Burkitt*

There are as many forms of temptation as there are Christians.

Edward Donnelly

Some temptations come to the industrious, but all temptations attack the idle.

C. H. Spurgeon

TEMPTATION — and Satan

There is a spark of hell in every temptation.

William Gurnall

All Satan's temptations . . . are so many 'welcome' notices along the broad road that leads to destruction.

J. I. Packer

TEMPTATION — and Sin

Temptation is the fire that brings up the sum of the heart. *Thomas Boston*

Let us beware of making light of temptations because

317

they seem little and insignificant. There is nothing little that concerns our souls.

J. C. Ryle

THANKSGIVING

(See also: Gratitude)

I give it as my testimony that there is a marvellous therapy in thanksgiving.

God's giving deserves our thanksgiving. *Anon.*

As the Lord loves a cheerful giver, so likewise a cheerful thanksgiver. *John Boys*

We should spend as much time in thanking God for his benefits as we do in asking him for them.

Vincent de Paul

The thankfulness of the receiver ought to answer to the benefit of the bestower as the echo answers to the voice.

Thomas Fuller

Thanksgiving is an act of self-denial. *William Gurnall*

Every stream should lead us to the fountain.

Matthew Henry

In thanking God, we fasten upon his favours to us; in praising and adoring God,

we fasten upon his perfections in himself.

Matthew Henry

Every virtue divorced from thankfulness is maimed and limps along the spiritual road. *John Henry Jowett*

Thankfulness is a flower which will never bloom well excepting upon a root of deep humility. *J. C. Ryle*

He enjoys much who is thankful for little.

William Secker

Our thanks should be as fervent for mercies received, as our petitions sought.

Charles Simmons

It is sad when there is nothing for which we feel grateful to God, but it is serious when there is something and we fail to show gratitude. *William Still*

Thanks must be given and held as still due.

John Trapp

Thanking God for whatever he gives us is one sure way of resisting the devil.

Spiros Zodhiates

THEOLOGY
(See also: Bible; Doctrine)

None but a theology that came out of eternity can carry you and me safely to and through eternity.
T. L. Cuyler

The basic questions of all theology are 'Who is God?' and 'Who is man?'
R. B. Kuiper

Let us come to Jesus — the person of Christ is the centre of theology. *H. B. Smith*

Theology is a rational necessity. *Augustus H. Strong*

The secret of life is theological and the key to heaven as well. *A. W. Tozer*

We being what we are and all things else being what they are, the most important and profitable study any one of us can engage in is without question the study of theology. *A. W. Tozer*

The plague of Christendom has been the passion of theology to define what God has not defined and to discover what he has kept secret. *Henry Van Dyke*

THOUGHTS
(See also: Mind)

Give burning thoughts time before they become flaming words. *Anon.*

Our minds are mental greenhouses where unlawful thoughts, once planted, are nurtured and watered before being transplanted into the real world of unlawful actions. *Jerry Bridges*

If you would voyage Godward, you must see to it that the rudder of thought is right. *W. J. Dawson*

The actions of men are the best interpreters of their thoughts. *John Locke*

Thoughts are the spies and messengers of the soul.
Thomas Manton

We grow like the things we think about.
Daniel L. Marsh

Thoughts, even more than overt acts, reveal character.
William S. Plumer

Ill thoughts are little thieves.
Richard Sibbes

Every normal person can determine what he will think about. *A. W. Tozer*

319

Thoughts

Whatever engages my attention when I should be meditating on God and things eternal does injury to my soul.   *A. W. Tozer*

What we think about when we are free to think about what we will — that is what we are or will soon become.   *A. W. Tozer*

TIME — and Eternity

Time is a file that wears and makes no noise.   *Anon.*

Time writes no wrinkle on the brow of the Eternal.   *Anon.*

If we look around us, a moment can seem a long time, but when we lift up our hearts heavenwards, a thousand years begin to be like a moment.   *John Calvin*

God doesn't rush men; he owns time.   *John Hercus*

God created time when he created finite things.   *J. Gresham Machen*

All space of time should be small to them that know the greatness of eternity.   *Thomas Manton*

Eternity depends upon this moment.   *Thomas Manton*

There is a time appointed by the Father when the whole machinery of creation shall stop, and the present dispensation shall be changed for another.   *J. C. Ryle*

We give so little thought to the fact that God made time as a preparation for eternity, and this earth the place where we acquire our entry either to heaven or hell.   *Spiros Zodhiates*

TIME — Misuse

Wasting time is a kind of unarmed robbery.

Time can be wasted, but it can never be re-cycled.   *Anon.*

As good have no time as make no good use of it.   *Thomas Fuller*

All that time is lost which might be better employed.   *Jean Jacques Rousseau*

TIME — Urgency

Time never takes time off.   *Augustine*

320

One today is worth two tomorrows.
Benjamin Franklin

There is not a single moment in life that we can afford to lose. *Edward M. Goulburn*

Time is urgency.
Paul S. Rees

We have much to do and little time in which to get it done! *A. W. Tozer*

TIME — Use

We are to redeem the time because we ourselves are redeemed. *Richard Chester*

The surest method of arriving at a knowledge of God's eternal purposes about us is to be found in the right use of the present moment. Each hour comes with some little faggot of God's will fastened upon its back. *Frederick W. Faber*

Have you time enough to eat, to drink, to sleep, to talk unprofitably, it may be corruptly, in all sorts of unnecessary societies, but have not time to live unto God?
John Owen

TITHING
(See also: Giving; Stewardship)

Shall we grudge the expenses of our religion, or starve so good a cause?
Matthew Henry

We are all congenitally allergic to tithing.
R. T. Kendall

If you are not a tither you are a robber.
Stephen Olford

TOLERANCE

Tolerance is seeing certain things with your heart instead of your eyes.
Anon.

In the great things of religion, be of a mind: but when there is not a unity of sentiment, let there be a union of affections.
Matthew Henry

We ought not to make any conditions of our brother's acceptance with us but such as God has made the conditions of their acceptance with him. *Matthew Henry*

TRIALS — Blessings
(See also: Pain; Sickness; Suffering)

For the Christian, trials and temptations are not only means for proving his faith but for improving his life.

The Christian's midnight is brighter than the sinner's noon.

Affliction is the school of faith.   *Anon.*

Afflictions are often God's best blessings sent in disguise.   *Anon.*

Some hearts, like evening primroses, open more beautifully in the shadows of life.
                    Anon.

The Christian justifies tribulation. Ten thousand times ten thousand saints . . . are ready to witness that their most manifest and rapid spiritual growth is traceable to their periods of trial.
                    Anon.

The darker the night, the brighter the stars; the hotter the fire, the purer the gold.
                    Anon.

The hammer shatters glass, but forges steel.   *Anon.*

The more a tree of righteousness is shaken by the wind, the more it is rooted in Christ.   *Anon.*

Trial is the school of trust.
                    Anon.

Where there are no trials in life, there are no triumphs.
                    Anon.

We have got more from Paul's prison-house than from his visit to the third heavens.   *Andrew Bonar*

It is the usual way of providence with me that blessings come through several iron gates.   *Thomas Boston*

Afflictions are blessings.
                    Thomas Brooks

Afflictions are the mother of virtue.   *Thomas Brooks*

Afflictions, they are but our Father's goldsmiths who are working to add pearls to our crowns.   *Thomas Brooks*

God's house of correction is his school of instruction.
                    Thomas Brooks

Stars shine brightest in the darkest night. Torches are the better for beating. Grapes come not to the proof till they come to the press. Spices smell sweetest when pounded. Young trees root the faster for shaking.

Vines are the better for bleeding. Gold looks the brighter for scouring; and juniper smells sweeter in the fire.   *Thomas Brooks*

The vinegar of adversity quickens our graces.
                    Thomas Brooks

The Lord uses his flail of tribulation to separate the chaff from the wheat.
                    John Bunyan

Our faith is really and truly tested only when we are brought into very severe conflicts, and when even hell itself seems opened to swallow us up.
                    John Calvin

The more we are afflicted by adversities, the more surely our fellowship with Christ is confirmed!   *John Calvin*

Affliction makes saints eminent.   *Chrysostom*

It is not until we have passed through the furnace that we are made to know how much dross there is in our composition.   *C. C. Colton*

There is no education like adversity. *Benjamin Disraeli*

Fiery trials make golden Christians.   *William Dyer*

Eminent virtue always shows brightest in the fire. Pure gold shows its purity chiefly in the furnace.
                Jonathan Edwards

Afflictions are continued no longer than till they have done their work.
                Matthew Henry

Afflictions are sent for this end, to bring us to the throne of grace, to teach us to pray and to make the word of God's grace precious to us.   *Matthew Henry*

Extraordinary afflictions are not always the punishment of extraordinary sins, but sometimes the trial of extraordinary graces.
                Matthew Henry

If we cry to God for the removal of the oppression and affliction we are under, and it is not removed, the reason is not because the Lord's hand is shortened or his ear heavy, but because the affliction has not done its work.   *Matthew Henry*

It has been the advantage of God's people to be afflicted.
                Matthew Henry

Many are taught with the briars and thorns of affliction that would not learn otherwise.
                Matthew Henry

Of the many that are afflicted and oppressed, few get the good they might get by their affliction. It should drive them to God, but how seldom is this the case!
Matthew Henry

Outward losses drive good people to their prayers, but bad people to their curses.
Matthew Henry

The injuries men do us should drive us to God, for to him we may commit our cause. *Matthew Henry*

Afflictions are the cause of eternal glory. Not the meritorious cause, but still the procuring cause.
Charles Hodge

Afflictions are unavoidable; they occupy a large proportion of life, and of godliness. *William Jay*

The Christian is more formed from his trials than from his enjoyments.
William Jay

As the wicked are hurt by the best things, so the godly are bettered by the worst.
William Jenkyn

Trouble is only opportunity in work clothes.
Henry J. Kaiser

Affliction is the Christian's theologian. *Martin Luther*

No man, without trials and temptations, can attain a true understanding of the Holy Scriptures.
Martin Luther

We should never see the stars if God did not sometimes take away the day.
Kenneth Macrae

God's children never gain so much honour as in their troubles. *Thomas Manton*

Trial is not only to approve, but to improve.
Thomas Manton

A dark hour makes Jesus bright.
Robert Murray M'Cheyne

No pain, no palm; no thorns, no throne; no gall, no glory; no cross, no crown.
William Penn

The hiding places of men are discovered by affliction.
S. I. Prime

Afflictions clarify the soul.
Francis Quarles

In the resurrection morning . . . we shall thank God for every storm. *J. C. Ryle*

Let us settle it firmly in our minds that there is a meaning, a needs-be and a message from God in every sorrow that falls upon us.
J. C. Ryle

Prosperity is a great mercy, but adversity is a greater one, if it brings us to Christ.
J. C. Ryle

There are no lessons so useful as those learned in the school of affliction.
J. C. Ryle

The tools that the great Architect intends to use much are often kept long in the fire, to temper them and fit them for work.
J. C. Ryle

Trials are intended to make us think, to wean us from the world, to send us to the Bible, to drive us to our knees.   *J. C. Ryle*

Poverty and affliction take away the fuel that feeds pride.   *Richard Sibbes*

When the afflictions of Christians are doubled, then they are commonly most humbled.   *Richard Sibbes*

Our troubles have always brought us blessings, and they always will. They are the dark chariots of bright grace.   *C. H. Spurgeon*

The tears of affliction are often needed to keep the eye of faith bright.
C. H. Spurgeon

Cold blasts make a fire to flame the higher and burn the better.   *George Swinnock*

God's rod, like Jonathan's, is dipped in honey.
George Swinnock

Despise not the desert. There is where God polishes his brightest gems.
R. A. Torrey

As the hotter the day the greater the dew at night; so the hotter the time of trouble the greater the dews of refreshing from God.
John Trapp

Better be pruned to grow than cut up to burn.
John Trapp

Affliction is God's flail to thresh off our husks.
Thomas Watson

There is more evil in a drop of sin than in a sea of affliction.   *Thomas Watson*

When God lays men on their backs, then they look up to heaven.   *Thomas Watson*

TRIALS — Certainty

God's people are not without trial — nor without God in time of trial. *Anon.*

No man has a velvet cross.
John Flavel

None are crowned till they have striven.
Thomas Goodwin

Christ went by the cross to the crown, and we must not think of going any other way. *Matthew Henry*

As the way to Canaan lay through a howling wilderness and desert, so the path to heaven lies through much affliction. *Thomas Manton*

Crosses seldom come single.
Thomas Manton

To hold on to the plough while wiping our tears, that is Christianity.
Watchman Nee

The grace of God exempts no one from trouble.
J. C. Ryle

God hath called you to Christ's side and the wind is now in Christ's face in this land; and seeing ye are with him, ye cannot expect the lee-side or the sunny side of the brae. *Samuel Rutherford*

How can I look to be at home in the enemy's country, joyful while in exile, or comfortable in a wilderness? This is not my rest. This is the place of the furnace and the forge and the hammer.
C. H. Spurgeon

While there is a devil and a wicked man in the world never expect a charter of exemption from trouble.
Thomas Watson

TRIALS — God the Sender

God sometimes puts us in the dark to show us he is the light.

God breaks the cistern to bring us to the fountain.
Anon.

God loves his people when he strikes them as well as when he strokes them.
Anon.

Those whom God loves he takes to pieces; and then puts them together again.
Anon.

Paradoxical as it may seem, God means not only to make us good, but to make us also happy, by sickness, disaster and disappointment.
C. A. Bartol

Our Father does not afflict to destroy or ruin us, but rather to deliver us from the condemnation of the world.
John Calvin

It is a great thing, when the cup of bitterness is pressed to our lips, to feel that it is not fate or necessity, but divine love working on us for our good ends.   *E. H. Chapin*

I had rather have God's vinegar than man's oil, God's wormwood than man's manna.   *John Donne*

God's pruning is purposeful.
Sinclair Ferguson

Trials . . . are not threats to God's purposes, but further indications of how meticulously faithful he is to that purpose.   *Sinclair Ferguson*

God retains his kindness for his people even when he afflicts them.
Matthew Henry

God's design in afflicting his people is their probation, not their destruction; their advantage, not their ruin.
Matthew Henry

Winds and clouds are in God's hands, are designed to try us, and our Christianity obliges us to endure hardness.   *Matthew Henry*

God sends us miseries, not to make us worse but to make us better.   *Thomas Manton*

I always feel much need of God's afflicting hand.
Robert Murray M'Cheyne

If nothing else will do to sever me from my sins, Lord send me such sore and trying calamities as shall awake me from earthly slumbers.
Robert Murray M'Cheyne

If we only saw the whole, we should see that the Father is doing little else in the world but training his vines.
Robert Murray M'Cheyne

Trials are medicines which our gracious and wise physician prescribes, because we need them; and he proportions the frequency and weight of them to what the case requires.   *John Newton*

Affliction is a talent . . . entrusted to us by God, which he expects us to improve to his glory and to our own everlasting good.
Brownlow North

An affliction at God's hands is better than a joy of our own creation.
William S. Plumer

By afflictions God is spoiling us of what otherwise might

have spoiled us. When he makes the world too hot for us to hold, we let go.
Thomas Powell

I bless the Lord that all our troubles come through Christ's fingers, and that he casts sugar among them.
Samuel Rutherford

I would wish each cross were looked in the face seven times, and were read over and over again. It is the messenger of the Lord and speaks something.
Samuel Rutherford

Every cross is a message from God and intended to do us good in the end.
J. C. Ryle

Affliction is not sent in vain from the good God who chastens those he loves.
Robert Southey

It is the Lord's way to tear before he heals. This is the honest love of his heart and the sure surgery of his hand.
C. H. Spurgeon

Our Lord's letters often come to us in black-edged envelopes. *C. H. Spurgeon*

God and adversity will be good company.
George Swinnock

A sculptor does not use a manicure set to reduce the rude, unshapely marble to a thing of beauty.
A. W. Tozer

God is ingenious in making us crosses. *A. W. Tozer*

If God has singled you out to be a special object of his grace you may expect him to honour you with stricter discipline and greater suffering than less favoured ones are called upon to endure.
A. W. Tozer

God never promises to save us from adversity, only to be with us in the midst of it.
David Watson

Whoever brings an affliction, it is God who sends it.
Thomas Watson

The God of circumstances will not place one upon us that is heavier than we can bear. *Spiros Zodhiates*

TRIALS — Response

Come then, affliction, if my Father wills, and be my frowning friend. A friend that frowns is better than a smiling enemy. *Anon.*

If you are swept off your feet, it's time to get on your knees. *Fred Beck*

Trials always change our relationship with God. Either they drive us to him, or they drive us away from him. *Jerry Bridges*

A gracious soul may look through the darkest cloud and see a God smiling on him. *Thomas Brooks*

If you would not have affliction visit you twice, listen at once to what it teaches. *James Burgh*

Lord, how happy it is when strong afflictions from thee raise in us strong affections for thee! *Francis Burkitt*

In every affliction, we ought immediately to review our past life. When we do so, we shall certainly find that we have deserved such chastisement. *John Calvin*

Learn how to suffer, for that is the most important of all lessons. *François Fenelon*

If the sun of God's countenance shine upon me, I may well be content with the rain of affliction. *Joseph Hall*

Perils and frights should drive us *to* God, not *from* him. *Matthew Henry*

Such is the nature of our trials that while they last we cannot see the end. *Martin Luther*

The cup which the Saviour giveth me, can it be anything but a cup of salvation? *Alexander Maclaren*

A Christian is a bird that can sing in winter as well as in spring. *Thomas Manton*

Seek holiness rather than consolation. *John Owen*

Saints must be best in worst times. *Samuel Rutherford*

Why should I start at the plough of my Lord, that maketh the deep furrows on my soul? I know he is no idle husbandman; he purposeth a harvest. *Samuel Rutherford*

Be it ours, when we cannot see the face of God, to trust under the shadow of his wings. *C. H. Spurgeon*

Faith always sees the bow of covenant promise whenever sense sees the cloud of affliction. *C. H. Spurgeon*

Let us love a chiding God. *C. H. Spurgeon*

TRIALS — Temporary Nature

The skirmish may be sharp, but it cannot last long. The cloud, while it drops, is passing over thy head; then comes fair weather and an eternal sunshine of glory.
William Gurnall

What matter in eternity the slight awkwardnesses of time?
Robert Murray M'Cheyne

He who has fixed the bounds of our habitation has also fixed the bounds of our tribulation. *C. H. Spurgeon*

The punishment of sin is everlasting, but the fatherly chastisement of it in a child of God is but for a season.
C. H. Spurgeon

The rod may make us smart, but the sword shall not make us die. *C. H. Spurgeon*

Affliction has a sting, but withal a wing; sorrow shall fly away. *Thomas Watson*

Correction may befall the saint, but not destruction.
Thomas Watson

TRUTH
(See also: Honesty)

Truth exists; only falsehood has to be invented.
George Braque

Keep the truth and the truth will keep you.
William Bridge

I thirst for truth, but shall not reach it till I reach the source. *Robert Browning*

The grandest homage we can pay to truth is to use it.
Ralph Waldo Emerson

The farther a soul stands from the light of truth, the farther he must needs be from the heat of comfort.
William Gurnall

Truth famine is the ultimate and worst of all famines.
Carl F. H. Henry

Without truth there is no goodness. *Matthew Henry*

O faithful Christian, search the truth, hear truth, learn truth, love truth, speak the truth, hold the truth till death. *John Hus*

Truth reforms as well as informs. *William Jenkyn*

According to Christianity, the acid test of truth and goodness is scripturalness.
R. B. Kuiper

Truths are concocted and ripened by meditation.
Thomas Manton

God and his truth cannot be changed; the gospel is not negotiable. *John Marshall*

Truth must not be suppressed because men are wicked and blind.
Wolfgang Musculus

Truth lives in the cellar, error on the doorstep.
Austin O'Malley

We have the truth and we need not be afraid to say so.
J. C. Ryle

Truth without godliness is a human knowledge of divine things. *Richard Sibbes*

It is in the way of truth that real peace is found.
C. H. Spurgeon

It is more to God's glory that the world should be conquered by the force of truth than by the blaze of miracles.
C. H. Spurgeon

Opinions alter, but truth certified by God can no more change than the God who uttered it.
C. H. Spurgeon

The practice of truth is the most profitable reading of it.
C. H. Spurgeon

Truth wears well.
C. H. Spurgeon

Truth engages the citadel of the human heart and is not satisfied until it has conquered everything there.
A. W. Tozer

We should never retreat before truth simply because we cannot explain it.
A. W. Tozer

Truth seldom goes without a scratched face. *John Trapp*

Truth is not ashamed of its name of nakedness; it can walk openly and boldly.
Ralph Venning

UNBELIEF
(See also: Atheism)

In all unbelief there are these two things: a good opinion of one's self and a bad opinion of God.
Horatius Bonar

Unbelief

Can any man perish more justly than they who refuse to be saved? *John Calvin*

The blindness of unbelievers in no way detracts from the clarity of the gospel; the sun is no less bright because blind men do not perceive its light. *John Calvin*

As faith is the greatest grace, so that which is opposite to it must be the greatest sin.
Stephen Charnock

Is not he as much guilty of his own death that rejects a medicine as he that cuts his own throat?
Stephen Charnock

When God is not believed we must needs give credit to the devil. *Stephen Charnock*

Christ distinguished between doubt and unbelief. Doubt says, 'I can't believe.' Unbelief says, 'I won't believe.' Doubt is honest. Unbelief is obstinate.
Henry Drummond

Unbelief is always conceited.
Richard Glover

Gospel light is justly taken away from those that endeavour to extinguish it.
Matthew Henry

Nothing is more offensive to God than disbelief of his promise and despair of the performance of it because of some difficulties that seem to lie in the way.
Matthew Henry

There are those who will trust Christ no further than they can see him . . . ; as if he were tied to our methods, and could not draw water without our buckets.
Matthew Henry

Unbelief is apt to mistake recruits for enemies, and to draw dismal conclusions even from comfortable premises.
Matthew Henry

Unbelief is the great obstruction to Christ's favours. *Matthew Henry*

Unbelief may truly be called the great damning sin, because it leaves us under the guilt of all our other sins; it is a sin against the remedy.
Matthew Henry

Unbelief, or distrust of God, is a sin that is its own punishment. *Matthew Henry*

Unbelief is a matter not only of the head but of the heart. The unbeliever's trouble is that his heart is not right with God. *R. B. Kuiper*

Unbelief is radically all other disobedience.
Robert Leighton

Birds lack faith. They fly away when I enter the orchard, though I mean them no ill. Even so do we lack faith in God.
Martin Luther

Unbelief is the mother of sin, and misbelief the nurse of it.
Thomas Manton

Unbelief is far, far more than entertaining an erroneous conception of God's way of salvation: it is a species of hatred against him.
A. W. Pink

Unbelief is not simply an infirmity of fallen human nature, it is a heinous crime.
A. W. Pink

If men do not have eternal life it is never because God did not love them, or because Christ was not given for them, but because they did not believe on Christ.
J. C. Ryle

No sin makes less noise, but none so surely damns the soul, as unbelief.
J. C. Ryle

Unbelief about the existence and personality of Satan has often proved the first step to unbelief about God.
J. C. Ryle

We can never be too much on our guard against unbelief. It is the oldest sin in the world. *J. C. Ryle*

Unbelief is so deeply rooted in the human heart that when God performs miracles on earth, unbelief doubts whether he can perform them in heaven, and when he does them in heaven, whether he can do them on earth. *Friedrich Tholuck*

Human unbelief cannot alter the character of God.
A. W. Tozer

I do not believe there is anybody who ever rejects Jesus Christ on philosophical grounds. The man who continues in his rejection of Christ has a pet sin somewhere — he's in love with iniquity. *A. W. Tozer*

The root of all apostasy is the primal sin of unbelief.
Geoffrey B. Wilson

URGENCY

Live your best, and act your best, and think your best each day, for there may be no tomorrows. *Anon.*

Urgency

Paul's calendar had only two days — 'today' and 'that day'.   *Anon.*

It is later than it has ever been before, and the smartest thing any man can do is to set his watch by God's clock.
Vance Havner

Opportunity is headlong bald behind, having never a lock to catch hold of.
Christopher Nesse

Opportunities are for eternity, but not to eternity.
William Secker

VANITY

Of all our infirmities, vanity is the dearest to us; a man will starve his other vices to keep that alive.
Benjamin Franklin

A vain mind is as bad, and as odious to God, as a vicious life.   *Thomas Manton*

It is hard to carry a full cup without spilling, and not to lift up ourselves when we are raised up by God.
Thomas Manton

Vanity is the fruit of ignorance.   *Alexander Ross*

VIGILANCE

Let us be as watchful after the victory as before the battle.   *Andrew Bonar*

Christian, seek not yet repose;
Cast thy dreams of ease away;
Thou art in the midst of foes:
Watch and pray.
Charlotte Elliott

All sins are rooted in love of pleasure. Therefore be watchful.   *Thomas Manton*

When we partake of the divine nature, we do not put off the human; we ought to walk with care, but yet with comfort.   *Thomas Manton*

If we know anything of true, saving religion, let us ever beware of the beginnings of backsliding.   *J. C. Ryle*

VIOLENCE
(See also: War)

Where violence reigns, reason is weak.
Sebastien Chamfort

Any man who knows the nature of his own heart realizes that violence is not another man's problem.
Os Guinness

334

Violence is normal in a fallen world.   *Os Guinness*

Violence is an involuntary quest for identity.
Marshall McLuhan

VIRTUE
(See also: Ethics; Goodness; Morality)

Virtue consists in doing our duty in the various relations we sustain to ourselves, to our fellowmen and to God, as it is made known by reason, revelation and providence.   *Archibald Alexander*

Virtue is the only true nobility.   *Anon.*

Negative virtue is not enough; we must do good.
William S. Plumer

Virtue is a state of war, and to live in it we have always to combat with ourselves.
Jean-Jacques Rousseau

VOWS

Many resolutions are like impressions made on the sand: the first wave washes them away.   *Anon.*

Christians are not to make vows to God. Sometimes the devil tempts us along this line, but it is only a shrewd attempt to get us back on the ground of law, where we can be dealt a heavy blow.
Donald Grey Barnhouse

Good resolutions are like cheques drawn on a bank where you have no account.
Oscar Wilde

WAR
(See also: Violence)

War is pleasant to those who never tried it.   *John Calvin*

Woes may come from peace but they must come from war.   *Thomas Fuller*

During war we imprison the rights of man.
Jean Giraudoux

The noise of war drowns the voice of laws.   *John Trapp*

WEALTH
(See also: Materialism; Money; Possessions; Prosperity; Riches)

Whenever wealth keeps a man from thinking about God it is not a blessing but a curse.

335

The two great tests of character are wealth and poverty. *Anon.*

It is only when the rich are sick that they fully feel the impotence of wealth.
C. C. Colton

Disquieting care is the common fruit of an abundance of this world, and the common fault of those that have abundance. *Matthew Henry*

Worldlings make gold their god; saints make God their gold. *Matthew Henry*

God gave us wealth, not that we should be hoarders but dispensers. *Thomas Manton*

Wealth often ends in pride.
Thomas Manton

Wealth is no mark of God's favour. Poverty is no mark of God's displeasure.
J. C. Ryle

Wealth ruins far more souls than poverty. *J. C. Ryle*

WILL
(See also: Free Will)

What the foot is to the body, the will is to the soul.
William Gurnall

What we call the will is just the whole person making choices. *J. Gresham Machen*

Will is character in action.
William McDougall

The will itself is not weak or strong; it is our motivation that is weak or strong.
John Powell

The root of all evil in human nature is the corruption of the will. *A. W. Tozer*

WILL OF GOD
(See also: Guidance; Providence)

A man in the centre of God's will is never 'just' anything.

God's will is the rule of righteousness, and his righteousness is the rule of his will. *Elisha Coles*

Inside the will of God there is no failure. Outside the will of God there is no success.
Bernard Edinger

It should be the aim of every Christian to have his will directed by the will of God revealed in Scripture.
Sinclair Ferguson

Only in obedience can we discover the great joy of the will of God.
Sinclair Ferguson

There is no avoiding, and no substitute for, the sometimes long, arduous experience of discovering the will of God in our own lives.
Sinclair Ferguson

The will of God is shaped in the image of his Son's cross.
Sinclair Ferguson

The will of God means death to our own will, and resurrection only when we have died to all our own plans.
Sinclair Ferguson

Wisdom and the will of God are intimately related . . . Nothing is more vital for practical knowledge of the purposes of God than wisdom.
Sinclair Ferguson

Seek neither more nor less than God's will for you.
Vance Havner

Doing the will of God leaves me no time for disputing about his plans.
George Macdonald

The choices of God's will are always — not sometimes, but always — determined by the ends which his infinite knowledge and his infinite wisdom place before him.
J. Gresham Machen

That soul shall have his will of God who desires nothing but what God will.
William Secker

Whether you shall live to reach home today or not depends absolutely upon God's will.   *C. H. Spurgeon*

Opposition to the divine will is the very essence of all sin.
David Thomas

The greatest folly in the universe is to oppose the will of God.   *David Thomas*

The will of God is the place of blessed, painful, fruitful trouble!   *A. W. Tozer*

WISDOM

True wisdom is a divine revelation.   *George Barlow*

Wisdom has never made a bigot, but learning has.
Josh Billings

Nearly all the wisdom we possess, that is to say, true and sound wisdom, consists of two parts: the knowledge of God and of ourselves.
John Calvin

Knowledge is the fountain of wisdom.   *Stephen Charnock*

Wisdom

There is no solid wisdom but in true piety.   *John Evelyn*

Wisdom and the will of God are intimately related ... Nothing is more vital for practical knowledge of the purpose of God than wisdom.   *Sinclair Ferguson*

Heavenly wisdom is better than worldly wealth, and to be preferred before it.
Matthew Henry

It is better to get wisdom than gold. Gold is another's, wisdom is our own; gold is for the body and time, wisdom for the soul and eternity.   *Matthew Henry*

Such is the degeneracy of human nature that there is no true wisdom to be found with any but those who are born again and who, through grace, partake of the divine nature.
Matthew Henry

Wisdom opens the eyes both to the glories of heaven and to the hollowness of earth.
J. A. Motyer

If the Lord Jesus Christ is a stranger to you, the best you can hope for is to become a philosopher, like Socrates of old. But apart from Christ there is no wisdom.
Spiros Zodhiates

The one who has wisdom in his head and heart does not need to shout at others.
Spiros Zodhiates

Wisdom, the wisdom of God, is not something that is acquired by man, but something that is bestowed by God upon his elect. It is a divine endowment and not a human acquisition.
Spiros Zodhiates

WITNESSING
(See also: Evangelism; Soul-Winning)

The secret of reaching men is to know the secret of reaching God.

We are called not merely to be advocates of Christianity but witnesses to Christ.

Anyone who is not doing personal work has sin in his life.   *C. M. Alexander*

We are not Christ's lawyers; we are his witnesses.
Anon.

Every believer is a witness whether he wants to be or not.   *Donald Grey Barnhouse*

Cry the gospel with your whole life.
Charles de Foucauld

Jesus, and shall it ever be,
A mortal man ashamed of thee,
Ashamed of thee, whom angels praise,
Whose glories shine through endless days?
Joseph Grigg

Witnessing is not just something a Christian says, but what a Christian is.
Richard C. Halverson

Wherever we go, let us not fail to take our religion along with us. *Matthew Henry*

In the New Testament we find the prophethood as well as the priesthood of all believers. *Geoffrey R. King*

A Christian is the world's Bible — and some of them need revising.
D. L. Moody

Our secrets are for sharing.
J. A. Motyer

I was never fit to say a word to a sinner, except when I had a broken heart myself.
Edward Payson

We are not responsible for conversion, but we are responsible for contact.
A. T. Pierson

Faithful witness is truth telling, not head counting.
Don Posterski

Love — and the unity it attests to — is the mark Christ gave Christians to wear before the world. Only with this mark may the world know that Christians are indeed Christians and that Jesus was sent by the Father. *Francis Schaeffer*

To be a witness does not consist of engaging in propaganda or in stirring people up. It means to live in such a way that one's life would not make sense if God did not exist. *Emmanuel Suhard*

The light of religion ought not to be carried in a dark lantern. *George Swinnock*

WORK

A lot can be achieved by an ounce of talent and a ton of hard work.

Every Christian should pursue excellence of workmanship and service in whatever vocational calling he finds himself.
Jerry Bridges

Service to God through service to mankind is the only motivation acceptable to God for diligence and hard work in our vocational calling. *Jerry Bridges*

He who disregards his calling will never keep the straight path in the duties of his work.   *John Calvin*

Do your work with your whole heart and you will succeed — there is so little competition!
Elbert Hubbard

The best preparation for good work tomorrow is to do good work today.
Elbert Hubbard

Throw your soul into the work as if your one employer were the Lord!
R. C. H. Lenski

Work for the world is done best when work for God is done first.
John C. Ryland

No labour is servile when the Lord's approval is the paramount consideration.
Geoffrey B. Wilson

WORLD

(See also: Worldliness)

The world counterfeits every Christian grace, but never is able to produce a coin with the right ring.
Donald Grey Barnhouse

As long as there are spots in the moon it is vain to expect anything spotless under it.
Thomas Fuller

The world's smiles are more dangerous than its frowns.
Matthew Henry

Enemy-occupied territory — that is what the world is.
C. S. Lewis

It is a hard matter to enjoy the world without being entangled with the cares and pleasures of it.
Thomas Manton

The world belongs to God and he wants it back.
David Pawson

The money, the pleasures, the daily business of the world are so many traps to catch souls.   *J. C. Ryle*

The earth is big in our hopes, but little in our hands.   *William Secker*

Thorns will not prick of themselves, but when they are grasped in a man's hand they prick deep. So this world and the things thereof are all good, and were all made of God for the benefit of his creatures, did not our immoderate affection make them hurtful.

Richard Sibbes

WORLDLINESS

(See also: World)

If you have a distorted view of the Christian life you have let the world develop the negative. *Anon.*

The Christian must live in the world, but he must not let the world live in him. *Anon.*

The stars which have least circuit are nearest the pole; and men whose earths are least entangled with the world are always nearest to God and to the assurance of his favour. *Thomas Brooks*

We are of the world, and until Christ rescues us from it, the world reigns in us and we live unto it. *John Calvin*

Nothing is more contrary to a heavenly hope than an earthly heart. *William Gurnall*

If you stand on the Word you do not stand in with the world. *Vance Havner*

Many Christians are still in the wilderness, longing for garlic instead of grace, melons instead of manna! *Vance Havner*

The path of the Word and the path of the world do not run parallel. *Vance Havner*

We cannot have a heavenly fellowship if we allow a hindering fellowship. *Vance Havner*

We must deal with the carnalities if we desire the spiritualities. *Vance Havner*

Worldlings make gold their god; saints make God their gold. *Matthew Henry*

To forsake Christ for the world is to leave a treasure for a trifle . . . eternity for a moment, reality for a shadow. *William Jenkyn*

Worldliness is a spirit, a temperament, an attitude of soul. It is life without high callings, life devoid of lofty ideals. It is a gaze horizontal, never vertical. Its motto is 'Forward', never 'Upward'. *John Henry Jowett*

God lays down one programme of life for his children; the world proposes another and totally incompatible programme for its servants. So love for the one excludes love for the other. *Robert Law*

The carnal mind sees God in nothing, not even in spiritual things. The spiritual mind sees him in everything, even in natural things.
Robert Leighton

A carnal Christian is the carcase of a true Christian.
Thomas Manton

The world and grace are incompatible.
Thomas Manton

Depend upon it, as long as the church is living so much like the world, we cannot expect our children to be brought into the fold.
D. L. Moody

The spirit of this world is devotion to the visible.
Andrew Murray

There is nothing the Christian life suffers more from than the subtle and indescribable worldliness that comes from the cares or the possessions of this life.
Andrew Murray

Being of the world means being controlled by what preoccupies the world, the quest for pleasure, profit and position.
J. I. Packer

Worldliness means yielding to the spirit that animates fallen mankind, the spirit of self-seeking and self-indulgence without regard for God.
J. I. Packer

To accommodate to the world spirit about us in our age is nothing less than the most gross form of worldliness in the proper definition of that word.
Francis Schaeffer

It strikes me that some people want only as much of God's salvation as will keep them out of hell, and they measure out with unconscious precision how much worldliness and sin they can still hang on to without jeopardizing their chances.
David Shepherd

He that loves the world is a worldling.   *Richard Sibbes*

The world's fashion is the worst fashion of all.
Richard Sibbes

A worldly Christian is spiritually diseased.
C. H. Spurgeon

Take care if the world does hate you that it hates you without cause.
C. H. Spurgeon

Worldly policy is a poor short-sighted thing, and when men choose it as their road it leads them over dark mountains.   *C. H. Spurgeon*

If I find anyone who is settled down too snugly into this world, I am made to doubt whether he's ever truly been born again.
A. W. Tozer

If men do not put the love of the world to death, the love of the world will put them to death. *Ralph Venning*

Identification with the world and its needs is one thing; imitation of the world and its foolishness is quite another. *Warren Wiersbe*

WORRY
(See also: Anxiety; Fear)

Fretting is the caressing of the old nature.
Donald Grey Barnhouse

Worry, like guilt, is a reflection of our human privilege as made in God's image. We are able to feel guilty because we have been given moral responsibility. We are able to feel anxiety because we have been given creative imagination by God. *Roy Clements*

Disquieting care is the common fruit of an abundance of this world, and the common fault of those that have abundance. *Matthew Henry*

Half our miseries are caused by things that we think are coming upon us.
J. C. Ryle

If a case is too small to be turned into a prayer it is too small to be made into a burden. *Corrie ten Boom*

WORSHIP — Essence

Worship is the sum total of all our response to God as his children.
Robert M. Horn

Worship is Christian living.
Dick Lucas

True worship seeks union with its beloved, and an active effort to close the gap between the heart and the God it adores is worship at its best! *A. W. Tozer*

WORSHIP — Importance
(See also: Awe; Fear of God)

Life ought not merely to contain acts of worship; it should be an act of worship.

The best eyes look inwards and upwards. *Anon.*

343

None reverence the Lord more than they who know him best. *William Cowper*

What greater calamity can fall upon a nation than the loss of worship? Then all things go to decay . . . literature becomes frivolous and society lives on trifles.
Ralph Waldo Emerson

As secret worship is better the more secret it is, so public worship is better the more public it is.
Matthew Henry

Those cannot worship God aright who do not worship him alone. *Matthew Henry*

Where we have a tent God must have an altar; where we have a house he must have a church in it.
Matthew Henry

Honest dealing becomes us when we kneel in God's pure presence. *David McIntyre*

What or whom we worship determines our behaviour.
John Murray

Where God is truly known, he is necessarily adored.
A. W. Pink

Worship requires us to be as adult, as responsible, as serious, as concentrated in our thoughts as we are capable of being.
Alwyn Pritchard

We must take our whole heart to the house of God, and worship and hear like those who listen to the reading of a will. *J. C. Ryle*

He whose soul does not worship shall never live in holiness. *C. H. Spurgeon*

Because we were created to worship, worship is the normal employment of moral beings. *A. W. Tozer*

God made us to be worshippers. That was the purpose of God in bringing us into the world. *A. W. Tozer*

God wants worshippers before workers; indeed, the only acceptable workers are those who have learned the art of worship.
A. W. Tozer

If you will not worship God seven days a week, you do not worship him on one day a week. *A. W. Tozer*

Man is a worshipper and only in the spirit of worship does he find release for all the powers of his amazing intellect. *A. W. Tozer*

Where there is not worship there is discord from the broken strings.
A. W. Tozer

Worship is a moral imperative. *A. W. Tozer*

Worship is the only fitting response to God's bounty.
Geoffrey B. Wilson

ZEAL

(See also: Abandonment; Consecration; Passion; Service — Wholeheartedness; Submission)

Zeal without knowledge is the sister of folly. *Anon.*

True zeal with knowledge only comes from the realization of God's valuation of a soul.
Donald Grey Barnhouse

I cared not when or how I lived, or what hardships I went through, so that I could gain souls for Christ.
David Brainerd

Zeal is like fire; in the chimney it is one of the best servants, but out of the chimney it is one of the worst masters. *Thomas Brooks*

Am I ignitable? God deliver me from the dread asbestos of 'other things'. Saturate

me with the oil of the Spirit that I may be a flame.
Jim Elliot

Those who in time past have wrought great things for God have possessed a sanctified energy totally devoid of sloth. *James R. Graham*

We cannot grow a harvest for God with one eye on the weather. *Vance Havner*

We need an outbreak of holy heartburn, when hearers shall be doers, when congregations shall go out from meetings to do things for God. *Vance Havner*

True zeal makes nothing of hardships in the way of duty.
Matthew Henry

Without Christ, not one step; with him, anywhere!
David Livingstone

A disciple can be forgiven if he does not have great mental ability. He can be forgiven also if he does not display outstanding physical prowess. But no disciple can be excused if he does not have zeal. If his heart is not aflame with a red-hot passion for the Saviour, he stands condemned.
William Macdonald

Zeal

I feel there are two things it is impossible to desire with sufficient ardour — personal holiness and the honour of Christ in the salvation of souls.
Robert Murray M'Cheyne

Oh, how I wished that I had a tongue like thunder, that I might make all hear; or that I had a frame like iron, that I might visit everyone, and say, 'Escape for thy life!'
Robert Murray M'Cheyne

Mix a conviction with a man and something happens!
Adam Clayton Powell

A zealous Saviour ought to have zealous disciples.
J. C. Ryle

I'd rather be a lean bird in the woods than a fat bird in a cage. *C. H. Spurgeon*

If by excessive zeal we die before reaching the average age of man, worn out in the Master's service, then glory to God, we shall have so much less of earth and so much more of heaven.
C. H. Spurgeon

Be extravagant for God or the devil, but for God's sake don't be tepid.
C. T. Studd

One live coal may set a whole stack on fire.
John Trapp

I have one passion only: It is he! It is he!
Nicolas von Zinzendorf

The world is my parish.
John Wesley

O Lord, make me an extraordinary Christian.
George Whitefield

Does our fire for God warm others, or does it burn them? If it burns them, it will burn us too. *Spiros Zodhiates*

Subject Index

Subject Index

Character
Charity
Chastening
Children — see Family Life
Christ — see Jesus Christ
Christian
Christianity — Characteristics
Christianity — Definition
Christianity — Uniqueness
Christlikeness
Church — Attendance and Membership
Church — Blemishes
Church — and Christ
Church — Divisions
Church — Duties
Church — Fellowship
Church — Glory
Church — Oneness
Church — Power
Church — Security in God's Purposes
Church Unity
Circumstances
Cleansing — see Forgiveness; Holiness
Clothing
Commitment — see Abandonment; Consecration; Submission; Zeal
Common Grace — see Grace — Common Grace
Communion with Christ
Communion with God
Communism
Companionship — see Fellowship; Friendship
Complacency
Complaining — see Murmuring
Compromise
Conceit
Confession

Confidence — see Assurance
Conflict — see Spiritual Warfare
Conformity — see Compromise
Conscience — and God
Conscience — Importance
Conscience — Power
Conscience — and Sin
Consecration
Consistency — see Faithfulness
Contempt
Contentment
Contrition
Controversy
Conversion
Conviction — see Assurance
Conviction of Sin
Courage
Courtesy
Covenant
Covetousness
Cowardice
Creation
Criticism by Others
Criticism of Others
Cross
Curiosity

Darkness — Spiritual — see Spiritual Darkness
Death — Anticipation
Death — Blessings
Death — Certainty
Death — and Heaven
Death — Indiscriminate
Death — and Judgement
Death — Meaning
Death — Preparation for
Death — Triumph over
Deceit — see Dishonesty; Lying
Democracy
Depravity
Desires

Forgiveness of Others
Formalism
Fortitude — see Patience
Free Will
Freedom — see Liberty
Friendship
Fruitfulness
Future

Generosity
Gentleness
Gifts — Spiritual — see
    Spiritual Gifts
Giving
Gloom — see Despair
Glory — see God — Glory
Gluttony
Goal — see Purpose
God — Eternity
God — Existence
God — Forgiveness — see
    Forgiveness by God
God — Glory
God — Goodness
God — Immutability
God — Independence
God — Inscrutability
God — Jealousy
God — Law — see Law of God
God — Love
God — Mercy — see
    Mercy from God
God — Name
God — Omnipotence
God — Omnipresence
God — Omniscience
God — Patience
God — Perfection
God — Promises — see
    Promises of God

God — Purposes
God — Sovereignty
God — Will — see Will of God
God — Wrath
Godhead
Godliness
Good Deeds
Good Works — see Good Deeds
Goodness
Gospel
Gossip
Grace — the Christian's
    Indebtedness to
Grace — Common Grace
Grace — Daily
Grace — Essence
Grace — and Heaven
Grace — Means — see
    Means of Grace
Grace — and Salvation
Grace — Supremacy
Graces
Gratitude
Greed
Grief — see Sorrow
Growth
Guidance
Guilt

Habit
Happiness
Hatred
Heart
Heaven — The Christian's
    Eternal Home
Heaven — Glory
Heaven — God's Presence
Heaven — Perfection
Heaven — Preparation for
Hedonism
Hell
Heresy

353

Righteousness — see Christlike-
    ness; Godliness; Holiness
Ritualism
Rumour

Sabbath — see Lord's Day
Sacrifice
Sadness — see Sorrow
Salvation
Sanctification — see Holiness
Satan
Saving Faith — see
    Faith — Saving
Science
Scripture — see Bible
Second Coming of Christ
Security
Self
Self-Control
Self-Crucifixion
Self-Delusion
Self-Denial
Self-Examination
Selfishness
Self-Pity
Separation
Sermons — see Preaching and
    Preachers
Service — Dignity
Service — God's Part
Service — Prayer
Service — Responsibility
Service — Rewards
Service — Wholehearted-
    ness
Sex
Sickness
Silence
Sin — and the Christian
Sin — Deceitfulness
Sin — Effects
Sin — Essence

Sin — Fact
Sin of Omission
Sin — Power
Sincerity
Sinful Nature
Slander
Sleep
Sloth — see Indolence
Social Responsibility
Sorrow
Soul
Soul-Winning
Speech
Spiritual Darkness
Spiritual Gifts
Spiritual Hunger
Spirituality
Spiritual Riches
Spiritual Warfare
Sport — see Amusements;
    Recreation
Stewardship
Stubbornness
Submission
Success
Suffering
Suicide
Sunday — see Lord's Day
Surrender — see Abandonment;
    Consecration; Submission;
    Zeal
Sympathy

Temptation — Avoiding
and Resisting
Temptation — Blessing
Temptation — Certainty
Temptation — and Satan
Temptation — and Sin
Testing — see Trials
Thanksgiving